Contents ■

# 1 *Company Structures*

**Key vocabulary** Most companies are made up of three groups of people: the **shareholders** (who provide the capital), the **management** and the **workforce**. The management structure of a typical company is shown in this **organisation chart**.

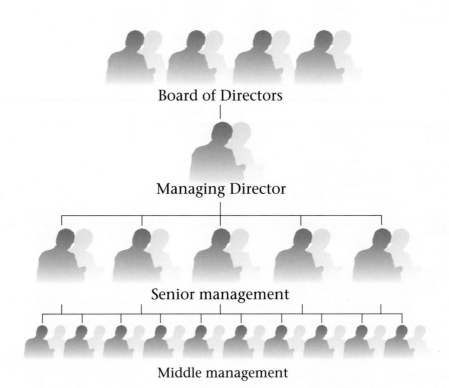

Board of Directors

Managing Director

Senior management

Middle management

At the top of the company hierarchy is the **Board of Directors**, headed by the **Chairperson** or **President**. The Board is responsible for policy decisions and strategy. It will usually appoint a **Managing Director** or **Chief Executive Officer**, who has overall responsibility for the running of the business. **Senior managers** or **company officers** head the various departments or functions within the company, which may include the following.

a **Marketing**

b **Public Relations**

c **Information Technology** or **IT**

d **Personnel** or **Human Resources**

e **Finance**

f **Production**

g **Research and Development** or **R and D**

WIL

NEW

STUDENTS' BOOK

Longman

# Contents

**Lead-in**

**1** 📼 Listen to seven people talking about their work and decide which department each one works for.

1 ☐    2 ☐    3 ☐    4 ☐    5 ☐    6 ☐    7 ☐

**2** Philips is a major multinational company which has almost 30,000 trademarks registered worldwide. In groups, study the organisation chart below.

**PHILIPS**

*Let's make things better.*

```
                    ┌─────────────┐
                    │  PRESIDENT  │
                    └─────────────┘
                           │
                ┌────────────────────┐
                │ BOARD OF MANAGEMENT │
                └────────────────────┘
```

(In charge of company strategy and general policy.)

```
┌──────────────────────────────────────────────────────┐
│ SUPERVISORY BOARD GROUP MANAGEMENT COMMITTEE           │
└──────────────────────────────────────────────────────┘
```

(Responsible for the general course of business.
Makes sure policy is implemented and advises the board of management.)

Corporate Departments

| Finance: Accounting & Control | Information Technology | Human Resource Management | Legal Affairs | Communication and Public Relations |
|---|---|---|---|---|

**Match these products to the sectors below which they come from.**

| faxes   mobile computing products   X-ray equipment   hairdryers   lamps |
|---|

Sectors

**Philips Business Electronics**

Products include:
■ digital video-communications systems
■ 1 _____
■ speech processing

**Philips Components**

Products include:
■ display components
■ general systems components

**Philips Consumer Electronics**

Products include:
■ video: TV, VCR
■ digital video DVD, internet, digital TV, digital cameras
■ mobile phones
■ 3 mobile computing products

**Philips Domestic Appliances and Personal Care**

Products include:
■ personal care: shavers, 2 _____, suncare
■ domestic appliances: vacuum cleaners, food processors, blenders, coffee makers

**Philips Lighting**

Products include:
■ 4 _____
■ lighting electronics and gear

**Philips Medical Systems**

Products include:
■ 5 _____
■ ultrasound

**Philips Semiconductors**

Products include:
■ telecom terminals
■ emerging business e.g. Trimedia

## Reading

**1 Before reading the text below about Philips, decide whether you think these statements are true (T) or false (F).**

1 It is the world's second biggest electronics company.  ☐

2 It has produced over 100 million TV sets.  ☐

3 Its headquarters are in Amsterdam.  ☐

4 It was the first company to produce compact discs.  ☐

5 It is active in a small number of specialised businesses.  ☐

6 It provides the lights for famous landmarks such as London's Tower Bridge.  ☐

**Read the text and check your answers.**

Netsite: http://www.news.philips.com

# The Philips Story

1 The foundations of the world's biggest electronics company were laid in 1891 when Gerard Philips established a company in Eindhoven, the Netherlands, to manufacture light bulbs and other electrical products. In the beginning, it concentrated on making carbon-filament lamps and by the turn
5 of the century was one of the largest producers in Europe. Developments in new lighting technologies fuelled a steady programme of expansion and, in 1914, it established a research laboratory to stimulate product innovation.

In the 1920s, Philips decided to protect its innovations in X-ray radiation and radio reception with patents. This marked the beginning of the diversification
10 of its product range. Since then, Philips has continued to develop new and exciting product ideas like the compact disc, which it launched in 1983. Other interesting landmarks include the production of Philips' 100-millionth TV set in 1984 and 250-millionth Philishave electric shaver in 1989.

## The Philips Company

15 Philips' headquarters are still in Eindhoven. It employs 256,400 people all over the world, and has sales and service outlets in 150 countries. Research laboratories
20 are located in six countries, staffed by some 3,000 scientists. It also has an impressive global network of some 400 designers spread over twenty-five locations. Its
25 shares are listed on sixteen stock exchanges in nine countries and it is active in about 100 businesses, including lighting, monitors, shavers and colour picture tubes; each day its factories turn out a total of 50 million integrated circuits.

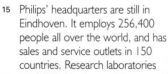

## The Philips People

30 Royal Philips Electronics is managed by the Board of Management, which looks after the general direction and long-term strategy of the Philips group as a whole. The Supervisory Board monitors the general course of business of the Philips group as well as
35 advising the Board of Management and supervising its policies. These policies are implemented by the Group Management Committee, which consists of the members of the
40 Board of Management, chairmen of most of the product divisions and some other key officers. The Group Management Committee also serves to ensure that business issues and
45 practices are shared across the various activities in the group.

The company creed is 'Let's make things better'. It is committed to making better products and systems and contributing to
50 improving the quality of people's work and life. One recent example of this is its 'Genie' mobile phone. To dial a number you just have to say it aloud. Its Web TV Internet terminal brings the excitement of cyberspace into the
55 living room. And on travels around the world, whether passing the Eiffel Tower in Paris, walking across London's Tower Bridge, or witnessing the beauty of the ancient pyramids of Giza, you don't have to wonder any more who lit these world
60 famous landmarks, it was Philips.

*http://www.news.philips.com*

**2** Read 'The Philips Story' again. Why are these dates important?

**a** 1891     **b** 1914     **c** the 1920s     **d** 1983     **e** 1984

**3** Read 'The Philips Company' again and find the figures that correspond to the following pieces of information.

Example: The approximate number of designers working for Philips: *400*

1  The number of people working for Philips worldwide
2  The number of countries with sales and service outlets
3  The number of countries where Philips has research facilities
4  The approximate number of scientists working in Philips' research laboratories
5  The number of integrated circuits produced every day

**Practise reading the figures aloud.**

◻ **Listen to the cassette and check your pronunciation.**

**4** ◻ **Listen and write down the numbers you hear.**

| 1 _____ | 3 _____ | 5 _____ | 7 _____ |
| 2 _____ | 4 _____ | 6 _____ | 8 _____ |

**Vocabulary**

**1** Match the words from the text with their corresponding definitions.

1  an innovation (*line 8*)          **a**  a planned series of actions
2  a patent (*line 9*)               **b**  main offices
3  diversification (*line 9*)        **c**  a place or address
4  a range (*line 10*)              **d**  the introduction of a new idea
5  headquarters (*line 15*)          **e**  a selection or series
6  a location (*line 24*)           **f**  making different types of products
7  a strategy (*line 32*)           **g**  an agreed course of action
8  a policy (*line 36*)             **h**  the right to make or sell an invention.

**2** In pairs, replace the words in italics with the words used in the text.

1  Gerard Philips *set up* (e s t a b l i s h e d) a company in Eindhoven.
2  The company initially *specialised in* (c _ _ _ _ _ _ _ _ _ _ _ _) making carbon-filament lamps.
3  Developments in new lighting technologies fuelled a steady *plan for growth* (p _ _ _ _ _ _ _ _ of e _ _ _ _ _ _ _).
4  In 1983 it *introduced* (l _ _ _ _ _ _ _) the compact disc *onto the market*.
5  Each day its factories *produce* (t _ _ _  o _ _) a total of 50 million integrated circuits.
6  Royal Philips Electronics is *run* (m _ _ _ _ _ _) by the Board of Management.
7  The Supervisory Board *carefully watches* (m _ _ _ _ _ _ _) the general course of business.
8  Policies are *put into practice* (i _ _ _ _ _ _ _ _ _) by the Group Management Committee.
9  The Group Management Committee consists of members of the Board of Management and chairmen of most of the product *sectors* (d _ _ _ _ _ _ _).
10 The Group Management Committee serves to ensure that *important matters* (i _ _ _ _ _) and *ways of doing business* (p _ _ _ _ _ _ _) are shared across the company.

**Now check your answers with the text.**

**3** Complete the passage using words from Vocabulary 1 and 2 in the correct form.

> The key to Philips' success can be described by two words. The first is
> ¹ _innovation_ ; the company designers are continually developing and creating
> new products. The second is ² _____; Philips is active in about 100 businesses
> varying from consumer electronics to domestic appliances and from security
> systems to semiconductors. With such a wide ³ _____ of products the
> company needs a complex system of management. Each product ⁴ _____ has
> its own chairman; most of these chairmen are members of the Group
> Management Committee, which ⁵ _____ all company decisions and plans.
> The Supervisory Board ⁶ _____ the general business of the group and it also
> advises and supervises the Board of Management.

## Vocabulary development: verbs and prepositions

Some verbs are always followed by the same preposition. Look at the examples from the text on page 6.

*In the beginning, it **concentrated on** making carbon-filament lamps. (line 4)*
(When a preposition is followed by a verb it always takes the *'ing'* form)

*These policies are implemented by the Group Management Committee, which **consists of** the members of the Board of Management. (line 39)*

**1**   Match the prepositions with the verbs below.

from    in (x3)    to (x4)    for    of    on (x2)

|   |   |   |   |
|---|---|---|---|
| a | apply _to_ somebody <br> _for_ something | f | refer ___ |
|   |   | g | succeed ___ |
| b | benefit ____ | h | belong ___ |
| c | approve ____ | i | depend ___ |
| d | result ____ | j | report ___ somebody |
| e | believe ____ |   | ___ something |

**2**   Complete the sentences using verbs and prepositions from exercise 1 in the correct form.

   **a** In the purchasing department there is a manager, and five employees who __report__ ___to___ her.

   **b** In this company, we firmly _____ _____ the value of creativity and innovation.

   **c** The development of computer technology has _____ _____ enormous changes in the way that people work.

   **d** Whether or not we succeed in creating and selling new products _____ _____ a number of factors.

   **e** Most of our staff _____ _____ at least one of the company's sports or leisure clubs.

   **f** The Personnel Manager thinks that we would all _____ _____ further training in how to use the office software.

**3**   Write three more sentences, using the verb and preposition combinations above.

**4**   What other verb and preposition combinations do you know?

## *Language Focus*

**Present perfect and past simple**

**Look at these sentences from the text on page 6.**

A *In the 1920s, Philips **decided** to protect its innovations.*

B *Since then, Philips **has continued** to develop new and exciting product ideas.*

1 What tense is the verb in bold in A and B?
2 Which tense has a connection with the present?
3 Which tense only tells us about the past?

▶▶ For more information on the present perfect and past simple, turn to page 164.

**Practice**

**Complete the company profile with either the present perfect or past simple tense of the verbs in brackets. Pay special attention to irregular verbs and the position of adverbs.**

## ⊕ COLGATE-PALMOLIVE COMPANY

William Colgate ¹ founded (found) the Colgate Company in 1806 as a starch, soap and candle business in New York City. For the first hundred years, the company ² _____ (do) all its business in the United States. However, in the early 1900s, the company ³ _____ (begin) an aggressive expansion programme that ⁴ _____ (lead) to the establishment of Colgate operations in countries throughout Europe, Latin America and the Far East. In more recent years it ⁵ _____ (set up) operations in Turkey, Pakistan, Saudi Arabia, Eastern Europe and China. Colgate-Palmolive ⁶ _____ (become) a truly global consumer products company, worth $8.7 bn and selling in more than 200 countries.

Colgate-Palmolive's five main sectors of business are: Oral Care, Body Care, Household Surface Care, Fabric Care and Pet Nutrition and Health Care. In the area of Oral Care, Colgate-Palmolive is the world leader in toothpaste. As a result of the company's heavy investment in research and technology, it ⁷ _____ (develop) many successful toothpastes, rinses and toothbrushes. To strengthen its presence in professional products, Colgate-Palmolive

⁸ _____ (buy) the Ora Pharm Company of Australia and the dental therapeutics business of Scherer Laboratories USA in 1990. For many years, the company ⁹ _____ (have) a strong dental education programme in schools throughout the world and ¹⁰ _____ (maintain) a close partnership with the international dental community. Recently it ¹¹ _____ (create) a web site for dental professionals.

The company ¹² _____ (always pay) close attention to the environment. It ¹³ _____ (already make) great progress in the use of recyclable bottles and packaging materials.

## Describing changes

The following verbs can be used to describe upward ( ↗ ) and downward ( ↘ ) movements in price, quantity and amount.

| Intransitive verbs (verbs which do not have an object) | Transitive verbs (verbs which have an object) |
|---|---|
| ↗ increase    rise    go up | ↗ increase    raise |
| ↘ decrease    fall    drop    go down    decline | ↘ decrease    reduce    drop |

*The population of the world is increasing.*
*The prices of electronic goods have fallen.*

*The government has increased income tax.*
*We have reduced our prices by 10 per cent.*

These corresponding nouns can also be used.

| | | | | |
|---|---|---|---|---|
| ↗ an increase | a rise | a raise (US = increase in salary) | | |
| ↘ a decrease | a fall | a drop | a decline | a reduction |

## Practice

**Complete these sentences using a noun or verb from the boxes above. Use each word only once.**

1 There are several competing companies entering the market and this has caused a 20% ___drop___ in prices.

2 Last year was a good year for the company and our sales _____ considerably.

3 The price of coffee has _____ as a result of the bad weather conditions.

4 As a result of the recession, we have had to _____ the amount of money we spend on research and development.

5 The _____ in profits is the result of poor management.

6 The recent _____ in overseas investment has been good for the economy.

7 Economists predict that interest rates will _____ if consumer spending continues to slow down.

8 Because of high profits last year, the company has announced a salary _____ for all its employees.

## *Skills Focus*

### Listening

**1 Complete the passage opposite about Mr Pat Guerin, Industrial Relations Manager of Guinness Ireland. Use these expressions.**

a This job involved …

b I reported directly to …

c I was employed as …

d I worked …

e The next position I held was …

f I was then promoted to …

g In this role …

h I've worked …

When I first started working in Guinness [1] I was employed as a general worker. For three years [2] _____ in the bottling plant as a machine operator. [3] _____ for a period of seven years in the engineering department as a maintenance assistant. This involved working with technically skilled personnel in maintaining plant and equipment. In both jobs [4] _____ a supervisor. Since then, however, the structure of the company has significantly changed and the supervisor layer no longer exists. General workers now report to a plant manager. [5] _____ the position of laboratory officer in the quality assurance laboratory. [6] _____ carrying out a wide range of analyses on all aspects of the brewing process. For the past year [7] _____ in the personnel department as an Industrial Relations Manager. [8] _____

I report directly to the Personnel Manager of the company.

**2** 🔲 **Listen to Mr Guerin and check your answers.**

**3** 🔲 **Listen to part 2 and answer the questions.**

1 What contributed to Mr Guerin's transition from general worker to a managerial position?
2 What is his principal role in the company?
3 What does this involve?
4 What does he think is the main skill that a manager needs today?

**4** 🔲 **Listen to part 3. How has the company changed since Mr Guerin joined? You may wish to check you understand these words before you listen.**

contract out
industrial unrest
consultation
negotiation
early retirement
compulsory redundancy

**Speaking**

**1** Work in pairs. Student A, look at the information below. Student B, look at the information on page 154.

**Student A (Susan Robertson)**

Read your profile. Prepare the questions that you will need to ask Student B (Giancarlo Peretto) in order to complete his profile.

Examples: *How long have you been with your present company?*
*What are you responsible for?*

Interview Student B and complete the profile. Then answer Student B's questions.

**Name:** Susan Robertson
**Age:** 29
**Nationality:** American
**Marital status:** Single
**Salary:** $48,000 per annum
**Company:** US Brands Incorporated
**Present position:** Brand Manager, works under the Director of Marketing

**Background:**
• MBA from the University of Pennsylvania
• Joined the company in 1999

**Present responsibilities:**
• In charge of determining national marketing strategy for a brand of paper towels.
• Heads a business team of 10 people which studies consumers' opinions of company products.

**Name:** Giancarlo Peretto
**Age:** _____
**Nationality:** _____
**Marital status:** _____
**Salary:** _____
**Company:** _____
**Present position:** _____
**Background:** _____
**Present responsibilities:** _____

**2** Work in pairs again. Student A, look at the information below. Student B, look at the information on page 155.

**Student A**
Read the company profile and answer Student B's questions about it.

# Virgin

is a leading international company based in London. It was founded in 1970 by Richard Branson, the present chairman. The group has seven main divisions: cinema, communication, financial services, hotels, investments, retail and travel. Its retail segment is led by Virgin Megastores, a network of music and entertainment stores. Virgin operates in 23 countries, including the United States, the United Kingdom, Continental Europe, Australia and Japan. In 1999, the combined sales of the different Virgin holding companies exceeded £3 bn.

Now ask Student B questions about the company that he or she has read about, and complete the notes below.

Name of company _____
Headquarters _____
Chairman _____
Business activities _____
Main markets _____
Sales in 1999 _____

**Writing**

Write a company profile for TESCO using the notes below. Use the examples in Speaking 2 to help you.

Name of company: TESCO plc

Established: 1924

Headquarters: Cheshunt, near London, UK

Chairman: John Gardiner

Business activities:
Superstores and hypermarkets - food, toys, clothes
Personal finance - banking, credit cards, loans, insurance
E-commerce - home shopping, books online
Internet service provider

Main markets: UK, Ireland, France, Czech Republic, Hungary, Poland, Slovakia, South Korea, Thailand (plans for Malaysia and Taiwan)

1999 sales: £18.5 bn

# 2 *Recruitment*

**Key vocabulary** When a company needs to **recruit** or employ new people, it may decide to advertise the job or **position** in the appointments section of a newspaper. People who are interested can then **apply for** the job by sending in a **letter of application** or **covering letter** (US **cover letter**) and a **curriculum vitae** or **CV** (US **résumé**) containing details of their education and experience. A company may also ask candidates to complete a standard **application form**. The company's Human Resources department will then select the most suitable applications and prepare a **short list** of **candidates** or **applicants**, who are invited to attend an **interview**. Another way for a company to **hire** is by using the services of a **recruitment agency** (US **search firm**) who will provide them with a list of suitable candidates.

**Lead-in**

**1** Read the advertisement opposite from the website of the American company Cognex, and match the information below with the corresponding red boxes in the advertisement.

1 Cognex provides evening entertainment for its employees.
2 There is a place for employees to play and unwind.
3 Employees are given the opportunity to travel to foreign countries.
4 Cognex likes to recognize and thank employees for their hard work.

**2** In pairs, discuss these questions.

1 What are the advantages and disadvantages of working for Cognex?
2 Would you like to work for a company like this? Why / Why not?
3 What do you think of this type of recruitment advertisement?
4 What kind of person is Cognex hoping to recruit?
5 What other ways can companies use to advertise for staff?

**3** Different methods may be used to recruit people. In groups, discuss the following.

Candidates may be asked to:
• tell a joke
• take part in a team game with employees from the company
• make a five-minute speech
• complete a probation period before being accepted

Employers may:
• offer a job to the husband or wife of a good candidate
• prefer to recruit people from the families of employees
• ask candidates to complete a personality test
• have candidates' handwriting analysed (graphology)

**Which methods do you think are acceptable / unacceptable? Why?**
**Would it be possible to recruit like this in your country?**

**Netsite:** www.cognex.com  What's Related

# COGNEX

## Vision for Industry

## Career Opportunities

### New Graduate Opportunities and Intern* Programs

About Our Company

Press Releases

Products

Vision Technology

Career Opportunities

Investor Relations

Customer Satisfaction

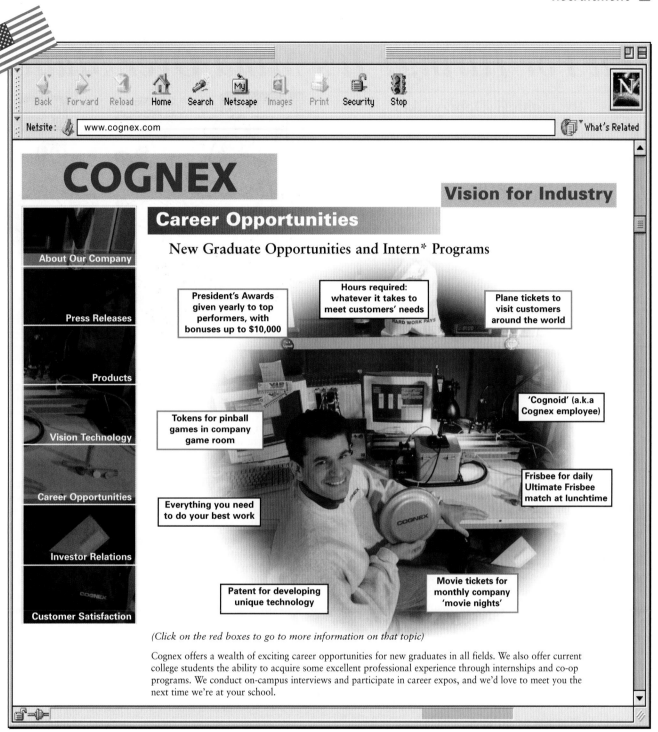

President's Awards given yearly to top performers, with bonuses up to $10,000

Hours required: whatever it takes to meet customers' needs

Plane tickets to visit customers around the world

Tokens for pinball games in company game room

'Cognoid' (a.k.a Cognex employee)

Everything you need to do your best work

Frisbee for daily Ultimate Frisbee match at lunchtime

Patent for developing unique technology

Movie tickets for monthly company 'movie nights'

*(Click on the red boxes to go to more information on that topic)*

Cognex offers a wealth of exciting career opportunities for new graduates in all fields. We also offer current college students the ability to acquire some excellent professional experience through internships and co-op programs. We conduct on-campus interviews and participate in career expos, and we'd love to meet you the next time we're at your school.

\* *an intern* (US): someone who works for a short time to gain experience

# Fit For Hiring? It's Mind Over Matter

## By Judith H. Dobrzynski

NEW YORK – Members of America's professional and managerial classes have always left college confident of at least one thing: they had taken their last test. From here on, they could rely on charm, cunning* and/or a record of
5 accomplishment to propel them up the corporate ladder.

But that's not necessarily true any longer. A growing number of companies, from General Motors Corp to American Express Co., are no longer satisfied with traditional job interviews. Instead, they are requiring
10 applicants for many white-collar jobs – from top executives down – to submit to a series of paper-and-pencil tests, role-playing exercises, simulated decision-making exercises and brainteasers*. Others put candidates through a long series of interviews by psychologists or trained interviewers.

15 The tests are not about mathematics or grammar, nor about any of the basic technical skills for which many production, sales and clerical workers have long been tested. Rather, employers want to evaluate candidates on intangible* qualities: Is she creative and entrepreneurial?
20 Can he lead and coach? Is he flexible and capable of learning? Does she have passion and a sense of urgency? How will he function under pressure? Most important, will the potential recruit fit the corporate culture?

These tests, which can take from an hour to two days,
25 are all part of a broader trend. 'Companies are getting much more careful about hiring,' said Paul R. Ray Jr., chairman of the Association of Executive Search Consultants.

Ten years ago, candidates could win a top job with the right look and the right answers to questions such as 'Why
30 do you want this job?'. Now, many are having to face questions and exercises intended to learn how they get things done.

They may, for example, have to describe in great detail not one career accomplishment but many – so that patterns
35 of behavior emerge. They may face questions such as 'Who is the best manager you ever worked for and why?' or 'What is your best friend like?'. The answers, psychologists say, reveal much about a candidate's management style and about himself or herself.

40 The reason for the interrogations is clear: many hires* work out badly. About 35 percent of recently hired senior executives are judged failures, according to the Center for Creative Leadership in Greensboro, North Carolina, which surveyed nearly 500 chief executives.

45 The cost of bringing the wrong person on board is sometimes huge. Searching and training can cost from $5000 for a lower-level manager to $250,000 for a top executive. Years of corporate downsizing, a trend that has slashed* layers of management, has also increased the
50 potential damage that one bad executive can do. With the pace of change accelerating in markets and technology,

companies want to know how an executive will perform, not just how he or she has performed.

'Years ago, employers looked for experience – has a
55 candidate done this before?' said Harold P. Weinstein, executive vice-president of Caliper, a personnel testing and consulting firm in Princeton, New Jersey. 'But having experience in a job does not guarantee that you can do it in a different environment.'

60 At this point, most companies have not shifted to this practice. Some do not see the need or remain unconvinced that such testing is worth the cost. But human-resource specialists say anecdotal* evidence suggests that white-collar testing is growing in popularity. What has
65 brought so many employers around to testing is a sense of the limitations in the usual job interview. With so little information on which to base a decision, 'most people hire people they like, rather than the most competent person,' said Orv Owens, a psychologist in Snohomish, Washington,
70 who sizes up executive candidates. Research has shown, he said, that 'most decision makers make their hiring decisions in the first five minutes of an interview and spend the rest of the time rationalizing their choice.'

Besides, with advice on how to land a better job about
75 as common as a ten-dollar bill, many people are learning to play the interview game.

Even companies that have not started extensive testing have toughened their hiring practices. Many now do background checks, for example, looking for signs of drug
80 use, violence or sexual harassment. But the more comprehensive testing aims to measure skills in communications, analysis and organization, attention to detail and management style; personality traits* and motivations that behavioral scientists say predict
85 performance.

*New York Times*

---

*cunning:* the ability to deceive people
*a brainteaser:* a problem which is fun to solve
*intangible:* s.th. that cannot be felt or described
*a hire* (US); *a recruit* (GB): someone who starts to work for a company

*to slash:* to cut
*anecdotal:* based on personal experience
*to bring around:* to persuade s.b. to agree with s.th.
*a trait:* a quality in someone's character

**Reading**

**Read the text opposite, and decide if the following statements are true (T) or false (F).**

1  Traditionally, candidates for executive positions have been evaluated on their technical skills. ☐

2  The principal aim of testing is to find out how candidates have performed in the past. ☐

3  Today, choosing the wrong person for a position can have more serious consequences than ten years ago. ☐

4  Most interviewers select candidates for their professional abilities. ☐

5  Candidates are now better prepared for interviews than they were in the past. ☐

**Dictionary skills**

Using an English dictionary to find the meaning of a word that you do not understand is a simple way to improve your vocabulary. When you look up a word in the dictionary, you can find information about:

- its pronunciation(s)
- its grammatical category i.e. noun (*n*), adjective (*adj*), verb (*vb*), adverb (*adv*), preposition (*prep*), phrasal verb (*phr v*) etc.
- its meaning(s)
- the way it can be used
- its suffixed forms
- its compound forms (when the word is used with another word)
- other ways it can be spelt

**Look at the sample entry for the word *survey* (line 44) and then complete the checklist below.**

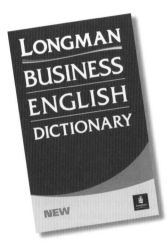

**survey²** /sə'veɪ‖ sər-/ *v* [T] 1 to ask a group of people a set of questions to find out about their opinions or behaviour: *The agency **surveys** executives in about 300 companies around the country.* | *Only 15% of **respondents surveyed** would admit to leaving the workplace early.*

**survey¹** /'sɜːveɪ‖ 'sɜːr-/ *n* [C] 1 a set of questions given to a group of people to find out about their opinions or behaviour: *People are becoming more pessimistic about the economy, according to the latest **consumer survey**.* +*of*: *A mild economic recovery starts this spring, according to a **survey** of 42 economists by the Wall Street Journal.*

**Dictionary checklist**

1  Are all forms of the word pronounced in the same way?
2  Does the word have one or more grammatical categories?
3  How many different meanings are given?
4  Can it be spelt in any other ways?
5  Does it have any suffixed or compound forms?
6  Which form of the word is the one that is used in the text?

**Vocabulary**

**1** Before using a dictionary, it is always a good idea to see if you can work out the meaning from the text. Find the following words in the article and see how many of the questions in the dictionary checklist you can answer:

*skill (line 16), employer (line 18), behavior (line 35), competent (line 68), rationalize (line 73).*

**2** Now see if you can answer any more questions in the dictionary checklist, using the entries below from the *New Longman Business English Dictionary*.

**behaviour** *BrE* **behavior** *AmE* /bɪˈheɪvjə‖-ər/ *n* 1 [U] the way that someone or something acts in different situations: *They have changed their buying behavior and are postponing major purchases.* | *The market's crash forced money managers to rethink basic assumptions about market behaviour.*

**competent** /ˈkɒmpɪtənt‖ˈkɒːm-/ *adj* 1 having enough skill, knowledge, or ability to do something to a satisfactory standard: *The farm would have to be run by a competent manager.* | *You need someone who is both competent at finance and honest.*

**employer** /ɪmˈplɔɪə‖-ər/ *n* [C] a person or company that pays people to work for them: *Every employer should spend money on training.* | *Who is your current employer?* | *Potential employers feel they can tell a lot about a person by looking at their handwriting.*

**rationalize** /ˈræʃənəlaɪz/ also **-ise** *BrE v* [I,T] to make a business or organization more effective by getting rid of unnecessary staff, equipment etc, or reorganizing its structure: *The company has been taking steps to rationalize its printing operations.*

**skill** /skɪl/ *n* [C,U] an ability to do something well, especially because you have learned and practised it: *You need computing skills for that job.* | *The successful applicant should be able to use their own initiative and have good communication skills.* | *There are still excellent jobs available for those with the right specialist skills and knowledge.* | *Unfortunately, listening may be the least practised management skill in today's workplace.* **+at/in**: *The Federal Reserve Chairman has demonstrated skill in adjusting interest rates.*

**3** Complete the following passage about the role of search firms in recruiting, using words from Vocabulary 1 and from the Key Vocabulary section. Change the form of the words where necessary.

> Headhunters or executive search firms specialise in finding the right person for the right job. When a company wishes to ¹ __recruit__ a new person for an important ² _____ it may use the services of such a firm. The advantages for the ³ _____ are that it does not have to organise the costly and time-consuming process of advertising, selecting and interviewing suitable ⁴ _____ . In some cases, the search firm may already have a list of people with the appropriate ⁵ _____ for the job. If this is not the case, then it may act as a consultant, advising on or even organising testing and simulations to evaluate the candidates' ⁶ _____ in order to select the most ⁷ _____ person for the job.

Now select three words from the text that you do not know and look them up in a dictionary.

**Vocabulary
development:
compound
nouns**

Compound nouns can be formed in different ways. *Decision maker* (*line 71*)
is formed by combining two nouns and refers to 'someone who makes
decisions'. The nouns in the two boxes below can be combined in the same way.

**1** Match one noun from each box to form a compound noun.

| | | | |
|---|---|---|---|
| 1 risk ʰ | 5 wage | a earner | e programmer |
| 2 computer | 6 wine | b winner | f solver |
| 3 problem | 7 law | c breaker | g importer |
| 4 award | 8 trouble | d shooter | h taker |

**2** Check your answers in a dictionary and note if the expression is written as two
words, with a hyphen (-) or as one word.

**3** Can you think of four more expressions like this?

**Discussion**

**On page 156 you will find four examples of questions from a personality test of
the type mentioned in the text.**

**1** Follow the instructions and answer each question.

**2** In pairs, discuss your answers to the questions. What do you think the answers
would tell an employer about your personality?

**3** What do you think of this type of testing?

## *Language Focus*

**Present simple
and present
continuous**

**Which sentence below refers to**

**1** a temporary situation? f

**2** an action that is happening at this moment?

**3** a permanent state or situation?

**4** a future arrangement?

**5** a regular or habitual action?

**6** a changing and developing situation?

**7** a future event based on a timetable?


**a** Candidates know what questions to expect.

**b** Companies are getting much more careful about hiring.

**c** Who is she talking to?

**d** I'm meeting the production manager this afternoon.

**e** The flight leaves at 18.00.

**f** James is working at home until the new office is ready.

**g** I get up at 7.00 most mornings.

**Which tense is used in each case?**

▶▶ For more information on the present simple and present continuous, and
for examples of verbs not normally used in the continuous, turn to page 164.

**Practice**

This is part of a report that a personnel manager wrote after interviewing a candidate for the position of Director of Software Development. Put the verbs in brackets into the present simple or present continuous tense.

### INTERVIEW ASSESSMENT

Articulate and well presented, Paul Sutherland is an excellent candidate for the post of Director of Software Development. He ¹___wants___ (want) to leave his present employer, a small computer company, because he ²_____ (feel) that he ³_____ (not use) his knowledge of software engineering to the full. He ⁴_____ (look for) a more challenging position where his field of specialisation can be exploited in a more stimulating environment. He ⁵_____ (realise) that our company ⁶_____ (grow) rapidly, and that he would be expected to contribute to that growth. He is familiar with our existing range of software and regularly ⁷_____ (read) our publications.

Although at present he ⁸_____ (live) in the south, he ⁹_____ (say) that he is willing to go wherever we ¹⁰_____ (decide) to send him. He occasionally ¹¹_____ (travel) to various European countries for trade fairs and exhibitions and ¹²_____ (enjoy) meeting people of different nationalities. At the moment he ¹³_____ (attend) a training course at the Goethe Institute in order to perfect his German.

*J Hargreaves*

Personnel Manager
27th January 2000

## Skills Focus

**Listening**

🔲 Look at the job advertisement below. You will hear a conversation in which Fiona Scott is telling a friend about the advertisement. Listen to the conversation and complete the missing information.

### 'PREFER A CAMPING TRIP TO A COCKTAIL PARTY?'

patagonia

**PATAGONIA has a new position open:**

¹_____ _____ **Associate**

Job is based in ²_____ . Candidates must have substantial ³_____ / _____ experience and strong ⁴_____ skills. They must have serious proficiency in technical sports (skiing, kayaking, climbing…) and outdoor experience. ⁵_____ mother tongue. Environmental background a plus. No glamor… it's a gritty job!

Patagonia is a ⁶_____ company which designs and distributes functional ⁷_____ _____ .

**Send CV with picture to:**

Nathalie Baudoin
Patagonia Gmbh
Reitmorstrasse 50
8000 Munich 22 – Germany

# patagonia®

The interviews will be in Munich during the last week of ⁸_____ .

## Preparation for writing

### 1 The curriculum vitae

**Fiona Scott decides to apply for the job at Patagonia. Study her CV carefully to see how she has presented the information about herself. Where do you think each of the following headings should be placed? Are CVs in your country presented differently?**

| | | |
|---|---|---|
| References | Activities | Personal Details |
| Education | Skills | Professional Experience |

## Curriculum Vitae

**1 Personal Details**

Fiona Scott
52 Hanover Street
Edinburgh EH2 5LM
Scotland
Phone: 0131 449 0237
E-mail: fiona.scott@caledonia.net

**2 _____**

| | |
|---|---|
| 1991–1992 | London Chamber of Commerce and Industry<br>Diploma in Public Relations |
| 1988–1991 | University of London<br>BA (Honours) in Journalism and Media Studies (Class II) |
| 1981–1988 | Broadfield School, Brighton<br>A levels in German (A), English (B), History (B) and Geography (C) |

**3 _____**

| | |
|---|---|
| 1995–present | Public Relations Officer, Scottish Nature Trust<br>Responsible for researching and writing articles on all aspects of the Trust's activities and ensuring their distribution to the press<br>Editor of the Trust's monthly journal<br>In charge of relations with European environmental agencies |
| 1992–1995 | Press Officer, Highlands Tourist Board<br>Preparation of promotional materials and brochures<br>Co-ordination of media coverage |
| Summers of 1990 and 1991 | The Glasgow Tribune newspaper<br>Two three-month training periods as assistant to the Sports Editor<br>Arranging and conducting interviews<br>Preparation of articles covering local community sports events |

**4 _____**

| | |
|---|---|
| IT | Office 2000 and Windows NT, Excel, Internet, Powerpoint |
| Languages | Fluent German and proficient in French |
| Additional | Driving licence (car and motorcycle) |

**5 _____**

Cross-country skiing, rock climbing and swimming
Ski Instructor (grade II)
Secretary of the local branch of 'Action', an association organising sports activities for disabled children

**6 _____**

| | |
|---|---|
| Geoffrey Williams<br>Professor of Journalism<br>University of London | Brenda Denholm<br>Sports Editor<br>The Glasgow Tribune |

## 2 The letter of application

**The letter of application can be as important as the CV in that it often provides the first direct contact between a candidate and an employer. If this letter is not well written and presented, it will make a poor impression. The letter of application normally contains four paragraphs in which you should:**

- confirm that you wish to apply and say where you learned about the job
- say why you are interested in the position and relate your interests to those of the company
- show that you can contribute to the job by highlighting your most relevant skills and experience
- indicate your willingness to attend an interview (and possibly say when you would be free to attend)

**Below you will find details from Fiona Scott's letter of application. Look at the outline of the letter on the left and indicate where the information below should go.**

1

(f)

2

3

4

5

6

7

8

9

Fiona Scott

10

(a) Although I am presently employed by a non-profit making organisation, it has always been my intention to work in a commercial environment. I would particularly welcome the chance to work for your company as I have long admired both the quality of the products that it provides and its position as a defender of environmental causes. As you will notice on my enclosed CV, the job you are offering suits both my personal and professional interests.

(b) I would be pleased to discuss my curriculum vitae with you in more detail at an interview. In the meantime, please do not hesitate to contact me if you require further information. I look forward to hearing from you.

(c) Dear Ms Baudoin     (d) 8th January 2000

(e) I am writing to apply for the position which was advertised last month in The Independent.

(f) 52 Hanover Street
Edinburgh
EH2 5LM
UK

(g) Nathalie Baudoin
Patagonia Gmbh
Reitmorstrasse 50
8000 Munich 22
Germany

(h) My work experience has familiarised me with many of the challenges involved in public relations today. I am sure that this, together with my understanding of the needs and expectations of sport and nature enthusiasts, would be extremely relevant to the position. Moreover, as my mother is German, I am fluent in this language and would definitely enjoy working in a German-speaking environment.

(i) Fiona Scott     (j) Yours sincerely

**3 Work in pairs. Refer back to the job advertisement, CV and letter of application. Do you think that Fiona has a chance of getting the job? What are her strengths and weaknesses?**

**Writing**

Clarke Hooper is advertising for graduates. Read the advertisement carefully, then prepare the CV and letter of application that you would send to Michelle Hocking. You may invent as many details as you wish, but note that the person who you present in your CV will not graduate until the end of this year.

---

2

# DON'T PASS

Not your degree, this ad. Got your attention though, didn't it? And that's our business. Promotional marketing involves everything from sales promotion to product launches, direct marketing to design. All of it involves grabbing people's attention. If you're interested in becoming an account handler, and you think you're capable of the kind of ideas that stand out in an increasingly media literate society, send your CV to Michelle Hocking at the address below.

**Check out our work and who we do it for at** www.chc.co.uk **You'll find more detail about what we expect from graduates at** www.chc.co.uk/gradrecruitment. **Whilst you're there you'll also find the questionnaire we'll be asking the best applicants to complete. If you want to get our attention, it might be a good idea to complete it now, and send it in with your CV.**

Clarke Hooper, St.Laurence Way, Slough, Berkshire, SL1 2BW. **E-mail:** michelle@chc.co.uk

---

**Listening**

You will hear David Smyth, the Personnel Manager of a major European insurance company, answering questions about the way he interviews and selects candidates.

1 ▭ In the first extract he talks about the four points listed below. Listen and number them in the order in which he mentions them.

**a** the mistakes a candidate can make in an interview

**b** the qualities a candidate must have

**c** his advice to interviewees

**d** the kinds of things a candidate is expected to know

▭ Listen again and make notes on each point.

**2** 🔲 In the second extract, David Smyth talks about the stages of an interview. Listen to what he says and complete the following chart.

1 | Interviewer is informed that the candidate has arrived

2 | 

3 | Candidate is asked what he or she knows about the job and the company

4 | 

5 | Interviewer gives candidate his views on the job and the company

6 | 

7 | 

**3** Look at the questions that David Smythe uses during an interview. In which section of the interview would each question appear?

a Have you ever been in a situation in which you lost your temper? ▢

b What sorts of projects did you work on during your time with them? ▢

c What do you know about our recent acquisitions in Latin America? [3]

d Did you have any trouble finding our building? ▢

e How do you deal with difficult people? ▢

f Which of the options that you took at university was the most interesting? ▢

g How ambitious are you? ▢

h Are there any questions that you'd like to ask me? ▢

**Speaking**

In pairs, look back at the job advertisement on page 23. You are going to interview a candidate for a place on the graduate recruitment programme. Swap your CVs and letters of application with another pair and prepare questions you would like to ask each of them.

When you have prepared the questions, interview one of the students whose CV you have read. After the interview, discuss the candidate with your partner. Would you employ him / her? Why? Why not?

# unit

# 3 *Retailing*

**Key vocabulary** **Retailing** is the business of selling products to the general public. Most **retailers** sell from **shops** or **stores** which are called **outlets**. Many countries have large retail **chains** which are organised nationally and sell a standardised selection of products. Their outlets are often in **shopping centres** (US **malls**), where there is a large variety of stores in the same location.

Many large retailers operate from out of town locations with parking facilities, known as either **hypermarkets** (over 30,000 square metres) or **superstores** (under 30,000 square metres). They may be on a **retail park**, where there are a number of large stores.

**Department stores** such as Harrods in London are large shops which sell a wide variety of products, usually from a city centre location. As the name suggests, they are organised in departments, each with its own manager.

**Lead-in**  **1** In groups, discuss the retail business in your country. How has the business changed in recent years? What do you think are the reasons for these changes?

**2** You will hear Janet Moore, a retail specialist, talking about the difficulties facing British retailers who try to penetrate the US market. She talks about four companies:

Habitat            The Virgin Group
The Body Shop      Next

**Listen to part 1. Which of the companies**

1  have been successful in the US?
2  have had to modify their US operations?
3  have abandoned the US market?

25

**3** Look at the list of potential problems for British retailers entering the US market. Which of these do you think are the actual problems?

1 assuming that American and British consumers have the same tastes
2 not investing enough money in their operations
3 offering too many products for sale
4 not advertising enough
5 taking too long to react to competition
6 not having high enough prices
7 sending UK managers to run the stores
8 choosing the wrong locations for stores

🔲 Listen to part 2 and tick the problems Ms Moore mentions.

**Reading**

**1** Look at the headline and introduction opposite. Write five questions you would like to ask about Richer Sounds.

**2** Read the text and see if you can find the answers to your questions. Can you guess the answers to your other questions?

**3** Read the text again and choose the best answer for each of the following questions.

1 Richer Sounds is
   **a** a single outlet retailer.
   **b** a privately-owned retail chain.
   **c** a department store.

2 Richer Sounds
   **a** sells ten times more than Marks and Spencer.
   **b** has more outlets than most UK retailers.
   **c** sells more per square foot than any other UK retailer.

3 Richer Sounds is cheaper than other hi-fi retailers because
   **a** it only sells old models of hi-fi equipment.
   **b** it buys equipment from manufacturers at special prices.
   **c** it sells second-hand equipment.

4 Manufacturers like doing business with Richer Sounds because
   **a** it can handle small numbers of items.
   **b** it has a large number of stores.
   **c** it accepts lower discounts than other retailers.

5 Richer Sounds
   **a** does all its advertising through brochures.
   **b** gets free publicity from newspaper and magazine articles.
   **c** buys advertising space at a low price.

6 At Richer Sounds, staff
   **a** regularly receive further training.
   **b** do not have to follow rules.
   **c** install equipment for their customers.

# RICHER
# Pickings

At hi-fi chain Richer Sounds 'we have a laugh', says founder Julian Richer. They also sell more per square foot than any other retailer in Britain.

## By Nigel Cope

Who is the busiest retailer in Britain? Marks and Spencer? Sainsbury perhaps, or Tesco? Wrong on all three counts. The answer is Richer Sounds, a
5 little-known, privately-owned, cut-price retailer of hi-fi equipment with 28 shops in the UK.

In the Guinness Book of Records, Richer Sounds warrants an entry for the highest
10 sales per square foot of any retailer in the UK – £17,000 – for its store on London Bridge Walk in the City. Even taking an average across all 28 stores, Richer Sounds still clocks up £5,780 per square
15 foot, ten times more than Marks and Spencer, six times the sales achieved by Sainsbury.

It is profitable too. Sales are up and its operating margin has soared from 3.4 per
20 cent in 1989 to almost thirteen per cent today. Last year Richer Sounds made profits of more than £3m on sales of almost £48 m.

The man behind Richer Sounds' success
25 is founder, managing director and 98 per cent shareholder Julian Richer, a 39-year-old Londoner who, at the age of 14, used to buy and sell candles during the energy crisis of 1974. A likeable bloke who wears
30 his blond hair in a pony tail and operates from a small converted Victorian vinegar factory in Bermondsey, south-east London, he raps out his sales pitch*.

"Even when I was at school I wanted to
35 go into business," he says, "but my age was against me. Property was out – I wasn't old enough to sign a contract. Cars were out – I couldn't drive. So I turned to hi-fi, which was catching on at school. I
40 bought a second-hand Bang and Olufsen for £10, did it up* and sold it for £22." In 1979, at the age of 19, he opened his first shop – the one on London Bridge Walk.

Since then little has changed. In simple
45 terms, Richer Sounds sells discounted hi-fi from tiny, basic shops with low overheads. Stock turnover is rapid and the company's smallness gives it flexibility to take advantage of deals offered by
50 manufacturers on end-of-line or surplus equipment.

The technique has enabled Richer Sounds to secure itself a lucrative niche in a £4 bn audiovisual market dominated by
55 independents.

While leading multiples stock mainly the mass market, volume selling midi systems which became popular in the early 1980s, Richer Sounds sells only hi-fi separates
60 such as tuners and amplifiers. It buys either end-of-line ranges which manufacturers are hoping to off-load before the next, cosmetically different model arrives from Japan, or small orders of current models
65 which, perhaps because of poor stock management, the manufacturer is prepared to sell at a reduced price. Now, as manufacturers' stock control improves, three-quarters of its stock is current
70 models.

Suppliers are keen to do business with this quirky* retailer. "People like Dixons and Comet have so many stores (344 and 262 respectively) that unless you've got 5,000 of
75 a model it's not worth their while putting it into their distribution system," says Clive Roberts, sales and marketing director of Akai. "With Richer, you can do a deal on 30."

Marketing is a key weapon. Richer
80 Sounds advertises regularly in national newspapers ("We buy late space at a discount," Richer says) and in alternative* magazines such as Private Eye and Viz. Every month it produces up to 350,000
85 copies of a brochure pushing the latest offers.

The shops are like walk-in warehouses. Outside, "bargain bins" tout special offers including audio cassettes for 59p. Inside,
90 compact disc players, tuners and speakers from leading names such as Sony, Akai and Marantz are stacked from floor to ceiling. Banners hanging from the ceiling proclaim: "If you've seen it cheaper, we'll beat that
95 price by up to £50."

Good service is another priority. At Richer Sounds staff are trained not to be pushy*. They all attend two training seminars a year at Richer's country house
100 in Yorkshire, where more attention is paid to following the correct administrative procedures.

First-time hi-fi buyers get a call to check that they have plugged in the equipment
105 correctly. Customer receipts include a freephone number they can dial if they have a problem. Richer's own name and office number are supplied too.

The emphasis is on fun. If it's raining,
110 customers are given a free umbrella. In summer they get a Chilly Willy (a type of ice lolly). Other seasonal gifts include mince pies at Christmas and hot-cross buns at Easter. "We have a laugh," Richer
115 says. "We don't take ourselves seriously, but we do take our customers seriously."

*Business*

---

*sales pitch:* what salespeople say to persuade you to buy s.th.
*to do s.th. up:* to repair s.th.

*quirky:* unusual, untypical
*alternative:* not traditional
*pushy:* rude in trying to get what you want

**Vocabulary**

**1** The following words can be used in more than one way. Underline the correct part of speech for each word as it is used in the text on page 27.

| | | | | | |
|---|---|---|---|---|---|
| 1 | stock (*line 47*) | **a** <u>noun</u> | **b** verb | | |
| 2 | deal (*line 49*) | **a** noun | **b** verb | | |
| 3 | surplus (*line 50*) | **a** noun | **b** adjective | | |
| 4 | secure (*line 53*) | **a** verb | **b** adjective | | |
| 5 | market (*line 54*) | **a** noun | **b** verb | | |
| 6 | model (*line 63*) | **a** noun | **b** verb | **c** adjective |
| 7 | order (*line 64*) | **a** noun | **b** verb | | |
| 8 | control (*line 68*) | **a** noun | **b** verb | | |

**2** Complete the passage using appropriate forms of the words in Vocabulary 1.

Sephora is a French beauty supermarket chain which has revolutionised the way that perfumes and fragrances are sold. Sephora operates in a ¹ _market_ that has traditionally been served either by small exclusive perfume stores or by department stores. It ² _____ a wide selection of top products from beauty houses like Chanel and Estée Lauder. Two years ago the original founder of Sephora, Dominique Mandonnaud, was approached by the luxury chain LVMH (Moet Hennessy – Louis Vuitton) with an offer to buy the company and one year later a ³ _____ was made. Today Daniel Richard, the new president, ⁴ _____ all aspects of the business. He has managed to ⁵ _____ the support of many of the big brands in the perfume business and has placed big ⁶ _____ with them. Sephora has ambitious plans for the future, and recently opened a store in New York.

**3** Read the text about the American company Wal-Mart, the world's largest retailer. Replace the words in italics with these words from the text on page 27.

| | | | | |
|---|---|---|---|---|
| **a** | profits (*line 22*) | | **d** | range (*line 61*) |
| **b** | overheads (*line 46*) | | **e** | suppliers (*line 71*) |
| **c** | niche (*line 53*) | | **f** | discount (*line 82*) |

Wal-Mart is already manoeuvring to bring its vision of retailing to the European consumer. In the United States the company operates stores that are often twice as big as their European equivalents and which sell a huge ¹ *selection* _range_ of quality products at a ² *significant price reduction* _____. However, duplicating its success on the old continent may prove to be just as difficult as conquering the New World's markets. Firstly, Europe with its limited space available for building new stores and its high ³ *operating costs* _____ may make it more difficult for the company to produce the same ⁴ *positive financial results* _____ that it has had in the US. In addition to that, it may be difficult to persuade ⁵ *companies that provide goods for retailers* _____ to do business with them in the same way as they do in the US. But with its purchase of the British supermarket chain ASDA, Wal-Mart clearly wants to establish a ⁶ *particular market* _____ for itself in Europe.

**Vocabulary development: compound nouns**

**1** Look at these compound nouns from the text on page 27.

*mass market* (*line 57*)          *special offer* (*line 88*)
*distribution system* (*line 76*)          *leading name* (*line 91*)

What other compounds do you know with these words?

**a** market     **b** system     **c** name     **d** special

**2** Match words from A and B to make compound nouns. Check your answers in a dictionary.

| A | | | B | | |
|---|---|---|---|---|---|
| 1 customer c | 4 sales | | a power | d margin | |
| 2 duty | 5 purchasing | | b goods | e figures | |
| 3 profit | 6 consumer | | c service | f free | |

**Discussion**

Read the extracts below from Julian Richer's book *The Richer Way*. What do you think of the company's approach to customer service? What experiences have you had of good or bad service in shops?

RICHER Sounds

We train our staff to take responsibility. If a customer has a complaint, the first thing the sales assistant does is apologise, even if he or she knows nothing about the circumstances. Then they go on to sort the problem out.

Every month the three winning shops in our customer service competition, the Richer Way League, win a car for a month. Two get Bentleys and one a Jaguar XJS convertible. The car is theirs to use as they wish, we pay the petrol.

At Richer Sounds we hand out gold aeroplane badges for our 'high flyers' – staff who have performed above and beyond the call of duty, perhaps by giving exceptional customer service, or having a really brilliant idea.

## *Language Focus*

**Make** and *do*

**Look at the sentences from the text on page 27.**

*Richer Sounds* **made profits** *of more than £3m. (line 21)*
*Suppliers are keen* **to do business** *with this quirky retailer. (line 71)*

▶▶ *Make* and *do* are very similar in meaning and it is not always easy to know which to use. Turn to page 165 for some guidelines.

**Practice**

**1** Which of the following words are used with *make*, and which with *do*? Use a dictionary to help you.

| | | | |
|---|---|---|---|
| 1 a complaint make | 5 a suggestion | 9 a decision | 13 the typing |
| 2 nothing | 6 a speech | 10 your best | 14 money |
| 3 an exam | 7 a loss | 11 research | 15 a job |
| 4 a mistake | 8 a trip | 12 plans | 16 good |

**2** Complete the questions with the correct form of *make* or *do* and words from exercise 1.

1 Have you ever had to __make__ a __speech__ in front of an audience?

2 What is the longest _____ that you've ever _____ to a foreign country?

3 Have you ever _____ a _____ about the poor quality of something you bought?

4 Is complaining useful? Do you think it _____ any _____ ?

5 Do you prefer to _____ _____ in a library or on the internet?

6 Have you ever _____ any _____ about how customer service could be improved in shops that you have visited?

7 How much _____ do you think you will _____ from your job next year?

8 What _____ have you _____ for the next summer holidays?

**3** In pairs, ask and answer the questions in exercise 2.

## Locating objects

at the front
at the back
at the top
at the bottom
in the middle
on the left
on the right

Do this quick-check exercise as preparation for the listening activity that follows. Look at the picture of a gift shop and complete the sentences with the words in the boxes.

The personal stereos are ¹ at the top of a large display cabinet, ² _____ of some small radios. The hi-fi systems are ³ _____ of the cabinet and the radio cassette recorders are ⁴ _____ . ⁵ _____ is a smaller display case containing a selection of jewellery: there are some earrings ⁶ _____ and some bracelets ⁷ _____ .

above
next to
between
in front of
below
inside
behind

8  The binoculars are on the shelf __below__ the video cameras.
9  The jewellery is _____ the perfume counter.
10  The scarves are _____ the perfume counter.
11  There are some video cassettes _____ a box.
12  There is a 'Sale' sign _____ the jewellery counter.
13  The watches are _____ the earrings and the bracelets.
14  The shop assistant is standing _____ the perfume counter.

## Skills Focus

**Listening**

**1** Where would you expect to find these items on the supermarket plan below?

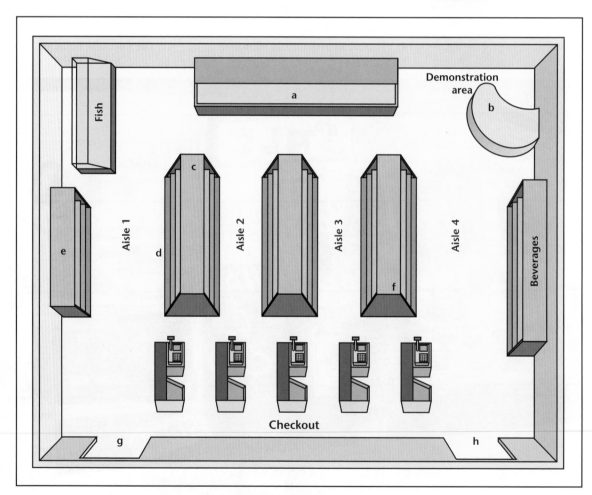

**2** 🖳 Listen to a British supermarket manager talking about the layout and design of her store. Indicate where the items are located on the floor plan.

**3** 🖳 Listen again. What reasons does she give for locating the items in this way?

**Writing 1**

You have been asked to prepare and test a questionnaire that will be used in a consumer survey of customers of a chain of retail bookshops. The questionnaire will be used in interviews with customers to collect the following information:

- customer profile
- customer satisfaction
- attitudes to mail order and e-commerce

In pairs prepare the questions to include in your survey, covering these areas:

| | |
|---|---|
| Customer profiles | • resident / visitor<br>• professional and social background<br>• income<br>• regular / occasional<br>• level of spending<br>• how they discovered the store |
| Customer satisfaction | • service<br>• product range<br>• prices<br>• communication of information<br>• suggestions for improvement |
| Customer attitudes | • experience and opinion of mail order<br>• experience and opinion of e-commerce |

Your questionnaire should contain a mix of question types. Look at the extract from the survey. Which question is:

a a multiple choice question?

b a closed question?

c an open question?

| | | |
|---|---|---|
| **1** | Do you live in this town? | Yes / No |
| **2** | What do you do? | _____ |
| **3** | How much money do you earn per year? | **a** £0 – 10,000 |
| | | **b** £10,000 – 30,000 |
| | | **c** more than £30,000 |

**Speaking**

**1** Student A, look at the photo on page 154. Student B, look at the photo on page 157. Prepare the answers that you think this person would give to each of the questions in the questionnaire.

**2** In pairs, take turns to interview each other.

**Writing 2**

Write a report for the chain of bookshops, based on the information you obtained in the interviews.

# 4 *Franchising*

**Key vocabulary** 🔲 **Franchising** is a business system in which a company (or **franchisor**) sells an individual (or **franchisee**) the right to operate a business using the franchisor's established system or format.

As part of the **franchise agreement** the franchisee pays an initial sum of money, a **franchise fee** or **front end fee**, to the franchisor and agrees to pay a **royalty** or **management services fee** for continuing advice and assistance, which is usually calculated as a percentage of annual turnover. The franchisee may also pay an **advertising fee** to contribute to the franchisor's annual advertising and marketing costs. The franchisee also has to find the necessary capital to open the business.

The franchisor provides an **operations manual** which contains all the information that the franchisee needs to run his or her business. A franchisor may appoint a **master franchisee** to supervise the business in a particular area.

**Lead-in**

1 In pairs, think of as many examples as you can of franchise operations in your country in the following sectors.

| Fast food | Clothing | Motor Trade |
|---|---|---|
| Burger King | Tie Rack | Hertz |
| ..................................... | ..................................... | ..................................... |
| ..................................... | ..................................... | ..................................... |
| ..................................... | ..................................... | ..................................... |
| ..................................... | ..................................... | ..................................... |

2 Student A, make a list of what you think are the principal advantages and disadvantages of the franchise system for a franchisee. Student B, do the same for a franchisor. Compare your lists.

**3** **In pairs, decide if the points below refer to (a) franchisees or (b) franchisors.**

1 They can easily get advice on how to deal with specific problems. `a`

2 They do not have to borrow large amounts of capital to expand.

3 They must respect certain rules.

4 They have to buy supplies from particular sources.

5 They are responsible for national advertising.

6 They can only sell certain products.

7 They have to seek approval before selling the business.

8 They provide regular reports on the level of sales.

9 They can develop their business without having to deal with the problems of recruiting and managing personnel.

⌨ **Listen to a business adviser talking about franchising, and check your answers.**

**Reading**

**1** **You are going to read a text about a typical day in the life of Vanessa Stein, a McDonald's restaurant franchisee. Using the categories given below, make a list of the things you think she has to do during the day.**

a people management

b time management

c networking

d administrative work

e unskilled work

f working at home

**2** **Read the text on the next page and compare your ideas with what she actually does.**

*Tom and Vanessa Stein meet Ronald McDonald.*

**3** **Read the text again and decide if the following statements are true (T) or false (F).**

1 Vanessa Stein starts to organise her day before she gets to work. `T`

2 In the future Vanessa will continue to work in exactly the same way as she does today.

3 The restaurant has not changed since the Steins bought it.

4 The majority of McDonald's restaurants in the UK are not franchises.

5 Vanessa's husband did his training after having been accepted as a franchisee.

6 Every two weeks they receive an independent evaluation of how their business is performing.

7 Vanessa feels that she is best at working directly with customers.

8 All of the administrative work is now done in electronic form.

9 If she didn't have children, she would probably stay longer at work.

# One day in my life

1 **T**hree years ago, Vanessa Stein and her husband Tom took up the fast food challenge: they bought the franchise for a
5 McDonald's restaurant near Leeds.

EARLY MORNING is always an effort for me. The alarm goes off at 6.30 a.m. and then I have 20 minutes' 'thinking time' to make some mental lists before I get
10 up. I live by lists, actually — it's the best way to keep things organised.

Recently I've been arriving at our McDonald's restaurant around 8.30 a.m. I've mastered the computerised accounts
15 now so I'm training one of our floor managers to help me with the administration. Eventually this should give me more time to get involved in other areas of the business such as
20 interviewing staff.

Our restaurant is in a retail park around five miles outside Leeds. Since we bought the franchise in 1995, we've already expanded the seating and now
25 we're looking to expand the restaurant itself. We have to conform to the McDonald's standards (quality, service, cleanliness and value) of course, but the restaurant is actually our own business.
30 We directly employ some 75 staff, order and pay for supplies (from 'preferred suppliers'), take care of any maintenance or refurbishment, arrange local marketing, and so on. Around a
35 quarter of all McDonald's 800 UK restaurants are franchised.

Buying this franchise was a big move for us. Tom (my husband) had to do nine months' training before we could
40 even be considered for a franchise. It paid off though, and we are delighted with this place — it boasts* what was the first Drive-Thru in Yorkshire! — and the surrounding countryside is truly
45 beautiful.

*University of Warwick Network*

By 9.30 a.m. I'm ready for a Bacon & Egg McMuffin and a cup of tea. I'll have a quick chat with our regular breakfast customers before opening the post. This
50 brings invoices from suppliers, marketing and training information from McDonald's (they run the training courses but we pay for our staff to attend), bookings for parties, or perhaps
55 the monthly report from the 'Mystery Diner'.

Mystery Diners make monthly checks on every restaurant and Drive-Thru in the country. All aspects are assessed —
60 food quality and presentation, atmosphere, quality and speed of service, restaurant cleanliness and so on. Staff are often commended by name, so I pass the news on to them and
65 make sure any problems are tackled. We're currently eighth in the UK league which is pretty good.

We have an ongoing dialogue with McDonald's. A field consultant visits us
70 every two or three weeks, and there are regular meetings with other franchisees to share ideas and experience.

Much of my morning is spent updating computer records. Tax office
75 queries, training records, payroll, etc, have to be organised. Staff turnover varies but we can sometimes lose our casual workers when they go to university or decide to go travelling.
80 There are McDonald's all over the world now, so their training here really can open distant doors.

The lunchtime rush* starts around noon. On the rare occasions that we're
85 short staffed (e.g. flu season), I'll muck in and serve customers (memories of my waitressing days at university!). I've even been known to cook fries when necessary. As with any small business,
90 one has to be flexible but I think it's also important to focus your energies where they are most effective. For me, this is behind the scenes admin work.

My own lunch is a salad or chicken
95 sandwich. By this time, my office looks like a bomb site* to the untrained eye. I've usually divided the masses of paperwork into piles ready to tackle them in priority order.
100 I have to head off around 3 p.m. to collect my two sons from school so I generally end up taking work home. I'll finish it in the kitchen, listening to Glenn Miller or the Moody Blues, while also
105 supervising the children's homework, music practice or whatever.

If I'm doing the end-of-month figures, I generally have to work into the early hours. Otherwise I'm in bed any
110 time after 10 p.m. I always have three or four books on the go, Walter Scott or Jane Austen for example, and usually one non-fiction — maybe an autobiography or a political work.
115 I'm glad to say Tom's snoring* was lasered away last summer, so now I can look forward to some undisturbed sleep before another busy day at the restaurant. Now I think of it, I used to
120 have cravings for McDonald's when I was pregnant. It must have been a premonition!

*Vanessa Stein and her second restaurant (under construction)*

| *to boast:* to have as a feature |
| --- |
| *a rush:* a busy period |
| *a bomb site:* a place where a bomb has exploded |
| *to snore:* to breathe noisily when sleeping |

## Vocabulary

**1** Match the words from the text with their corresponding definitions.

| | | | |
|---|---|---|---|
| 1 | a challenge (*line 3*) | **a** | a reservation |
| 2 | maintenance (*line 33*) | **b** | a list of employees and the wages they are paid |
| 3 | a booking (*line 54*) | **c** | work involving written or printed documents |
| 4 | a report (*line 55*) | **d** | to review and include recent changes |
| 5 | to tackle (*line 65*) | **e** | a piece of writing giving information on a particular subject |
| 6 | to update (*line 74*) | | |
| 7 | records (*line 74*) | **f** | to pay special attention |
| 8 | a payroll (*line 75*) | **g** | a difficult but exciting thing to do |
| 9 | to focus (*line 91*) | **h** | keeping equipment in good condition |
| 10 | paperwork (*line 98*) | **i** | to deal with |
| | | **j** | written documents containing information about the past |

**2** Complete the following questionnaire using words from Vocabulary 1.

## Managing your time

① When working with other people do you <u>focus</u> on the work that you can do best?

Yes ☐    No ☐

② When preparing a written _____ do you list the different sections then make a brief summary of what you will include in each?

Yes ☐    No ☐

③ Do you _____ your address book as soon as people move?

Yes ☐    No ☐

④ Do you organise your _____ so that documents are grouped according to subjects?

Yes ☐    No ☐

⑤ Do you enjoy the _____ of doing new and perhaps more complicated work?

Yes ☐    No ☐

⑥ Do you regularly do _____ work to make sure that equipment works efficiently?

Yes ☐    No ☐

⑦ Do you keep clear _____ of the work that you have already done?

Yes ☐    No ☐

⑧ Do you _____ the most difficult pieces of work first?

Yes ☐    No ☐

Change the form of the words where necessary.

**3** In pairs, interview each other. Suggest how your partner could manage his or her time better.

## Vocabulary development: suffixes

Look at the way these nouns are formed.

| noun | stem | suffix |
|---|---|---|
| assessment | assess (*verb*) | + ment |
| effectiveness | effective (*adjective*) | + ness |
| regularity | regular (*adj*) | + ity |
| administration | administer (*verb*) | + ation |

1 Say the nouns and stems. Which nouns have the same main stress as their stem? Which nouns have a different main stress?

2 Using a dictionary, check that you understand the meaning of the words below. Put the words into the correct columns in the table. In which ones does the stress change?

| | | | |
|---|---|---|---|
| confidential | willing | prepare | require |
| organise | similar | present | invest |
| disagree | careless | popular | aware |

| -ment | -ness | -ity | -ation |
|---|---|---|---|
| | | confidential | |

3 What other nouns do you know with these suffixes? Add two more to each column.

## *Language Focus*

### Adverbs

Look at these adverbs expressing time from the text on page 36.

| | |
|---|---|
| *Early morning is **always** an effort for me.* | (line 6) |
| ***Recently** I've been arriving around 8.30 a.m.* | (line 12) |
| ***Eventually** this should give me more time.* | (line 17) |
| *We've **already** expanded the seating.* | (line 24) |
| *We're **currently** eighth in the UK league.* | (line 66) |
| *We can **sometimes** lose our casual workers.* | (line 77) |
| *I've **usually** divided the masses of paperwork.* | (line 87) |

**Match the adverbs to their corresponding definitions.**

1 not long ago          recently

2 after a long time      _____

3 by or before now      _____

4 at the present time      _____

5 on some occasions but not all      _____

6 on most occasions or in most situations      _____

7 all the time      _____

▶▶ **For more information on adverbs and frequency, turn to page 165.**

*Used to do; be used to doing*

**Look at the two photos of the same person.**

**A** *He **used to go** to school in a small village.*

**B** *He's **used to** making presentations.*

**Complete the rules with *used to* + infinitive or *be used to* + *-ing*.**

- _____ is used for things that happened regularly or for a long time in the past but which no longer happen.
- _____ is used when talking about something which is familiar and no longer strange.

▶▶ **For more information on *used to do* and *be used to doing*, turn to page 166.**

Practice

**1 Complete the following sentences about Vanessa Stein by combining the verb in brackets with the appropriate form of *used to* or *be used to*.**

a She ___used to go___ (go) to university.

b She _____ (help) her children with their homework.

c She _____ (chat) with regular customers.

d She _____ (attend) meetings with other McDonald's franchisees.

e Her husband _____ (snore).

f She _____ (work) as a waitress at university.

g The restaurant _____ (have) fewer seats.

h She _____ (take) work to do at home.

**2 Write a short description of a typical day in your life, using *used to*, *be used to* and time adverbs. Try to show how your life today is different to what it was before.**

## Skills Focus

Reading **1** Match the words and examples below with their definitions from *The New Longman Business English Dictionary*.

① **working capital** also **operating capital** *We will have to make our entire technical staff redundant because we have run out of operating capital.* | *the need for working capital to expand operations*

② **return** *n* **3** [C] *Over 12.2 million taxpayers filed federal returns electronically this year.* | *allegations that the company had falsified its corporate tax return.*

⑤ **charge**[1]*n* **1** [C,U] *Vodafone is cutting its call charges by 15%.* | *You can search the D&B database free of charge.* **+for**: *Politicians are opposing higher charges for electricity.* C usually plural] *concern at the level of bank charges charged by some of the High Street banks*

③ **fixtures and fittings** *BrE* abbreviation **f & f**; **fixtures** *AmE n* [plural] *Ask the seller of the house to list the smaller fixtures and fittings that are to be left.*

⑥ **gross margin** also **gross profit margin** *n* [C] *Selling, general and administrative expenses were more than 30%, so IBM needed a gross margin of around 40% just to make any reasonable profit.*

④ **trademark** *n* [C] *The company used names similar to well-known trademarks to sell cheap imitations.*

⑦ **market research** also **marketing research**; abbreviation **MR** *Market research showed "good potential" for marketing the aftershave to Hispanic men.* | *Performance Research, a sports marketing research company*

---

ⓐ LAW, PROPERTY things such as lights etc that are fixed or fastened to a house or building and are included as part of the property when it is sold:

ⓓ the difference between the price that a product or service is sold for and the cost of producing it, without including OVERHEADS (=general costs not related to particular products or services):

ⓑ MARKETING the activities involved in obtaining information about a particular market, including how much of a product is being sold, who is buying it, why they are buying it etc, or information about what they might buy:

ⓔ money used by a business to carry on production and keep trading, for example to pay employees and suppliers before money is received for goods sold:

ⓕ a name, sign, or design used on a product to show it is made by a particular company. Trademarks are protected by law:

ⓒ an amount of money paid for services or goods: money charged by a bank for services such as paying cheques, sending out bank statements etc:

ⓖ TAX an official form that is filled in and sent to the tax authorities so they can calculate how much tax is owed:

**2** Bang & Olufsen is a Danish franchisor which manufactures and sells hi-fi and television equipment in 40 countries. Use the words from exercise 1 to complete the franchisee brochure opposite.

## Your Investment

£

**OPENING STOCK / WORKING CAPITAL**
Purchase of display and back-up stock
General [1] _working capital_     43,000

**SHOPFITTING**
Installation costs / contractors
An allowance for fitting the shop:
Security systems, air-conditioning, [2] _____
ISDN and telephone lines     30,000

**FRANCHISE FEE PACKAGE**
[3] _____ and territory evaluation, property search and survey
5 weeks of induction training in Denmark and UK for two people, retail
software package, operations manual, intensive opening support     11,000

**MARKET LAUNCH FEE**
Promotional launch package
Bang & Olufsen profiled customer base for direct marketing purposes
Opening event, public relations support
Launch programme defined by franchisee and Bang & Olufsen     7,500

**LEGAL AND BANK COSTS**
Lease negotiations, bank [4] _____     4,000

**TRAVEL AND ACCOMMODATION**
Subsistence expenses for the initial training period for two people     2,000

**FRANCHISE FEE**
The leasing of the right to operate a Bang & Olufsen Franchise and the
use of [5] _____ and know-how     NIL

| **TOTAL INVESTMENT** | **97,500** |
|---|---|

**VALUE ADDED TAX**
Reclaimable on the first VAT [6] _____, estimated
to be sufficient to cover additional working capital     17,000

| **TOTAL FUNDING REQUIREMENT** | **114,500** |
|---|---|

**FUNDING**
Up to 70% of finance can be provided by the clearing banks
(subject to status)     80,000

| **MINIMUM CASH INJECTION BY OWNER** | **34,500** |
|---|---|

## Your Reward

| | Year 1 | Year 2 | Year 3 |
|---|---|---|---|
| Sales | 378,000 | 510,000 | 612,000 |
| [7] _____ | 34.9% | 34.9% | 35.9% |
| Total Operating Costs | 79,000 | 96,000 | 116,000 |
| Management Fee (1% of turnover) | 3,780 | 5,100 | 6,000 |
| **Result** | **49,000** | **76,000** | **98,000** |

**Listening**

**1** ▭ Listen to Janis Errickson, a franchisee with Dunkin' Donuts, talking about the organisation that she is a part of. Complete the diagram below.

# DUNKIN' DONUTS®

# Baskin (31) Robbins

# ALLIED DOMECQ

| Parent company: |
| --- |
| 4 _____ |

| Franchise company: | Dunkin' Donuts | 5 | 8 |
| --- | --- | --- | --- |
| Specialises in: | 1 | 6 | sandwiches |
| First franchise: | 2 | 1950 | 9 |
| Minimum capital required: | 3 | 7 | $100,000 |

**2** ▭ Now listen to Janis talking about how to run a franchise successfully. What reasons does she give for paying particular attention to the following things?

1 Preparation

2 Management

3 Money management

4 Vision

5 Faith

**Speaking**

Work in pairs. Student A, read the franchise profile on page 156 and Student B, read the one on page 161. Use the information to make a short presentation of the business to your partner, explaining how it operates and what investments are required from franchisees. When you have finished your presentations, compare the two franchises and decide which you would be most interested in and why.

**Writing**

e-mail

The tone of an e-mail message can be like writing or speaking. If you are writing to someone you don't know then you should address this person as *Dear Mr/Mrs/Ms X*. You should keep the style of your message quite formal and finish with *Yours sincerely* or *Best regards*. However, if you are writing to a friend, you can start with *Hi* or *Hello* and write as if you were speaking to the person directly.

**1** You have decided to e-mail the International Franchise Association, a non-profit making advisory organisation, for more information on the franchise that your partner told you about.

Look at the screen for sending an e-mail and match the labels to the corresponding sections.

a e-mail address of people you wish to send a copy of the message to

b key words that describe the message you are sending

c the text of your e-mail

**d** the icon for transmitting your message

**e** the icon that allows you to include a file with your message

**f** e-mail address of people you wish to send a copy of your message to, without them knowing that it is a copy

**g** the icon for sending a message that you have received to another person

**h** the icon for sending an answer to a message you have received

**i** the address of the person you are writing to

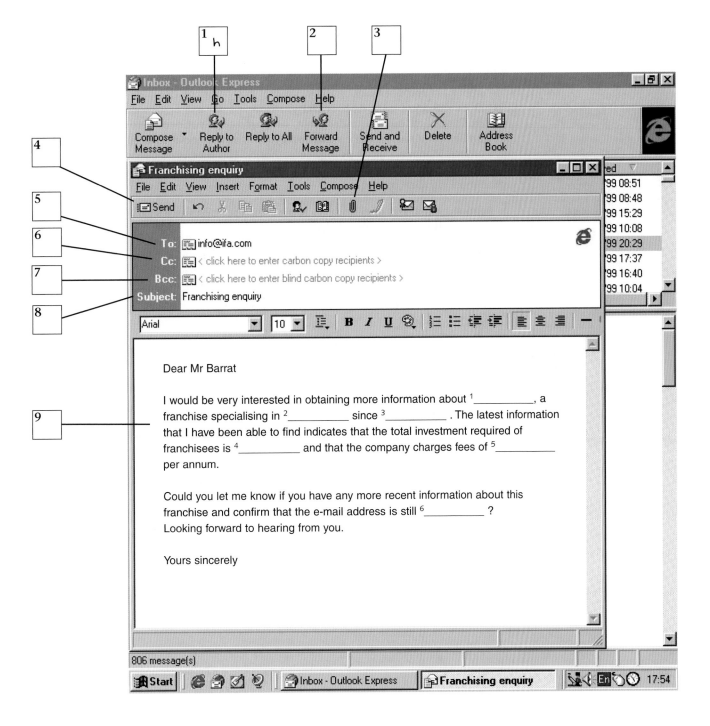

**2** Complete the e-mail message using information from Speaking on page 42.

# *International Business Styles*

Key vocabulary The characteristics of management often vary according to **national culture**, which can determine how managers are trained, how they lead people and how they approach their jobs.

The amount of responsibility of any individual in a company depends on the position that he or she occupies in its **hierarchy**. Managers, for example, are responsible for leading the people directly under them, who are called **subordinates**. To do this successfully, they must use their **authority**, which is the right to take decisions and give orders. Managers often **delegate** authority. This means that employees at lower levels in the company hierarchy can use their **initiative**, that is make decisions without asking their manager.

**Lead-in**  **1** **Read the portraits of managers in five different countries and decide which country each one corresponds to.**

- Germany
- Poland
- Sweden
- The United Kingdom
- The United States

**1**
**Managers from this country**

- consider professional and technical skills to be very important.
- have a strong sense of authority.
- respect the different positions in the hierarchy of their companies.
- clearly define how jobs should be done.
- are very loyal to their companies and expect their subordinates to obey them.
- are often older than in other countries.

**2**
**Managers from this country**

- receive a general education.
- delegate authority.
- take a practical approach to management.
- have relatively formal relationships at work.
- encourage their employees to work individually.
- believe it is important to continue education and training at work.

**3**
**Managers from this country**

- consider social qualities to be as important as education.
- encourage their employees to take an interest in their work.
- pay close attention to the quality of working life.
- do not use as much authority as in other countries.
- appreciate low-level decision-making.
- are often women.

**4**
**Managers from this country**

- generally attend business schools.
- communicate easily and informally at work.
- admire the qualities of a leader.
- expect everyone to work hard. Individual performance is measured and initiative is rewarded.
- have competitive and aggressive attitudes to work.
- often accept innovation and change.

**5**
**Managers from this country**

- have either gained their experience in state-owned enterprises or are competitive self-starters.
- older managers hold technical degrees rather than business qualifications.
- work very long hours and expect their subordinates to do so.
- are extremely innovative, optimistic and determined.
- are quick to invest in the development of new products, market techniques and methods of production and distribution.

**2** In groups, discuss the advantages and disadvantages of each approach to management, and say which one you would find the most attractive. Do any of these profiles correspond to management practices in your country?

# Learning to cope with corporate culture clashes

1 The dos and don'ts of travelling abroad are a potential minefield for the unprepared traveller. If you spit in some countries, you could end up in prison. In others, spitting is a competitive sport.

2 *The Centre for International Briefing has spent 40 years preparing the wary traveller for such pitfalls.* Though it may sound like a covert operation for aspiring secret agents, what the Centre does is prepare travellers for encounters with new social and business customs worldwide. To date, over 50,000 people have passed through its headquarters at Farnham Castle in Surrey. 'There are two broad tracks to our training programme,' explains Jeff Toms, Marketing Director. 'One covers business needs, the other social etiquette*. For example, business travellers need to know how decision-making works.'

3 _____ In China, it may be necessary to have government involved in any decisions taken. And in India, people are sometimes late for a scheduled appointment.

4 _____ While we are familiar with the short firm handshake in this part of the world, in the Middle East the hand is held in a loose grip for a longer time. In Islamic cultures, showing the soles of your feet is a sign of disrespect and crossing your legs is seen as offensive.

5 _____ Jeff Toms tells the story of a British employee asked to post a letter by her Indonesian employer. 'She knew the letter was too late for the six o'clock post, so she decided to hold it until the eight o'clock one. Her boss saw the letter on her desk and sacked her for not posting it immediately. In Western cultures, we believe in empowering* people and rewarding them for using initiative, but other cultures operate on the basis of obeying direct orders.'

6 _____ 'For them, the most senior person at the meeting will say very little, and the person doing most of the talking is not very important.' Doherty has spent 12 of his 16 years with the IDA working abroad in the USA, Germany, South-East Asia and Japan.

7 _____ 'With a population of 125 million condensed into a narrow strip of land, private space for the Japanese is virtually non-existent. You can't worry about your personal space in a packed train when people are standing on your feet.'

## Tiptoeing through the minefield

8 *Do*
- Show an interest in, and at least an elementary knowledge of the country you are visiting;
- Learn a few words of the language – it will be seen as a compliment;
- Be sensitive to countries who have bigger and better-known neighbours, and try not to confuse Canadians with Americans, New Zealanders with Australians, Belgians with French;
- Familiarise yourself with the basics of business and social etiquette. As a starting point, learning how to greet people is very important.

*Don't*
- Assume you won't meet any communication problems because you speak English. You may think you are paying somebody a compliment by telling them their business is going a bomb*, Americans will infer you think it is failing.
- Appear too reserved. As Americans are generally more exuberant* than their European colleagues, they may equate reserve with lack of enthusiasm.

*The Irish Independent*

---

*to empower: to give s.b. more control
*to go a bomb (GB): to be successful
*etiquette: polite behaviour

*to bomb (US): to go badly
*exuberant: happy, cheerful, full of energy

**Reading**

**1** **Read the text opposite about The Centre for International Briefing, which runs training courses for business people travelling to other countries, and complete the paragraphs using the sentences below.**

**a** 'In a country like Japan, the notion of personal space which we value so much simply has no meaning,' he says.

**b** In Asian cultures most of it takes place behind the scenes.

**c** The difference between understanding a culture and ignoring its conventions can be the measure of success or failure abroad.

**d** The Centre for International Briefing has spent 40 years preparing the wary traveller for such pitfalls.

**e** John Doherty, International Marketing Director with the Irish Industrial Development Authority, explains how you can easily talk yourself into trouble at a business meeting in Japan:

**f** Greetings, gestures and terms of address are all potential hazards abroad.

**2** **In pairs, discuss these questions.**

**a** What social etiquette is important for business travellers to your country?

**b** In your experience, what can be difficult about dealing with British or Americans?

**Vocabulary**

**1** **Match the words from the text with their corresponding definitions.**

| | | | |
|---|---|---|---|
| **1** | abroad (*para 1*) | **a** | something done in a society because of tradition |
| **2** | a minefield (*para 1*) | **b** | able to understand others' feelings |
| **3** | a pitfall (*para 2*) | **c** | in or to a foreign country |
| **4** | a custom (*para 2*) | **d** | something that expresses admiration |
| **5** | etiquette (*para 2*) | **e** | to show or represent |
| **6** | scheduled (*para 3*) | **f** | rude or insulting |
| **7** | to be a sign of (*para 4*) | **g** | a situation with hidden dangers |
| **8** | offensive (*para 4*) | **h** | formal rules for polite behaviour in society |
| **9** | a compliment (*para 8*) | **i** | a likely problem |
| **10** | sensitive (*para 8*) | **j** | arranged for a certain time |

## 2 Complete the passage using words from Vocabulary 1 in the correct form.

**Gift giving in the international business context**

In Great Britain and the United States corporate gift giving is not a very popular
¹ _custom_ ; people can spend their entire working lives without ever receiving a
corporate gift. However, gift giving is sometimes an integral part of the
negotiation process when doing business ²_____ . It is important to learn
about the ³_____ of gift giving before sending or taking a gift to an
international client or business partner, or you may find that your gesture appears
⁴_____ . For example, in China a desk clock ⁵_____ bad luck or death.
It is also interesting to note that the receiver never opens a gift in front of the
giver as that would signify that the content was more important than the act of
giving. Waiting for the person to open your gift would show
that you were not ⁶_____ to Chinese culture. In France,
don't give something with your company logo, as they find
items like this impersonal and in bad taste. Giving knives in
Italy, Russia or Argentina could lead to problems in
establishing a deal as this signifies cutting off the relationship!
Giving flowers is another possible ⁷_____ . In England,
Australia and Canada, some people see white lilies as a
symbol of death while in Germany, yellow and white
chrysanthemums could be seen this way.

**Vocabulary development: prefixes**

In the text on page 46, the word *non-existent* (*para 7*) consists of the prefix *non-*
and the main word *existent*. The prefix gives the word the opposite meaning.

**1** Match the prefixes with the groups of adjectives.

| dis- | il- | im- | in- | ir- | un- |
|------|-----|-----|-----|-----|-----|

| a | _im_ | possible | probable | precise |
|---|------|----------|----------|---------|
| b | _____ | honest | similar | organised |
| c | _____ | popular | economical | manageable |
| d | _____ | legible | legal | logical |
| e | _____ | complete | expensive | efficient |
| f | _____ | regular | relevant | responsible |

In which of the six lists do the adjectives have something in common?

**2** Add prefixes to the following adjectives.

| a | _un_likely | b | respectful | c | polite | d | rational |
|---|------------|---|------------|---|--------|---|----------|
| e | literate | f | frequent | g | lawful | h | proportionate |
| i | resistible | j | liberal | k | mature | l | helpful |

**3** Add one more adjective to each group above.

## *Language Focus*

**The imperative**

The imperative has the same form as the infinitive without *to*. It is used:

- to give orders or instructions, for example on packaging, labels or documents.
  **Fill in** *the form in block capitals.*
  **Empty** *the contents into boiling water.*

- to give strong advice.
  **Avoid** *showing the soles of your feet in the Middle East.*

If you want to be emphatic you can use *do* or *always*.
**Do learn** *a few words of the language.*
**Always familiarise** *yourself with the basics.*

The negative is formed by using *don't* or *never*.
**Don't appear** *too reserved.*
**Never cross** *your legs in the Middle East.*

▶▶ **For more information on the imperative, turn to page 166.**

**Practice**

**Complete the sentences below using the expressions in the box in the correct imperative form, positive or negative.**

| study | invest | be flexible |
|---|---|---|
| expect (x 2) | assume | judge |
| increase | beware | leave |

1 <u>Leave</u> attitudes like 'my way is the only way' behind.
2 _____ , be curious and fascinated instead.
3 _____ some time in preparing yourself for encounters with other business and cultural styles.
4 _____ your understanding of the countries and cultures you are visiting by attending cross-cultural seminars.
5 _____ the general protocol and etiquette of the country or countries you are visiting.
6 _____ delays, frequent changes in plans and cancellations.

7 _____ to have easy access to your e-mail while on the road. In some cases it may be impossible to log on to your internet server remotely.

And I thought overseas travel was fun...

8 _____ when negotiating prices.
9 _____ that market or sales techniques that work in your country, work in others.
10 _____ of drinking too much alcohol over a business lunch; you might need to make important decisions.

## Adjectives of nationality

Look at these examples from the text on page 46.

**Country:** *In China, it may be necessary to have government involved.* (*para 3*)
**Nationality:** *Jeff Toms tells the story of a British employee.* (*para 5*)
**Inhabitant:** When talking about the inhabitants of a country we generally use the adjective of nationality.
*Private space for the Japanese is virtually non-existent.* (*para 7*)

▶▶ For more information on adjectives of nationality, turn to page 166.

## Practice

Match the words from the three columns below to make sentences. Transform the names of the countries into adjectives.

Example: *IBM is an American computer company.*

| | | | | |
|---|---|---|---|---|
| 1 | Hola | Denmark | furniture retailer |
| 2 | Ferrari | Norway | newspaper |
| 3 | Evian | France | computer company |
| 4 | Mateus Rosé | Holland | beer |
| 5 | IBM | Spain | electronics company |
| 6 | AGFA | Finland | industrial company |
| 7 | Philips | USA | mineral water |
| 8 | Carlsberg | Britain | seaport |
| 9 | IKEA | Turkey | airline |
| 10 | BBC 1 | Portugal | car manufacturer |
| 11 | Olympic | Russia | photographic company |
| 12 | Pravda | Germany | wine |
| 13 | Aker AS | Greece | mobile phone company |
| 14 | Istanbul | Italy | weekly magazine |
| 15 | Nokia | Sweden | television channel |

## *Skills Focus*

### Writing

#### A memo

A memorandum (or memo) is a very common form of business communication which is exchanged between members of the same organisation. The memo usually focuses on one message or piece of information, and often requests action to be taken. It may be sent to a single person or a group of people.

There are many different techniques used in memo writing, but several basic rules should always be applied:

- Since memos are a little less formal than business letters, it is best to use simple language and a neutral tone.

- Keep your memo clear. Use short, simple sentences.

- A memo should not be any longer than one page. Most people do not have time to read long memos.

- The opening and closing formula can be more direct, and less formal than in a letter.

Pharmatec Pharmaceuticals is sending a delegation of executives to Japan for the first time to negotiate an important contract, so the executives are going to attend a series of seminars given by Tomomi Moriwake, a Japanese consultant.

**Read the memo from the Managing Director to the Human Resources Manager and match the parts of the memo (1–6) with the descriptions (a–f)**

# Memorandum

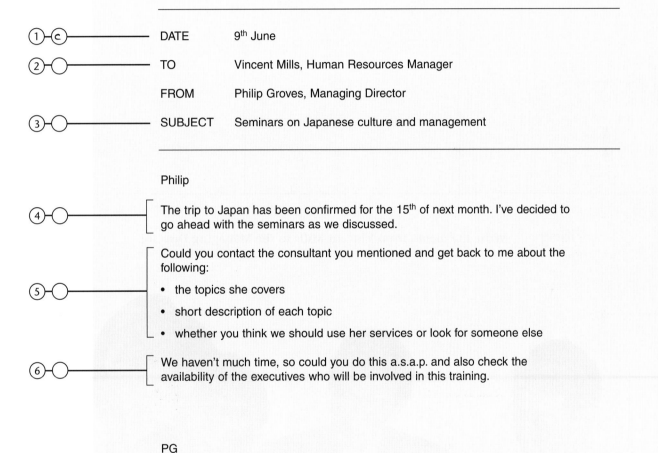

① —c——————— DATE　　　9th June

② —O——————— TO　　　　Vincent Mills, Human Resources Manager

　　　　　　　　　　FROM　　　Philip Groves, Managing Director

③ —O——————— SUBJECT　　Seminars on Japanese culture and management

Philip

④ —O——— The trip to Japan has been confirmed for the 15th of next month. I've decided to go ahead with the seminars as we discussed.

　　　　　Could you contact the consultant you mentioned and get back to me about the following:

⑤ —O———
* the topics she covers
* short description of each topic
* whether you think we should use her services or look for someone else

⑥ —O——— We haven't much time, so could you do this a.s.a.p. and also check the availability of the executives who will be involved in this training.

PG

    **a** The 'body' of the memo.
    **b** A short heading which tells you what the memo is about.
    **c** When the memo is sent.
    **d** The conclusion of the memo, which often recommends a course of action.
    **e** Name of the person to whom the memo is sent.
    **f** A brief introduction to the memo giving the most important information.

Listening    🔊   Listen to the Japanese consultant discussing the content of her seminars and make notes under the following headings. These notes will help you to organise the memo which you will be writing.

| Emphasis on the group | Human relationships | Japanese managers |
|---|---|---|
| | | |

Writing    Write the memo from Vincent Mills to the Managing Director.

**Role-play**  Giving and asking for advice

**Student A**

You are a cross-cultural consultant hired by a foreign executive who is going to do business for the first time in your country or a country you know well. Prepare some advice to give your client about business practices. Use these topics to help you.

**Use of language:**  addressing / greeting (formal? informal?)

**Non-verbal communication:**  handshaking, gestures and silence?

**Business negotiations:**  punctuality / respecting the agenda?
negotiating styles; direct? indirect? When is the right moment to mention money?

**Socialising:**  attitudes: gift giving, eating, humour?
conversation topics (religion? politics? salaries?)

The following structures will help you to answer the questions that your client (Student B) will ask.

*You should always / never …*
*I would advise you to …*
*Don't forget …*
*Never …*
*Do …*
*Always …*
*It is important / essential to …*
*It would be a good idea to …*

**Student B**

You are a business person going to negotiate in a foreign country. As part of the preparation for your trip, you have arranged to meet a consultant (Student A) who is an expert on the culture of the country. Using the headings below, make a list of questions to ask him / her.

**Use of language**
**Non-verbal communication**
**Business negotiations**
**Socialising**

Examples:
*first name?*
*greetings?*
*business cards?*
*topics to avoid?*

# Review 1

## Grammar check

**1 Underline the correct forms of the words in italics.**

My name is Alexander Herrbach, I'm a 27-year-old mechanical engineer and at the moment I [1] _am working_ / _have worked_ for a company in the South of Germany where I [2] _am_ / _have been_ since I [3] _have left_ / _left_ France last July. Actually I have [4] _already_ / _recently_ spent most of my life here in Germany because that is where I [5] _complete_ / _completed_ my secondary and university education.

Before I [6] _have graduated_ / _graduated_ I went on a European study programme in [7] _Britain_ / _British_ for one year. After university I [8] _join_ / _joined_ an American company in Berlin and subsequently I [9] _moved_ / _have moved_ to France when the headquarters were transferred there.

In my present job my duties [10] _are including_ / _include_ supervising our activities in what we call 'the rest of the world'. Basically this [11] _means_ / _is meaning_ that I'm responsible for giving our representatives there our commercial and technical support. It's a new job for me so I'm [12] _currently_ / _usually_ learning exactly what it [13] _involves_ / _is involving_. However, there are many new things that I'm still not [14] _used to do_ / _used to doing_.

At present our company [15] _is expanding_ / _has expanded_ its activities outside of its main market, which is Europe, and we [16] _develop_ / _are developing_ our network of agents, particularly in South Africa and Brazil.

I [17] _used to think_ / _am used to thinking_ that it was enough to speak two foreign languages but I now realise that the more languages you speak the better you communicate. That is why I [18] _always_ / _sometimes_ take every opportunity to develop my language skills.

In order to prepare for my future as a manager I [19] _intend_ / _have intended_ to study for an MBA. In fact my boss [20] _has agreed_ / _agrees_ to give me one day a week off work for this.

**2 Underline the mistake in each sentence, and correct it.**

1 We have received several applications for the position; one of the best ones is from a <u>French</u>.
   French person

2 Credit cards can be used in the checkout.

3 The company was founded in Germany and is still faithful to its Dutch origins.

4 Have you received the letter I sent about the mistake your company did?

5 I'm not very tall, so it's difficult to reach items at the bottom in the supermarket.

6 What did you like most about the last work you did?

7 The position of Marketing Director is below that of sales assistant.

8 The Finn company Nokia is one of the leaders in the mobile phone sector.

9 A well-written covering letter can do the difference between a successful and an unsuccessful application.

10 The Ireland President announced her intention to encourage foreign investment.

**3 Complete the sentences below, using the words in the box to show what changes have occurred between last year and this year. Use each word once.**

| decline | drop | increased |
|---------|------|-----------|
| raised | risen | rise |
| gone up | fell | reduction |
| reduced | | |

1 Tax last year: 10%  Tax this year: 12%
   The government has __raised__ tax.

2 Cars last year: 2 million
   Cars this year: 1.8 million
   There has been a _____ in car production.

3 Price last year: $50  Price this year: $35
   The price of this product has been _____ .

4 Employees last year: 40
   Employees this year: 75
   There has been a _____ in the number of employees.

5 Orders last year: 10 million
   Orders this year: 8 million
   Orders _____ this year.

6 Investment last year: $500,000
   Investment this year: $650,000
   The company has _____ investment in new equipment.

7 Franchisees last year: 120
   Franchisees this year: 300
   The number of franchisees has _____ .

8 Budget last year: 100%
   Budget this year: –25%
   There has been a _____ in the budget.

9 Franchise fees last year: £30,000
   Franchise fees this year: £35,000
   Franchise fees have _____ .

10 Sales per outlet last year: $1,000,000
   Sales per outlet this year: $850,000
   There has been a _____ in sales per outlet.

## Vocabulary check

**1** Complete the boxes with the words and expressions from the list below that are most commonly associated with each theme.

| Company Structure | Recruitment |
|---|---|
| _____ | _____ |
| _____ | _____ |
| _____ | _____ |
| _____ | _____ |

| Retailing | Franchising |
|---|---|
| *department store* | _____ |
| _____ | _____ |
| _____ | _____ |
| _____ | _____ |

| Management |
|---|
| _____ |
| _____ |
| _____ |
| _____ |

department store
operation manual
organisation chart
corporate culture
applicant
authority
interview
headquarters
front end fee
discount

mass market
royalty
IT
subordinate
CV
subsidiary
head-hunter
management services fee
range
decision-making

**2** Replace the words and expressions in italics with words from exercise 1 which are similar in meaning, in the correct form.

There were hundreds of [1] *people who sent letters of application* __*applicants*__ for the post of Chief Buyer in one of our [2] *large city centre outlets selling a variety of different products* _____. Our Personnel Department couldn't possibly study all the [3] *documents containing education and employment history* _____ which we received. They had to call on the services of a [4] *search firm* _____ to help them compile a short list of the most suitable people to [5] *meet with to talk about their experience and qualifications* _____ . We were looking for someone with good communication and organisational skills. Furthermore this is a position that requires someone who is capable of [6] *deciding what action to take* _____ and can get [7] *the people who work under him / her* _____ to reach their objectives. The job involves monitoring performance and ensuring that our large [8] *variety of products* _____ is always up to date. The final selection process was organised at our [9] *main office* _____ . The successful candidate is now being given extensive training in order to help him to adapt to our [10] *company philosophy and style of working* _____ .

**3** Complete the extract from the letter of application below, using an expression from A in the correct form and a preposition from B.

| A | B |
|---|---|
| to believe | from |
| to collaborate | in (x4) |
| to result | to |
| to report | on |
| to benefit | for (x2) |
| to apply | with |
| to work | |
| to be responsible | |
| to be involved | |
| to succeed | |

I am writing to [1] __*apply for*__ the position of Senior Computer Programmer. As you can see in my enclosed curriculum vitae, I already hold the position of Team Manager where I [2] _____ three programmers who [3] _____ me directly. As an additional part of my job I have to [4] _____ other Team Managers from different divisions of the company. I have recently [5] _____ a major research and development project where my team was asked to [6] _____ a new network application for the company's accounts department. During this project we [7] _____ solving a number of complex technical problems. This programme is now in the final stages and once complete will [8] _____ considerable savings in both cost and time. While I am happy in my present position, I would welcome the challenge of managing a bigger team. I firmly [9] _____ the value of teamwork and power sharing which I know are important elements in the working environment of your company. Moreover, I feel sure that on both a personal and professional level I would be able to [10] _____ the opportunity of working for a company with such a well-established international reputation.

# 6 *Banking*

**Key vocabulary** 📼 The banking sector in the United Kingdom is made up of a variety of institutions supervised by the country's central bank, **The Bank of England**. This bank looks after the government's finance and monetary policy and acts as banker to other banks. However, for the general public and many businesses, banking services are provided by **commercial banks**, or **clearing banks**, which have branches throughout the country. These banks offer a wide range of services which include accepting deposits, making loans and managing customers' accounts. **Merchant banks**, on the other hand, do not deal with the public but specialise in services for companies or corporate customers. They are particularly active in arranging mergers and acquisitions and in advising on aspects of corporate finance.

**Lead-in**

**1** **In pairs, make a list of the different services that banks in your country provide for the general public. Tick the services that you use.**

Example: *current account* ✓

**HSBC** ◆X◆

**2** 📼 **Listen to Eleanor Stevens, an HSBC Bank branch manager, describing the bank that she manages. Make notes under these headings.**

Location
_____

Number of customers
_____

Opening hours
_____

Services offered
_____

Number of employees
_____

Role in the community
_____

**How do the services offered by this bank compare with those available from a bank of a similar size in your country?**

## 3 Match the banking words with the illustrations below.

1 chequebook (US checkbook) ز
2 bank statement
3 credit card or debit card
4 bill (US check)
5 traveller's cheques
    (US traveler's checks)

6 bank notes (US bills)
7 coins
8 keyboard
9 screen
10 cash machine or cashpoint
    (US ATM)

(a)

(b)

(c)

(d)

(e)

(f)

(g)

(h)

(i)

(j)

## 4 Which of the items would you use if you needed to

1 check how much money you had in your bank account several weeks ago?
2 take money with you for a visit to a foreign country?
3 see how much you have to pay for the electricity you used last month?
4 send payment by post?
5 take money out of your account on a Sunday?

**Reading**

**1** In pairs, make a list of the services that a company would expect from a bank.

**2** Read the text which describes the Bank of Scotland's Home and Office Banking System (HOBS), and see which points in your list are mentioned.

# PICTURE
## *the scene*

1 *It's 6.30 on Monday morning. You're on a shuttle en-route for London and a crucial meeting that will play a large part in deciding the future of your business. You need the most up-to-date financial information you can get, including*
5 *details of cheques presented\* today. But it's an hour and a half until the bank opens.*
*Now you can unlock all the information you need for the meeting quickly and simply. Just boot up your laptop and, using data downloaded from Bank of Scotland's central*
10 *computers, the information is there at your fingertips. You can group accounts to give you an overall view of your business's financial position, focus on the net position of a particular area of the business – even prepare reports.*
*HOBS, Bank of Scotland's Home and Office Banking Service,*
15 *is perfect for people like you who are too busy running their business to worry about fitting in to banking hours.*

THE KEY TO ...financial control... (1)

With HOBS in your office, you can

- access comprehensive, up-to-the-minute
20   information on all your sterling, foreign currency and credit card accounts.

- initiate BACS\* payments to pay salaries, wages, suppliers etc.

- initiate CHAPS\* and International payments.

25 - transfer money instantly between your accounts.

- check all your standing orders and direct debits.

- locate specific transactions quickly using a range of search criteria.

- open an exclusive HOBS Investment Account to
30   make surplus\* funds work really hard for you.

THE KEY TO ............................................. (2)

With HOBS, you no longer have to devote valuable time to routine transactions, or fit your business into banking hours. Control your accounts whenever it suits you, 24 hours a day,
35 7 days a week.

THE KEY TO ............................................. (3)

Connecting to HOBS costs just the price of a local phone call from anywhere in the UK. Further built-in features, such as off-line\* processing, mean that the amount of time you
40 need to be connected to HOBS is kept to a minimum.

THE KEY TO ............................................. (4)

A series of advanced, built-in features maintained in your PC allow you to restrict access to designated users, and to specify exactly what information each individual can access
45 and what transactions they may carry out.

THE KEY TO ............................................. (5)

Corporate HOBS has been designed to dovetail\* with your existing financial software, giving you a choice of account reporting and payment processing facilities and a smooth
50 transfer of account information to and from other packages such as Sage ® or Pegasus ® .
The BACS Direct facility is ideal for the distribution of wages, salaries or expenses, and the template function saves you from having to re-key similar data each week / month. A
55 database of beneficiaries [suppliers, employees] is maintained on your PC.

THE KEY TO ............................................. (6)

When you have urgent payments to make, the CHAPS function enables you to send funds for same-day credit
60 subject to a cut-off time of 3pm.

*The Bank of Scotland*

---

\**to present a cheque:* to pass a cheque from the receiver's bank to the payer's bank, for payment
\**surplus:* extra
\**off-line:* not connected to the Internet
\**to dovetail:* to fit together perfectly

\**BACS:* Bankers Automated Clearing Services. This company works with the banks to initiate computerised payments.
\**CHAPS:* Clearing House Automated Payment System. This is a system for dealing with high-value payments.

3 **Complete the headings in the text with these words.**

a  Security
b  Cost-effectiveness
c  Financial Control

d  Flexibility
e  Convenience
f  Priority Payments

4 **Read the text again and decide if the following statements are true (T) or false (F).**

1  You can only use HOBS during normal banking hours. ☐

2  HOBS cannot provide information about accounts in dollars. ☐

3  The telephone charges for using HOBS are the same all over the UK. ☐

4  You can control who can obtain information from the system. ☐

5  Using CHAPS, you can make a payment to someone and they will always receive it on the same day. ☐

**Vocabulary**   1 **Complete the crossword using words from the text.**

## CLUES

### Across

1  (*n*) Regular payments from a bank account to an organisation. (*line 26*) (2 words)

4  (*n*) Money your employer pays you every month. (*line 22*)

6  (*adj*) The amount that remains after everything else has been deducted. (*line 12*)

9  (*n*) Money you make when you work, usually paid weekly, in cash. (*line 22*)

10  (*adj*) Ordinary and boring. (*line 33*)

12  (*v*) The calls are cheap; they don't _____ much. (*line 37*)

17  (*n*) The currency unit of the United Kingdom, based on the pound. (*line 20*)

18  (*v*) To find the space or time for something. (*line 33*)

20  (*n*) Money used in another country. (*line 20*) (2 words)

### Down

1  (*n*) Giving things to a large group of people. (*line 52*)

2  (*n*) The business of looking after people's money. (*line 33*)

3  (*n*) Movements of money into or out of customers' accounts. (*line 33*)

5  (*n*) Giving information. (*line 49*)

7  (*adj*) Very important, needed very quickly. (line 58)

8  (*n*) Information or facts. (*line 9*)

11  (*v*) To make something do what you want it to. (*line 34*)

13  (*v*) To move something from one place to another. (*line 25*)

14  (*n*) Amounts of money. (*line 30*)

15  (*n*) The amount of money for which something is sold or bought. (*line 37*)

16  (*v*) First you need to _____ an account. (*line 29*)

19  (*v*) To give money. (*line 22*)

**2** Complete the passage using words from the box and the information in the bank statement below.

| | | | |
|---|---|---|---|
| credit | account | cash | transactions |
| payment | balance | deposit | |
| cheque | debit | debit card | |

Jane Sadler opened her ¹ _account_ with the Medway Bank on 28th January with a cash ² _____ of £300. On 15th February she wrote a ³_____ for £53.25 and this appeared as a ⁴_____ on the bank statement on 20th February. On 22nd February she took out £60 in ⁵_____ from a cashpoint machine. On the following day the bank debited £33.50 from her account for a ⁶_____ she had made using her ⁷_____. Her monthly salary was paid directly into her account and this appeared as a ⁸_____ of £802.20 on 26th February. There were no further ⁹_____ on her account and she finished the month with a ¹⁰_____ of £955.45.

| ACCOUNT NUMBER | 548634396 | PAGE 1 | **Medway** |
|---|---|---|---|
| STATEMENT NUMBER | 01 | | **Bank**plc |
| STATEMENT DATE | 1 MAR 2000 | | |

Ms Jane Sadler
75 Ebury Mews
London SW5

53 The Mews Road
London
L34 PY6

| Date | Particulars | | Debits | Credits | Balance |
|---|---|---|---|---|---|
| 28 Jan | Opening deposit | (CSH) | | 300.00 | 300.00 |
| 20 Feb | Cheque 000001 | (CHQ) | 53.25 | | 246.75 |
| 22 Feb | Autobank AB69301 | | | | |
| | Oxford Street | (CSH) | 60.00 | | 186.75 |
| 23 Feb | Maitland and Co | (DC) | 33.50 | | 153.25 |
| 26 Feb | Bennet and Sons | (CSH) | | 802.20 | 955.45 |

| Date | Particulars | Debits | Credits | Balance |
|---|---|---|---|---|
| 1 Mar | | 146.75 | 1102.20 | 955.45 |

ABBREVIATIONS: CHQ – CHEQUE    CSH – CASH    DC – DEBIT CARD    TR – TRANSFER

**3** Underline all the words and expressions related to computers in the text on page 58. Match the words and expressions with the definitions below.

1 to make a computer ready to be used      b _oot_ u _p_

2 a small computer that you can carry with you      l_____

3 to move information or programs from one part of a computer system to another      d_____

4 the key words used to find information in a database      s_____ c_____

5 the analysis of information by a computer program      p_____

6 the sets of programs in a computer      s_____

7 to type information into a computer again      r_____

**Vocabulary development: abbreviations**

A number of abbreviations are used in the text, for example *PC* (*line 56*) for personal computer.

**1** Put each business abbreviation below into one of these categories.

| time | money | people | companies | other |
|------|-------|--------|-----------|-------|

**VAT**   i.e.   Ltd   p.a.   asap   e.g.

IOU   MD   AGM   SFr   Corp   N/A

AOB   **PAYE**   **CEO**   plc   *GMT*   a.m.

**2** What other abbreviations do you know for each category?

## Language Focus

**Allow, enable, let**

The verbs *allow* and *enable* can be used to express possibility. Look at the following examples from the text on page 58.

> *Features maintained in your PC **allow** you to restrict access to designated users. (line 43)*

> *The CHAPS function **enables** you to send funds. (line 59)*

The same idea can be expressed using the verb *let*.

> *HOBS **lets** you group information from different accounts.*

While *allow* and *enable* are followed by an object and an infinitive with *to*, *let* is followed by an object and an infinitive without *to*.

**Practice**

**Write a sentence about each invention using *allow, enable, let*. Use each verb twice.**

Example: *A credit card allows you to buy goods and pay for them later.*

1  A fax machine
2  A laptop computer
3  A mobile phone
4  A modem
5  A credit card
6  E-mail

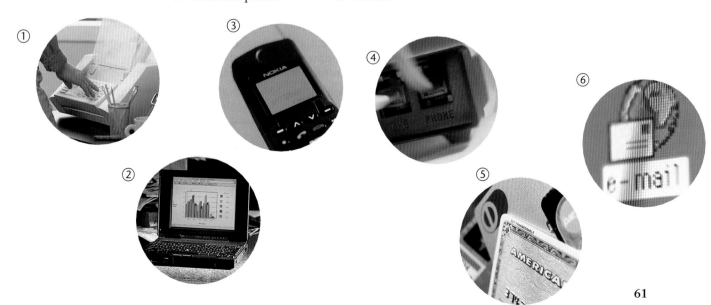

## First and second conditional

Look at these sentences, then complete the explanations that follow, using the words in the box.

**A** *If you transfer your money to a deposit account, you'll (you will) earn more interest.*

**B** *If I had more money, I'd (I would) invest it on the Stock Exchange.*

| | | |
|---|---|---|
| second conditional | first conditional | is unlikely to happen |
| may possibly happen | is unreal | |

1 Sentence **A** is an example of the _____ . The conditional clause (*if ...*) refers to a situation that _____ .

2 Sentence **B** is an example of the _____. The conditional clause (*if ...*) refers to a situation that _____ or _____ .

▶▶ For more information on the first and second conditional, turn to page 166.

## Practice

**1** Decide which of these things may happen to you and which are unlikely to happen. Write complete sentences using the appropriate verb forms.

1 If / go abroad next summer / change / some money into traveller's cheques.

*If I go abroad next summer I'll change some money into traveller's cheques*

or

*If I went abroad next summer I'd change some money into traveller's cheques*

2 If / lose / credit card / inform / the bank immediately.

3 If / need some money / ask / the bank manager for a loan.

4 If / find / mistakes on my bank statement / change / to a different bank.

5 If / earn / more money / be able to / save more.

6 If / order / chequebook / get / it before the end of the week?

**2** Read the problems below. In pairs, discuss what you would do in each situation.

1 You have spent the last month preparing a report for head office. You have just learned that your boss has taken all the credit for the work.

2 Your boss gave you a highly confidential report to read over the weekend. Now you cannot find it and you think you may have left it on the train.

3 You have been sent to negotiate an important new contract for your firm. During the negotiations your counterpart makes it clear that he expects a personal cash contribution (a bribe) from you if your company is to win the contract.

4 In your CV you lied about your qualifications in order to get the job you wanted. You have just been offered the job, but your new employer has asked to see your certificates.

5 Two years ago your company signed an agreement to become the exclusive importer of kitchen equipment from a Swedish supplier. You have just received confirmation that another company is selling the same products at a lower price.

6 You have just seen in your bank statement that your employer has paid you £500 more than your monthly salary.

## *Business Skills Focus: Negotiating*

Reading    1 Complete the following questionnaire.

# Are you a good
# negotiator?

*1 = strongly disagree*     *10 = strongly agree*

- **1**   I can stay cool when I am in the middle of a conflict.
- **2**   I am willing to compromise when I have to.
- **3**   I realise that others have needs.
- **4**   I am very patient.
- **5**   I can identify the most important issues quickly.
- **6**   If necessary, I can remain calm when I am being personally attacked.
- **7**   I am willing to research and analyse issues carefully.
- **8**   I believe in, and work towards, situations where both sides can win.
- **9**   I can deal with stressful situations.
- **10**   I am a good listener.

**TOTAL**

If your total score was 80 or above, you are aware of most of the important issues in negotiation and have the makings of a good negotiator. If you scored between 60 and 79, you will make a good negotiator but there are some areas that you need to improve. If your score was below 60, you may want to rethink some of your attitudes about negotiation and get some additional training.

2 Discuss the scores with your partner and suggest areas for improvement.

**Listening**  Mark Cowan is the owner of a new shopping service called 'The Pedigree Page', specialising in providing a variety of products for pet owners which can be ordered on the Internet.

**1** 📼 Listen to the dialogue between Mark Cowan and his bank manager and answer the following questions.

**a**  Why is Mark Cowan meeting the bank manager?

**b**  What is the bank manager's response?

**2** 📼 Listen to the dialogue again. Which speaker does the following things? Write 'M' for Mark Cowan, and 'B' for the bank manager. Note the language used in each case.

| | | |
|---|---|---|
| 1  Making a proposal | M | ... I'd like to know if you'd be prepared to... |
| 2  Rejecting a proposal | ☐ | _____ |
| 3  Asking for clarification | ☐ | _____ |
| 4  Imposing conditions | ☐ | _____ |
| 5  Accepting a proposal | ☐ | _____ |
| 6  Confirming an interpretation | ☐ | _____ |

**Roleplay**  This is a meeting between a bank employee (Student A) and a business person applying for a loan (Student B).

**1** Prepare your role with a student who has the same role as you. Student A, turn to page 162. Student B, turn to page 157.

**2** In pairs, hold your meeting.

**Writing**  Student A:  Write a short report for the director of the loan department of the bank, summarising the decisions that were reached and outlining the action that you would recommend.

Student B:  Write a short report for your business partner, summarising the decisions that were reached and outlining the action that you would recommend.

# unit

# 7 Business and the Environment

**Key vocabulary** 🔊 It is often said that we live in a **consumer society**; we consider it important to buy products and services. Companies need to be aware of the impact of this on the **environment**, the natural world around us. Many companies use **packaging** (boxes, bottles, etc.) which has been **recycled**, that is made using old materials. **Pollution**, such as smoke in the air, can be reduced if companies use trains instead of road transport.

**Lead-in** **1 In groups, look at the cartoons below and discuss these questions.**

- Which environmental threat does each cartoon refer to?
- Which cartoon do you think is the most effective?
- Which environmental cause do you think is the most important today?

These words will help you.

| ozone layer | global warming | oil spills |
|---|---|---|
| chemical / nuclear waste | rubbish bin (GB) | trash can (US) |

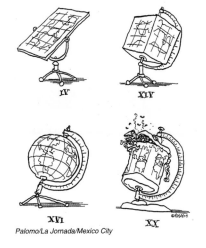

XVI XX
*Palomo/La Jornada/Mexico City*

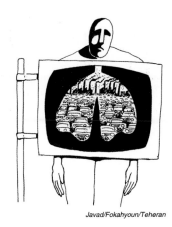

*Javad/Fokahyoun/Teheran*

*Ewk/Aftonbladet/Stockholm*

*Cummings/Free Press/Winnipeg*

65

**2** In groups, discuss these statements made by Anita Roddick, founder of The Body Shop International. Do you agree with any of them? Why? Why not?

'A good business should be part of society, and you have to have pride in what you do. There's no pride in making millions of pounds, but there is pride in helping people and the environment.'

'The idea now is global responsibility. Businesses are the true planetary citizens, they can push frontiers, they can change society.'

'In the next decade, environmentalism will be the most important issue for business.'

**3** As consumers become increasingly concerned about the environment, more and more companies claim to be producing 'environmentally-friendly' products. Read the claims below and match each one to the company that you think made it.

| a cosmetics firm | a fast food chain |
|---|---|
| a car manufacturer | a sports footwear firm |

1  'We provide refills for all our bottles.'
2  'All our packaging is made of biodegradable materials.'
3  'When you've finished with our products bring them back, we recycle them.'
4  'Our latest model is much less polluting.'

What other companies with environmentally-friendly policies do you know?

## Reading

**1** Read the text below and write three questions you would like to ask about Patagonia.

**patagonia**® is a Californian company. Its corporate culture has its roots in the 1960s Californian counterculture of climbers and surfers with the ethic of radical environmentalism. Although its CEO, Yvon Chouinard, is dedicated to social change he also insists on disciplined management and sound business practices. As a previous CEO of Patagonia said, 'The one thing I'm clear about is that Chouinard demands 10% pretax profit.' For him, it is not a question of social good or business profit, but social good and business profit.

*Yvon Chouinard*

**2** Read the text opposite and see if you can find the answers to your questions. Can you guess the answers to your other questions?

**3** Read the text again and answer these questions.

1  According to the text, why are Patagonia's customers so loyal?
2  In what ways does Patagonia make efforts to explain its products' 'earth-friendliness'?
3  What is the overall objective of Patagonia's environmental education policy?
4  How does Patagonia reassure customers who might question their claims to be environmentally-friendly?
5  How do customers react to Patagonia's grants projects?

# Proven environmental commitment helps create committed customers

## Jacquelyn Ottman

1 When self-proclaimed 'Patagonics' dial up Patagonia, they know they will receive more than a high-quality fleece anorak or a waterproof pair of hiking boots. Thanks to the California-based retail firm's outdoor clothing catalog and its exemplary method of communicating its corporate environmentalism, customers are not only knowledgeable about the company's environmental progress, they are loyal*, too.

2 When purchasing products from Patagonia, customers also buy into a commitment to environmental restoration. Patagonia's example demonstrates good green-marketing strategies.

### Educate consumers on environmental product attributes and benefits.

3 Patagonia takes pains to explain its products' earth-friendliness and show customers the big picture. For example, in the mid-1990s, Patagonia began using organically-grown cotton exclusively. In addition to highlighting the organic* merchandise in product descriptions in catalogs, essays explained why organically-produced products are environmentally preferable.

4 Other essays expanded the issue beyond individual products and processes. In a 1996 catalog essay, for example, CEO Yvon Chouinard explained the rationale behind the company's switch to organically-grown cotton, including the problems associated with producing conventional cotton, the larger long-term benefits of investing in organically-grown products and the need to think about long-term sustainability issues when choosing products.

5 One might assume that explaining the benefits of organic cotton in catalogs was a strategic move, since the company had to justify the $2 to $10 premium per garment. But other essays, for instance, addressed environmental issues not directly linked to company profit.

6 Broad environmental education teaches consumers that although thinking and buying green is more expensive, environmentalism is less taxing on the earth in the long run, and therefore, on individuals.

### Use a variety of media.

7 Patagonia's advertising and company literature aim to educate. Instead of a catalog packed only with sales information, Patagonia's catalog is more like National Geographic. Demonstrations in Patagonia's retail stores engage* customers with interactive displays of the earth's processes. Annual reports, pamphlets and other company literature explain new ideas in environmentalism. And Patagonia was one of the first companies to discuss sustainability in paid media.

### Demonstrate tangible corporate environmental progress.

8 Patagonia realizes that customers sometimes doubt corporate environmental claims. To avoid consumer backlash*, Patagonia publishes the results of its internal environmental assessment.

9 This report reviews all office, production and merchandising activities and uncovers opportunities to cut waste and reduce energy. Readers can see how Patagonia tries to conduct business in a socially responsible manner, from choosing long-lasting efficient light bulbs to providing on-site child care for employees' children. The grounds around the company's headquarters even feature edible landscaping – banana trees.

10 Through an environmental grants program, dubbed* Earth Tax, Patagonia pledges 1% of its sales or 10% of its pre-tax profit, whichever is greater, to small, local preservation and restoration efforts. Through* April 1997, Patagonia had contributed more than $8m to hundreds of such organizations.

11 Believing that grass roots* efforts do the most to raise community awareness of local problems, the Earth Tax program targets smaller grass roots organizations committed to issues such as biodiversity*, old-growth forests, environmentally preferable methods of resource extraction*, alternative energy and water, social activism and environmental education. By funding more than 350 of these efforts each year, Patagonia helps raise community awareness nationwide.

### Empower consumers to take action.

12 An annual Earth Tax Report invites customers to apply for grants for local projects. Participants are quick to apply and inform the company about environmental successes. One recent catalog featured a customer sporting an insulated Patagonia guide jacket as she rescued a calf born during a Colorado snow storm.

13 With powerful communication, meaningful corporate environmental progress and avenues for consumer activism, it is no wonder that even skeptics become Patagonia customers and customers become 'Patagonics'.

*Marketing News*

---

*loyal: always supporting
*organic: made without artificial chemicals
*to engage s.b.: to attract s.b. and keep their interest
*a backlash: a strong reaction against s.th.
*to dub: to give an 'unofficial' name

*through (US): until (GB)
*grass roots: at the level of ordinary people
*biodiversity: many different plants and animals existing in one area
*resource extraction: taking natural products from the earth

**Vocabulary**

**1** Complete the passage below using these words from the text.

**a** sustainability (*para 4*)    **d** empower (*para 12*)

**b** product descriptions (*para 3*)    **e** commitment (*para 2*)

**c** catalogs (*para 3*)    **f** organic (*para 3*)

> Patagonia is an outdoor clothing firm with a strong [1] _commitment_ to environmental causes. It sells its products through retail outlets and by mail order. Patagonia is renowned for its spectacular [2]_____ which are filled with unusual and dramatic photos (all taken by customers) displaying the clothing in exciting ways. They also contain detailed [3]_____ which include definitions of materials and explanations of manufacturing processes.
>
> The company makes jackets from recycled plastic bottles and produces clothing from [4]_____ materials. It offers courses to its employees on non-violent demonstrations and even pays bail for employees who get arrested. It also donates money to environmental groups and generally supports efforts that [5]_____ consumers to take action. Patagonia's strategy isn't just to give away money to good causes but to pioneer new, long-term practices of [6]_____ in business, prove their economic viability and persuade other businesses to follow.

**2** Find words in the text which have the opposite meaning to the words below.

**1** imperfect (*para 1*) **exemplary**    **5** separate (*para 5*)

**2** uninformed (*para 1*)    **6** taken (*para 10*)

**3** innovative (*para 4*)    **7** locally (*para 11*)

**4** uncalculated (*para 5*)    **8** failures (*para 12*)

**3** Match the nouns and verbs as they are used in the text.

**1** address    **a** business

**2** doubt    **b** awareness

**3** publish    **c** results

**4** conduct    **d** issues

**5** raise    **e** claims

**4** Replace the words in italics with expressions from Vocabulary 3 in the correct form.

**1** The speaker will *talk about the difficulties* we are likely to encounter.

**address the issues**

**2** The company *runs its affairs* in an ethical and honest manner.

**3** The government will *make public the conclusions* of the environmental study next month.

**4** We are running a campaign designed to *increase* public *knowledge* of the current crisis.

**5** Many consumers *don't believe statements* made by companies about their products.

**Vocabulary development: word building**

With some words it is possible to create several new words by adding suffixes. Look at these examples.

| Verb | Noun (idea) | Noun (person) | Adjective |
|---|---|---|---|
| – | environment | environmentalist | environmental |
| activate | activism activity | activist | active |

**1** Complete the table below, using a dictionary. Some words may have two forms with the same spelling.

| Verb | Noun (idea) | Noun (person) | Adjective |
|---|---|---|---|
| produce | a _____ (efficiency) | b _____ | c _____ (making a lot) |
| d _____ | progress | – | e _____ (supporting new ideas) |
| manage | f _____ | g _____ | h _____ (relating to senior staff) |
| direct | i _____ | j _____ | k _____ |

**2** What suffixes can you add to these words?
  a develop    b commit    c sustain    d employ

**Discussion**

**In groups, discuss these questions.**

1 What do you think of Patagonia's approach to business?
2 Are consumers in your country concerned about the environmental policies of businesses?
3 Would you pay more for things produced in an environmentally-friendly manner? If so, how much more?

## Language Focus

**Expressing contrast**

Look at the following sentence from the text on page 67.

***Although*** *thinking and buying green is more expensive, environmentalism is less taxing on the earth in the long run. (para 6)*

**1** Join the sentence halves below.

| | | | |
|---|---|---|---|
| **1** | In spite of the present recession, | **a** | we still haven't reached our target. |
| **2** | Despite rising costs, | **b** | people are still buying them. |
| **3** | Even though our products are expensive, | **c** | they are keeping their prices low. |
| **4** | Although profits are increasing, | **d** | we can reach our output deadline. |
| **5** | Despite the fact that our supplies were late, | **e** | the long-term economic outlook is optimistic. |

**2** In pairs, underline the expressions of contrast in exercise 1.
**Which are followed by:**

**a** subject + verb?

**b** noun or verb + *-ing*?

▶▶ For more information on expressing contrast, turn to page 167.

**Practice**

Join the pairs of sentences using an expression of contrast. Use each expression once.

Example:
Patagonia sales fell in the 90s. Their reputation for high quality didn't decline.

*In spite of a fall in sales in the 90s, Patagonia's reputation for high quality didn't decline.*

**1** Young people are concerned about the environment. They can't always afford environmentally-friendly products.

**2** Patagonia makes efforts to convince other companies to use organically-grown cotton. Many companies resist because it costs more.

**3** Pollution is rising in Paris. People still prefer to take their cars to work.

**4** Many countries organise separate waste collections for glass, paper, metal and plastic. Many others don't.

**5** Most beauty products carry the label 'against animal testing'. Some of the components may have been tested on animals.

**The passive**

Look at the following extracts from a Patagonia brochure.

**A** *Patagonia **saves** thousands of gallons of oil by diverting millions of plastic bottles from landfills to recycling plants.*

**B** *For every 3,700 (2-litre) bottles that **are recycled**, a barrel of oil (42 gallons) **is saved**.*

**What form is the verb in bold in each sentence?**

**What is the difference in emphasis?**

▶▶ For more information on the passive, turn to page 167.

**Practice**

**1** The following extract describes how Patagonia uses recycled plastic bottles to make material for jackets. Put the verbs in brackets in the passive form to complete each stage of the process.

**PCR Fleece Story**

## Soda Bottles to Synchilla Fleece

**patagonia**®

Bottles
¹ _are brought_
(bring) to the local
recycling centre.

From Bottles to Fiber

to Fabric to Clothes

The plastic
² _____ ( convert)
into small pieces and
³ _____ (chop)
into flakes.

The flakes
⁴ _____
(melt) and shaped into
fine fibers.

They ⁶_____
(make) into clothes known
as 'PCR synchilla clothing'.

The recycled fibers
⁵ _____ (ship) to
the mill.

**2** Rewrite the following sentences using a passive form. Omit the agent if it is not important.

Example:
Patagonia introduced recycled fleece into its range in 1993.
*Recycled fleece was introduced in 1993.*

1 Consumers will buy more and more 'environmentally-friendly' products.
2 Consumers should take plastic bottles to the local recycling centre.
3 Patagonia can make 150 synchilla garments from 3,700 bottles.
4 The company has recently added a new item to the product range.
5 Many companies are developing green-marketing strategies.

**Listening**

## *Skills Focus*

The Body Shop International is a highly successful franchise skincare retailer. It is against using animals in testing cosmetics, very active in community projects, and particularly well known for its involvement in environmental causes.

🔲 Listen to eight customers in a London Body Shop branch, and note the reason(s) each customer gives for buying Body Shop products.

**Speaking**

## Convincing a sponsor

Like Patagonia, many companies sponsor, or contribute money towards, events or activities to maintain their image or to create a new image. Sponsorship can cover a whole range of activities including sport, education and local community projects depending on the type of image the company wants to project. For example, IBM sponsored the 2000 Olympic Games in Sydney, and Coca-Cola sponsors 151 American college students every year.

1 In pairs, make a list of companies which sponsor activities like those mentioned above. What kind of image does each company want to project through its sponsorship?

2 In groups, choose one of the following projects which need sponsorship.

**1 A charity organisation**
You are in charge of fundraising activities for the charity 'People in Need'. You want companies to make regular contributions to fund a hot meal delivery service to old and disabled people in your town. Local journalists have agreed to write articles aimed at raising awareness of the scheme. These articles could feature profiles of the companies willing to make contributions.

**2 An environmental cause**
You are members of a local environmental group which plants trees in urban areas. You are organising a 'tree planting' ceremony in the main square of your town centre. You need sponsorship to pay for the planting and upkeep of the trees. You plan to put the sponsors' names on plaques mounted in front of each tree. The mayor and other important local politicians will be at the ceremony.

**3 An international exhibition of children's art**
You represent the National Art Gallery and are organising an exhibition of children's art from all over the world. You are looking for sponsorship to finance programmes, catalogues, reproductions etc. You have invited a famous artist to open the exhibition, and children and teachers from various countries will be available for a press conference.

**4 A TV documentary**
You are directors of a video company. You have been commissioned to make a programme for national TV about the effects of pollution on marine life in the Pacific, as part of a wildlife series. It is also your job to find a sponsor to finance the sophisticated equipment and specialised crew members necessary to make this programme.

3 Choose an international company to approach for sponsorship. Discuss what your project can offer them and prepare the arguments that you will use to persuade them to sponsor your project. Look at the checklist of questions opposite that a company will ask itself before sponsoring a project. How will your project satisfy the company with respect to these questions?

① Will the project appeal to our customers?

② Does it have a logical link with our company? If not, could one be developed?

③ Is it unique or one of many similar things on offer?

④ Will there be other sponsors? If so, are they our competitors?

⑤ What kind of media coverage does the project offer? (for example, local press, TV, company name / logo on T-shirts, programmes etc.)

⑥ What are the chances of it being successful? (We don't want negative publicity.)

⑦ If our sponsorship is a success, will there be future opportunities to continue our connection with the project?

⑧ Does it present an opportunity to invite our employees or shareholders as observers or participants?

⑨ Are any of our customers involved directly or indirectly in this project?

**Writing**

**1** **In the same groups, write a letter to the company asking them to consider your request for sponsorship. Use the guidelines below to help you.**

Dear ...

(*Opening paragraph*) I am a member of a team ... (*give details*) currently working on (*present the project in general terms*). I am contacting you because ... (*introduce the idea of their possible interest in the project*)

(*In the second paragraph, outline the project giving dates, times and activities. Give specific reasons why the project should interest the company, including possible media coverage, customer appeal, etc.*)

(*In the closing paragraph, say how you hope the project will be of interest to the company.*)

(*Closing formalities and signature*)

**2** Read the other groups' letters. Consider each one as if you were the company directors. Which project would you choose and why?

# 8 *The Stock Market*

**Key vocabulary**  A company can raise money on the **stock market** or **stock exchange** (a market place for buying and selling shares) in two different ways.

It can **issue shares** (US **stocks**), or units of its capital, to **institutional investors** or the general public. Different types of shares or **equities** are available, but the most common are known as **ordinary** or **common shares** (US **common stock**). When an investor buys a share, using the services of a specialist company or **broker**, he or she becomes a **shareholder** (US **stockholder**) and owns a part of (or has a **stake** in) a company. Shareholders can make money by receiving **dividends**, paid as a proportion of a company's annual profits, and when the value of their shares increases.

A company can also borrow money from investors by issuing **bonds**, loans for fixed periods with fixed interest rates.

**Securities** refers to both shares and bonds. Each year billions of shares and bonds are sold or **traded** on the world's major stock exchanges.

**Lead-in**

**1** Many companies are authorised to use the stock exchange to trade their shares. Every day, the press gives prices and other information about the shares of these listed companies. Read the following newspaper headlines. In groups, decide whether each one reflects a good or poor performance of the company's shares on the stock exchange.

Example: GENERAL CINEMA SEES $20 MILLION GAIN

*The shares of this company are doing well since there has been a gain.*

① **XIR sales improve in second quarter**

② AMD TO CUT JOBS IN DRIVE TO RESCUE FALLING PROFITS

③ INTERNATIONAL COMPUTING RISES

④ JONES AND SHIPMAN PROFITS REACH RECORD HIGH

⑤ Belle Cosmetics sees fall in first quarter

⑥ Scottish and Newcastle report slight losses

⑦ SELECT WINES HAVE CAUSE TO CELEBRATE

⑧ Simmons and Simmons face disastrous year as sales continue slide

**2** 🔲 You will hear Isobel Mendelson talking about investments that she has made on the stock market and her reasons for doing so. Listen to part 1 and complete the table.

| Types of investment | Reasons for investing |
|---|---|
| •  | •  |
| •  | •  |

🔲 Listen to part 2. How does she check on her shares?

**Reading**

**1** You are going to read a text with the headline '*Europeans Log On To Investment Fever*'. In pairs, discuss what you think the text is about.

**2** Read the text on the next page and see if your ideas were correct.

# Europeans Log On To Investment Fever

## US Brokers Start to Target Continent

*By John Tagliabue*

*LONDON – Alan English has an addiction, and he is not ashamed to discuss it.*

'I log on every day, sometimes from the office, in the morning and in the evening,' said Mr English, 51, a computer consultant who is still
5 hooked* a year and a half after he began shopping for stocks over the Internet. 'Some days I trade four or five times a day.'

Mr English is one of a growing
10 number of Europeans with on-line investment fever. There is a stock market boom at the moment, and as Web surfing gains popularity across Europe, more and more people are
15 logging on to shop for financial products, and buying and selling stocks.

Compared with the United States, where about 20 percent of all stock
20 trades are entered from the Internet, the movement in Europe is still in its infancy. But as the trend gathers pace*, American Internet brokers have begun moving into Britain and
25 increasingly are setting their sights on the Continent as well.

Their arrival poses a challenge for new European on-line trading firms. Analysts expect it to accelerate* vast
30 changes in the securities business that are already under way here as Europe becomes a single market.

Nowhere is the trend more apparent than in Britain. In April,
35 Charles Schwab Corp set up an on-line trading service, and in June, the E-Trade Group, based in California, announced a joint venture with a British partner, as well as licensing
40 agreements in Germany. Other Internet brokers such as Ameritrade and DLJ Direct, are studying moves to catch up.

'American brokers, under
45 competitive pressure back home that is driving down profit margins, are being drawn to the lucrative potential of Europe, where the idea of a discount broker
50 is still rather novel*,' said Stephen Eckett, the author of *Investing Online*, a guide to Internet investments.

Mr Eckett said that fees at full-
55 service brokers in Britain for the purchase of $10,000 of stock in a British company would amount to about $120, while the going commission for making a similar
60 trade on the World Wide Web could be as low as $9.

Though European investors can already use US on-line brokers to buy shares in the United States, the
65 American companies do not actively promote this business for fear of annoying European securities regulators. Thus, at the start, the American on-line brokers operating
70 in Europe, like Schwab, are offering their customers the chance to trade only on individual European exchanges. The long-range goal, however, is to expand the system into
75 a truly global marketplace where investors in any country will be able to trade freely in stocks across national boundaries. While European Internet usage still lags behind* the
80 United States, it is expected to grow rapidly in the next several years and Europe's single currency will foster* the spread of stock trading across national boundaries. The American
85 on-line firms, despite their aggressive plans, will not have it easy.

Barclays plc, one of the largest British banks, will be the first to fight off the competition when it launches
90 its own on-line service in September,

complete with financial information and real-time share trading service.

Philip Bungey, Head of Research and Development at Barclays
95 Stockbrokers, said Barclays would let customers trade in about 2,000 companies on the London Stock Exchange and the Alternative Investment Market, a small-
100 companies market. In the future, he said, Barclays wants to enable its customers to trade electronically on American exchanges, like NASDAQ*.

105 Increasingly, American on-line brokers will be squeezed* by the very revolution they have helped start. Mr Eckett predicts a 'major collapse' of commission fees. He
110 noted that in the United States, commissions for Internet trades have dipped as low as $5 a transaction since Web trading surfaced about four years ago. 'The same will
115 happen in Europe,' he said, 'as consumers surf the Internet in search of cheaper financial services.'

*New York Times*

---

*hooked:* addicted
*to gather pace:* to move faster and faster
*to accelerate:* to make s.th. happen more quickly
*novel:* new, unusual and interesting

*to lag behind:* to move more slowly than
*to foster:* to help s.th. develop
*NASDAQ:* A US electronic stock exchange
*to squeeze:* to make it difficult for s.b. to do business

**3** **Read the text again and answer the questions.**

1 Why are more people taking an interest in the stock exchange?
2 What will make European markets change more quickly?
3 Why do American on-line traders operating in Europe restrict their dealings to European exchanges?
4 How are the European traders reacting to American competition?
5 What will the long-term effect on American brokers be?

**Vocabulary**

**1** **Match the words from the text with their corresponding definitions.**

| | | | |
|---|---|---|---|
| 1 | to log on (*line 1*) | **a** | profitable |
| 2 | a boom (*line 12*) | **b** | a dramatic reduction |
| 3 | to surf (*line 13*) | **c** | an authority that supervises an industry |
| 4 | a move (*line 42*) | **d** | to reach a total of |
| 5 | to catch up (*line 43*) | **e** | to connect |
| 6 | lucrative (*line 48*) | **f** | money that a customer pays for a service, usually a percentage of the total |
| 7 | to amount to (*line 57*) | | |
| 8 | commission (*line 59*) | **g** | a tactical change of position |
| 9 | a regulator (*line 68*) | **h** | to move between different websites on the Internet |
| 10 | a collapse (*line 110*) | | |
| | | **i** | a rapid expansion or development |
| | | **j** | to reach the person in front |

**2** **Complete the passage about a transaction on the stock exchange using words from Key Vocabulary and Vocabulary 1. Some words may be used more than once.**

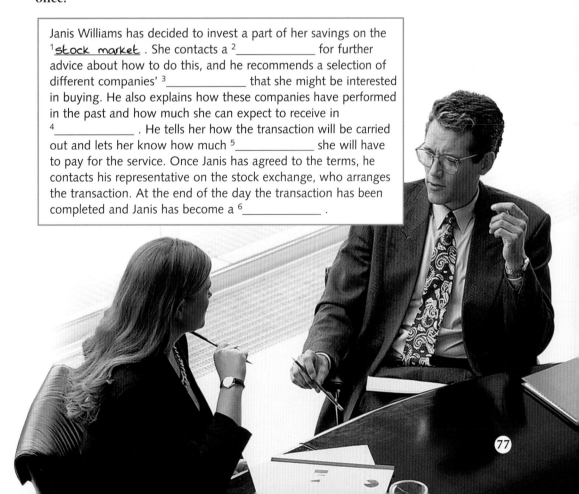

> Janis Williams has decided to invest a part of her savings on the
> ¹<u>stock market</u> . She contacts a ²_____ for further
> advice about how to do this, and he recommends a selection of
> different companies' ³_____ that she might be interested
> in buying. He also explains how these companies have performed
> in the past and how much she can expect to receive in
> ⁴_____ . He tells her how the transaction will be carried
> out and lets her know how much ⁵_____ she will have
> to pay for the service. Once Janis has agreed to the terms, he
> contacts his representative on the stock exchange, who arranges
> the transaction. At the end of the day the transaction has been
> completed and Janis has become a ⁶_____ .

Vocabulary
development:
phrasal verbs 1

Look at these examples of phrasal verbs from the text.

*In April, Charles Schwab Corp* **set up** *an on-line trading service... (line 35)*

*Barclays plc ... will be the first to* **fight off** *the competition... (line 89)*

1   Are the verbs in bold

  **a** transitive (followed by an object)?

  or

  **b** intransitive (not followed by an object)?

2   Replace the words in italics with a verb from **A** and a particle from **B** in the correct form.

| A | | B | |
|---|---|---|---|
| point | buy | out | on |
| think | look | over | about |
| call (x2) | let | off | down |
| go | | up | after |

  **a**  The meeting has been *cancelled* because several people are unable to attend. called off

  **b**  We already own 30% of the company's shares and we intend to *purchase* at least another 20% in the coming year.

  **c**  The new subsidiary in Bahrain will be *supervising* our operations in the Middle East.

  **d**  It will be a difficult conference to organise. How shall we *start doing* it?

  **e**  We'll need some more time to *reflect upon* your proposal before we can give you an answer.

  **f**  In her presentation she *drew attention to* some of the problems that the new project would involve.

  **g**  One of our sales representatives will *visit* you next week.

  **h**  This year the company has *disappointed* investors by announcing an unexpected loss.

  What other verbs of this type do you know?

## *Language Focus*

**The third conditional**

**Look at these sentences and answer the questions.**

A *If I **had sold** my shares after six months, I **would have made** a lot of money.*

1 Does this sentence refer to the past or now?
2 Did the person sell the shares?
3 Did the person make a lot of money?

B *If I **hadn't taken** so many risks, I **wouldn't have** lost so much.*

1 Does this sentence refer to the past or now?
2 Did the person take risks?
3 Did the person lose money?

▶▶ **For more information on the third conditional, turn to page 167.**

**Practice**

**Look at the charts and graphs and write complete sentences using the prompts.**

Example: I spent £10,000 on a holiday this year.
If / open a savings account / receive …

*If I had opened a savings account with £10,000, I would have received 9.35% interest.*

| Premium Savings account | |
| --- | --- |
| Gross Rate | p.a.(%) |
| £25,000 plus | 9.65 |
| £10,000-£24,999 | 9.35 |
| £500 – £9,999 | 8.65 |

1 In 1998 you were a cashier at Fashion World Clothing.
If / be / assistant manager / earn …

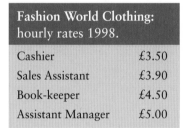

| Fashion World Clothing: hourly rates 1998. | |
| --- | --- |
| Cashier | £3.50 |
| Sales Assistant | £3.90 |
| Book-keeper | £4.50 |
| Assistant Manager | £5.00 |

| London Gatwick Airport: | | |
| --- | --- | --- |
| **Flight Arrivals 23 May 2000.** | | |
| FLIGHT | TO | COMMENTS |
| AF615 | PARIS | delayed |
| BD493 | PARIS | on time |
| AA6132 | NEW YORK | delayed |

2 I took flight AF615 to Paris and was late.
If / take flight / BD493 / arrive …

3 I sold my Renault in 1999.
If / sell it / 1997 / get …

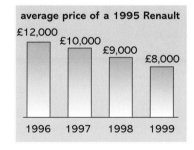

average price of a 1995 Renault
£12,000   £10,000   £9,000   £8,000
1996   1997   1998   1999

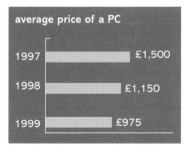

average price of a PC
1997   £1,500
1998   £1,150
1999   £975

4 I bought my PC in 1997.
If / wait until 1999 / pay …

5 I sold my M&S shares in 1998.
If / not sell / receive … in 1999.

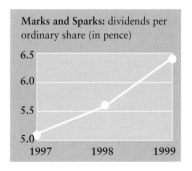

Marks and Sparks: dividends per ordinary share (in pence)
6.5
6.0
5.5
5.0
1997   1998   1999

## Yet, still, already

**Look at these sentences.**

1 *Mr English is **still** hooked a year and a half after he began.*
2 *Have you bought shares in your company **yet**?*
3 *I've **already** checked the FTSE 100 prices.*
4 *He **still** hasn't subscribed to the internet dealing service.*
5 *I haven't made any profit on my shares **yet**.*
6 *European investors can **already** use US on-line brokers.*

**Complete the rules using *still, already, yet*.**

a We use _____ to emphasise that a situation continues at the time of speaking.

b We use _____ to emphasise that a situation started, or something was done, before the time of speaking.

c We use _____ (at the end of the sentence) to emphasise that something hasn't happened after some time.

d We use _____ when asking questions about whether something has happened or not.

## Practice

**Correct the mistakes in these sentences.**

1 Have you made any money ~~already~~? yet
2 I am yet thinking about investing on the stock market but can't make up my mind.
3 I have contacted a broker still and he has given some very good advice.
4 He already hasn't bought anything on the European exchanges.
5 I'm very pleased with my shares; they've gone up yet.
6 Now that you've lost so much money, do you yet think it's a good idea to invest on the stock exchange?

## Skills Focus

### Reading

**Many newspapers have a financial section which includes information about the share prices of listed companies. This information enables you to follow the progress of any shares that you own or may be thinking of buying. Read the explanation of the listing opposite and answer the questions.**

1 What was the closing price for each of the following shares?
  a Cadbury-Schweppes 915.0    c Black Arrow
  b Allied Zurich    d Care UK

2 For each of the five sectors, which shares had the greatest change in price (increase or decrease) compared with the previous day's price?

3 Which of the following household goods companies is furthest from its highest price for the year?
  a Allied Text    c Reckitt and C
  b Cornwell Pkr    d Stoves

4 Which insurance company has
  a the highest yield?
  b the lowest yield?

5 What is the price / earnings ratio for each of the following shares?
  a International Energy Group    c Isotron
  b Cox Insurance    d Associated British Foods

**Stock**
The name of the share.

**Price-Earnings ratio**
This figure refers to the relationship between the current market price of a share and the profit earned by the company over the most recent year. For example the price of a Unilever share is 38.7 times the earnings per share for the most recent year. The P-E is often used to compare companies in the same industry.

**Sector**
Companies are grouped according to sector, for example Insurance, Building, Banks, Electricity.

| High | Low | Stock | Price | Chg | Yld | P/E |
|---|---|---|---|---|---|---|
| | | **FOOD PRODUCERS** | | | | -1.252% |
| 287 | 135 | Acatos & Hutch | 155.0 | 0.0 | ... | ... |
| 39 | 6 | Albert Fisher | 7.0 | 0.0 | ... | 18.0 |
| 96 | 27 | Anglo East | 40.0 | 0.0 | 10.0 | 4.2 |
| 668 | 433 | **Assc Brit Fds** | 560.0 | -38.0 | 2.2 | 18.5 |
| 305 | 155 | Banks Syd C | 217.0 | 0.0 | 6.6 | 9.2 |
| 513 | 379 | Barr A G | 440.0 | 0.0 | 6.8 | 8.5 |
| 193 | 83 | Bertam Hldgs | 87.5 | 0.0 | 5.9 | 7.0 |
| 360 | 92 | Booker | 121.5 | -4.0 | 20.5 | 6.6 |
| 1078 | 527 | Brake Bros | 660.0 | 0.0 | 2.2 | 18.0 |
| 993 | 573 | **Cadbury-Schw** | 915.0 | 25.0 | 2.0 | 24.9 |
| 245 | 184 | Rob Wiseman | 184.0 | -1.0 | 2.7 | 12.4 |
| 103 | 48 | Rowe Evans | 50.5 | 0.5 | 8.6 | 4.0 |
| 585 | 256 | Tate & Lyle | 350.0 | 11.0 | 4.9 | 15.5 |
| 153 | 103 | Terranova Fds | 118.5 | 0.0 | | ... |
| 739 | 428 | Unigate | 521.5 | 24.0 | 5.3 | 11.2 |
| 712 | 400 | **Unilever** | 600.0 | 15.0 | 1.8 | 38.7 |
| 304 | 180 | Utd Biscuits | 235.0 | 2.0 | 5.6 | 40.5 |
| 63 | 37 | WT Foods | ... | ... | ... | 17.5 |
| | | **GAS DISTRIBUTION** | | | | -1.145% |
| 60 | 46 | Carlo Grp | 57.7 | 0.8 | 1.4 | 18.7 |
| 125 | 79 | **Centrica** | 116.0 | -0.5 | | ... |
| 428 | 247 | **BG** | 391.5 | -5.5 | 2.6 | ... |
| 147 | 98 | Intl Energy Grp | 134.0 | 0.0 | 3.7 | 12.5 |
| | | **HEALTH CARE** | | | | 2.449% |
| 603 | 263 | Alliance UniChem | 575.0 | -1.5 | 2.2 | 25.4 |
| 1025 | 638 | Bespak | 827.5 | 22.5 | 2.1 | 20.8 |
| 647 | 62 | Biocompatibles | 75.5 | -1.0 | ... | ... |
| 167 | 78 | Biotrace Intl | 97.5 | | 0.0 | 54.2 |
| 248 | 133 | Care UK | 185.5 | 0.5 | 0.9 | 23.8 |
| 101 | 22 | Celsis Intl | 28.0 | 0.0 | ... | ... |
| 551 | 388 | Comnty Hosp | 430.5 | 0.0 | 3.8 | 14.5 |
| 130 | 54 | Drew Scientific Gp | 80.5 | 0.0 | | ... |
| 173 | 128 | Gyrus Grp | 130.0 | 0.0 | | ... |
| 244 | 131 | Huntleigh | 215.0 | -1.5 | 1.9 | 23.4 |
| 593 | 400 | Isotron | 512.5 | 0.0 | 1.7 | 15.9 |
| 232 | 143 | London Intl | 205.5 | 3.0 | 1.6 | 41.1 |
| 388 | 160 | Nestor-BNA | 373.5 | 10.0 | 1.4 | 40.2 |
| 577 | 305 | **Nyce Amersham** | 419.5 | 13.5 | 1.2 | ... |
| 835 | 455 | Seton Scholl | 755.0 | 24.0 | 1.7 | 26.0 |
| 810 | 280 | Shield Diagn | 452.5 | -15.0 | | 196.7 |
| 241 | 99 | Sinclair Montrose | 102.5 | -1.0 | 0.2 | 36.6 |
| 200 | 118 | Smith & Neph | 166.0 | 6.0 | 4.1 | 15.2 |
| 83 | 13 | Tepnel Life | 15.0 | 0.0 | ... | ... |
| 413 | 254 | Westm H'care | 257.5 | 1.0 | 3.4 | 17.2 |

| High | Low | Stock | Price | Chg | Yld | P/E |
|---|---|---|---|---|---|---|
| | | **HOUSEHOLD GOODS** | | | | -1.949% |
| 178 | 73 | Airsprung | 73.5 | -3.0 | 12.5 | 3.8 |
| 220 | 165 | Alba | 169.5 | 0.0 | 4.8 | 9.1 |
| 167 | 82 | Alexandra | 110.0 | 5.5 | 8.0 | 10.3 |
| 188 | 79 | Allied Text | 97.5 | 0.0 | 11.0 | 5.9 |
| 233 | 146 | Aquarius Grp | 165.5 | 0.0 | 6.9 | 9.2 |
| 25 | 7 | Armour Tst | 10.0 | -0.5 | ... | ... |
| 286 | 101 | Baird (Wm) | 117.5 | 0.0 | 15.3 | 5.8 |
| 422 | 233 | Black (Peter) | 241.0 | 2.5 | 3.6 | 12.6 |
| 150 | 87 | Black Arrow | 107.5 | 0.0 | 5.8 | 8.3 |
| 615 | 103 | Churchill China | 117.5 | 0.0 | 13.2 | 2.9 |
| 93 | 13 | Claremont | 18.3 | 0.0 | ... | ... |
| 115 | 30 | Coats Viyella | 31.5 | -1.3 | 7.9 | ... |
| 133 | 71 | Colefax & Fowler | 74.0 | 2.0 | 4.7 | 92.5 |
| 183 | 94 | Cornwell Pkr | 93.5 | -1.5 | 5.3 | 6.2 |
| 203 | 174 | Pifco A | ... | ... | ... | 8.8 |
| 358 | 165 | Portmeirion | 167.5 | 0.0 | 9.9 | 4.8 |
| 48 | 23 | Readicut | 25.3 | 0.3 | 12.8 | 7.2 |
| 1333 | 806 | **Reckitt & C** | 1033.0 | 24.0 | 2.5 | 19.4 |
| 620 | 280 | Relyon | 301.5 | 11.0 | 6.4 | 9.7 |
| 228 | 76 | Royal Doulton | 83.5 | 5.0 | 15.0 | 12.3 |
| 48 | 27 | Sherwood Gp | 43.0 | -0.5 | 10.5 | 10.8 |
| 295 | 165 | Silentnight | 189.5 | -2.5 | 7.8 | 7.6 |
| 71 | 51 | Sirdar | 59.5 | 0.5 | 11.9 | 7.2 |
| 53 | 27 | Stirling | 28.5 | 0.0 | 11.0 | 5.3 |
| 263 | 90 | Stoves | 94.0 | 0.5 | 8.5 | 6.1 |
| 279 | 75 | Swallowfield | 78.5 | 0.0 | 11.0 | 3.7 |
| 165 | 68 | Vymura | 86.5 | 1.5 | 7.9 | 6.1 |
| 87 | 11 | Walker GBank | 53.0 | 0.0 | ... | 8.0 |
| 106 | 48 | Waterfd Wedg | 56.0 | 3.5 | 2.6 | 69.3 |
| 73 | 57 | Worthington Grp | 59.0 | 1.5 | 6.6 | 8.1 |
| 145 | 78 | Yorklyde | 80.0 | 0.0 | 6.0 | 12.7 |
| | | **INSURANCE** | | | | 1.695% |
| 900 | 461 | **Allied Zurich** | 714.0 | 29.0 | | ... |
| 150 | 96 | Amlin Ordinary | 112.5 | 8.0 | 12.2 | ... |
| 162 | 105 | Benfield & Rea | 111.0 | 1.0 | 7.3 | ... |
| 79 | 34 | Bradstock Gp | 48.5 | 0.0 | 12.4 | 6.5 |
| 1297 | 725 | CGU | 946.5 | 8.5 | 3.5 | 18.2 |
| 278 | 199 | Charles Taylor | 216.0 | 0.0 | 2.8 | 24.0 |
| 167 | 120 | CLM Insur Fnd | 127.0 | -0.5 | 12.9 | ... |
| 525 | 222 | Cox Insce | 349.0 | 1.5 | 1.4 | 26.8 |
| 610 | 430 | Dom & Genl | 460.0 | 10.0 | 3.0 | 15.7 |
| 168 | 97 | Euclidian | 126.0 | 0.0 | 14.9 | 4.2 |
| 162 | 116 | GoshawkinsurHldgs | 118.0 | 0.0 | 3.1 | 11.8 |
| 497 | 229 | **GRE** | 289.5 | 6.8 | 4.5 | 4.4 |

*The Independent*

**High / Low**
These columns show the highest and lowest prices (in pence) for the shares during the current year. For example, when this information was published the highest price at which Unilever shares had been bought and sold was 712 and the lowest price at which they had been bought and sold was 400 pence.

**Change**
This shows how much the closing price of the share changed in comparison with the previous day's closing price. For example, Unilever closed 15 pence higher than the previous day.

**Price**
This shows the price of the share as it stood at the close of business yesterday. For example, Unilever closed at 600 pence.

**Yield**
The yield shows how much shareholders can expect to receive as a dividend, in pence, for every £1 invested (based on the current share price). In other words, if you own £100 worth of shares in Unilever and the share price remains constant, you can expect to receive a dividend of £1.80.

Listening

**1** Complete the sentences with one of these words.

down    to (x2)    by    from    of    at    up

| Name of the share | Yesterday's closing Price | Today's closing price | Change |
|---|---|---|---|
| Barclays | 1399 | 1451 | +52 |
| Boots | 1049 | 1035 | -14 |
| British Airways | 402 | 404 | +2 |
| Marks & Spencer | 448 | 442 | -6 |
| Pearson | 1080 | 1103 | +23 |
| Sainsbury | 533 | 522 | -11 |
| Stanley Leis | 261.5 | 261.5 | – |

1  Shares in Boots fell ___from___ 1049p ___to___ 1035p.
2  British Airways shares rose 2p _____ 404p.
3  Sainsbury's shares were_____ 11p at 522p.
4  Shares in Stanley Leis stood _____ 261.5p.
5  Shares in Pearson increased _____ 23p.
6  Barclays shares were _____ 52p at 1451p.
7  There was a drop _____ 6p in Marks & Spencer shares.

**2** 📼 Listen to a radio stock market report and complete the table.

| Name of the share | Yesterday's closing price | Today's closing price | Change |
|---|---|---|---|
| Avis Europe | 246p | 253p | +7p |
| British Energy | | 654p | |
| _____ | 245p | _____ | _____ |
| Cookson | _____ | _____ | +7p |
| Tesco | 178p | _____ | _____ |
| _____ | _____ | 512p | _____ |
| BSkyB | _____ | 510p | _____ |
| Alsthom | 140p | _____ | _____ |

Calculate any prices which are not given.

**Speaking**

**1** Work in pairs or small groups. You have £1,000 and are thinking of investing it on the stock market. Decide which of the shares listed on page 81 you would buy, and calculate how many you could afford. Choose a maximum of four different companies.

Example:

| | | |
|---|---|---|
| Tate & Lyle (food producers) | 100 shares @ | 350p = £350.00 |
| Inter. Energy Group (gas distribution) | 150 shares @ | 134p = £201.00 |
| Allied Zurich Insurance | 25 shares @ | 714p = £178.50 |
| Seton Scholl (health care) | 35 shares @ | 755p = £264.25 |
| | | Total = £993.75 |

**2** After consideration, you decide not to purchase any shares. However, you are curious to know whether or not you did the right thing. Look at the prices for the same shares six months later on page 158. Calculate how much money your group would have made or lost if you had bought the shares.

*If we had bought _____ , we would have made/lost _____ .*

**Writing**

**1** Read the headline and discuss possible reasons for the change in share prices.

# Motorola stock falls $3 to close at $52

**2** Read an extract from the newspaper article and see if any of your suggestions are mentioned.

Motorola Inc, the world's top maker of cellular phones, said Wednesday it planned to cut more jobs in a drive to improve falling profits after reporting a loss for the second quarter.

Late on Tuesday they posted a net loss of $1.33 bn for the quarter to June 27, compared with a net profit of $268 m a year ago. Sales slipped to $7.02 bn from $7.52 bn. Although the results were slightly better than analysts expected, Motorola stock fell $3, to close at $52.

**3** Correct the mistakes in this summary of the article.

> Motorola is currently experiencing financial difficulties. Sales fell considerably and consequently profits are up. The company has decided to cut costs by increasing the number of employees. Share prices have suffered as a result of this situation. They rose in value from $55 to $52 in one day.

**4** Look through the financial pages of a newspaper and choose three short articles about events that have caused companies' share prices to change. Write a brief summary describing what happened to each company and showing how its shares were affected. Use the example above to help you.

# Import Export

Key vocabulary  International trade is the exchange of goods and services between different countries. Depending on what a country produces and needs, it can **export** (send goods to another country) and **import** (bring in goods from another country).

Governments can control international trade. The most common measures are **tariffs** (or **duties**) and **quotas**. A tariff is a tax on imported goods, and a quota is the maximum quantity of a product allowed into a country during a certain period of time. These measures are **protectionist** as they raise the price of imported goods to 'protect' domestically produced goods.

International organisations such as the **WTO** (World Trade Organisation) and **EFTA** (European Free Trade Association) regulate tariffs and reduce trade restrictions between member countries.

Lead-in **1** Listen to an economist from the Organisation for Economic Co-operation and Development (OECD) explaining why countries trade, and answer the questions.

1  What does the speaker compare countries to?
2  What activity does he give as an example?
3  Why does it make sense for countries to trade?

**2** Look at this history of the European Union.

| | |
|---|---|
| **1957** | The European Economic Community (EEC) was founded in order to create a common market in which tariffs and quotas between member countries would be progressively eliminated. The six original member countries were Belgium, France, Italy, Luxembourg, the Netherlands and West Germany. |
| **1973** | Denmark, Ireland and the UK joined. |
| **1981** | Greece joined. |
| **1981** | Portugal and Spain joined. |
| **1987** | The Single European Act created a single economic area from 1st January 1993, called the European Community (EC). |
| **1991** | The Maastricht Treaty was signed, reinforcing economic and monetary union. |
| **1993** | In November the organisation became the European Union (EU). |
| **1995** | Membership increased to 15 countries as Austria, Finland and Sweden joined the Union. |
| **1999** | The single European currency, the euro, was launched. |

**Have any other countries joined?**

In pairs, do the following quiz.

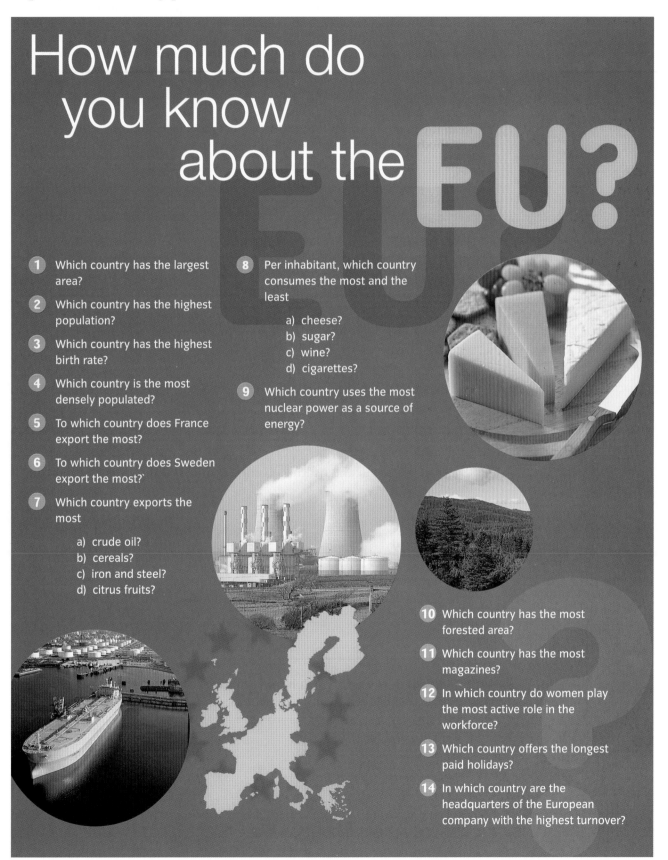

# How much do you know about the EU?

1. Which country has the largest area?

2. Which country has the highest population?

3. Which country has the highest birth rate?

4. Which country is the most densely populated?

5. To which country does France export the most?

6. To which country does Sweden export the most?`

7. Which country exports the most
   a) crude oil?
   b) cereals?
   c) iron and steel?
   d) citrus fruits?

8. Per inhabitant, which country consumes the most and the least
   a) cheese?
   b) sugar?
   c) wine?
   d) cigarettes?

9. Which country uses the most nuclear power as a source of energy?

10. Which country has the most forested area?

11. Which country has the most magazines?

12. In which country do women play the most active role in the workforce?

13. Which country offers the longest paid holidays?

14. In which country are the headquarters of the European company with the highest turnover?

**Reading**

Companies can choose from various methods to establish their products in a foreign market. One option is to start by working with **local experts** such as **sole agents** or **multi-distributors**, who have a specialist knowledge of the market and sell on behalf of the company. This often leads to the company opening a **local branch** or **sales office**. Another option is to sell, or give permission to use, **patents** and **licences** for their products. They may wish to start by manufacturing in the export market, in which case they can either set up a **local subsidiary** or a **joint venture** with a local partner.

**1** Read the text opposite about BARCO, a Belgian electronics firm. Which of the methods mentioned above did BARCO use to establish itself on the Indian market?

**2** Read the text again and list the advantages and disadvantages of exporting to India.

| Advantages | Disadvantages |
|---|---|
| The market is growing | High import duties |

**Vocabulary**

**1** Find words in the text which have a similar meaning to the words and expressions listed below.

1 complicated (*para 1*) complex
2 put together (*para 1*)
3 a change (*para 2*)
4 particular segment (*para 3*)
5 take advantage of (*para 6*)
6 difficulties (*para 6*)
7 a complicated official system (*para 6*)
8 lateness (*para 7*)

## Profile:

# BARCO

## of Belgium

*The statue outside the BARCO main building*

1 After three years travelling around Asia as head of BARCO's activities in the region, Joost Verbrugge is convinced that India is one of the most exciting long-term market opportunities in the world and one of the most complex. Since 1994, BARCO, best-known for its digital projectors for computers, has gone from a relatively low level of exports to India to selling about BFr 200m of products there a year, half exported from Europe, half assembled on the spot*. That is a small but significant part of its total BFr 23bn turnover last year.

2 Expansion in India has taken place at the same time as a shift in BARCO's strategic focus, and its emergence* as one of Belgium's fastest-growing companies.

3 Created in 1934 as the Belgian American Radio Corporation, the company moved out of consumer products in the 1980s. It concentrated instead on high-value niche markets such as computer projectors and specialist display systems.

4 From its base in Kortrijk, Flanders – Belgium's Dutch-speaking region – it has exported to India for more than a decade, originally selling kits for video monitors to the national television station, through local agents. Four years ago, it set up its own sales and services office in New Delhi.

5 It now has a smaller sales office in Bangalore, a software house in Chennai and a projector assembly plant in Noida, near New Delhi.

Having invested about BFr 100m, and now employing 150 people in India, it plans a further sales office in Mumbai and a components factory in Noida. 'That is quite a lot for a small company like BARCO,' says Mr. Verbrugge. 'It's mainly investment for the future. The market is partly there now, and we are convinced it will definitely be there in a few years.'

6 But for those wanting to exploit the potential*, obstacles remain. Although India has made efforts to open its economy in recent years, Mr. Verbrugge says it remains more closed than other fast-growing markets such as China when it comes to bureaucracy, import duties and tax barriers.

7 'It is not unusual to have import duties of 40% on things that you would consider normal working tools, like a printer for a PC,' he says. 'As well as the high import duties, you have a famous – or should I say infamous – bureaucracy.' This can have important practical effects. Mr. Verbrugge says that BARCO would like to assemble more of its products within India, but this would mean importing components* from 20 different countries, creating huge amounts of paperwork and delays.

8 Although India is welcoming to foreigners, Mr. Verbrugge says there are also cultural hurdles which can initially be deceptive. 'On a first visit India seems easier than China or Japan because

people speak English. Only after you start operating there do you see all the complexities. There are sensitivities between states, between religions, between strata* of society.' Such differences also make the country fascinating. 'India is a hundred different worlds living next to each other in the same country,' Mr. Verbrugge says.

9 These practical and cultural complexities were largely behind BARCO's decision to set up its own sales office in the subcontinent. 'Much more is needed than just having an agent with a fax and a phone. You have to understand the marketplace, how Indian business works.'

10 But the opportunities presented by India outweigh* any disadvantages. 'If you can afford to miss a fifth of the world's population, you can afford not to be there,' says Mr. Verbrugge. 'I think any company serious about having a worldwide market share can't be absent from India.'

*The Financial Times*

---

*on the spot:* in the place mentioned
*emergence:* appearing for the first time
*potential:* possible opportunities

*a component:* a part used to make s.th.
*strata:* levels
*to outweigh:* to be more important than

**2** Complete the following passage, which describes the experience of the French car manufacturer Peugeot in the Indian market, with words from Key vocabulary, Reading and Vocabulary 1, in the correct form.

> Peugeot signed a joint venture agreement to produce cars in India in 1994. They saw this as a great opportunity for them to [1] _exploit_ this vast and quickly growing market. They planned to [2]_____ 22,000 cars by 1997 and 60,000 by the year 2000. In reality production in 1997 was just 2,000.
>
> Automotive group Maruti, which had been working with Suzuki since 1984, had established an extraordinary dominance in the country's economy car sector. The strongest [3]_____ _____ for a foreign competitor therefore, appeared to be in the market for upper-range cars. Peugeot opted for its 309, a mid-range car in Europe but one which represents between 40 and 60 months' salary for the average worker in India. In spring 1995 [4]_____ occurred when Indian authorities argued that certain parts imported for production were still on a list of banned products which are taxed separately and Peugeot had to pay high [5]_____ to import them.
>
> But in spite of all the [6]_____ this market presents, Peugeot has not given up on the country. As one executive explains 'We will expand by granting [7]_____ to local manufacturers in the future.'

## Vocabulary development: compound adjectives 1

Adjectives can be formed by combining two words, for example *long-term* (*para 1*). These adjectives are hyphenated only when they come before a noun.

**1** Complete the phrases below, using words from **A** and **B**. There is sometimes more than one correct answer, and some words may be used more than once.

| A | B |
|---|---|
| environmentally | fashioned |
| old | term |
| short | budget |
| low | known |
| well | friendly |
| high | level |
| user | trained |

a _environmentally_ _friendly_ packaging
b _____ _____ typewriter
c _____ _____ opportunities
d _____ _____ advertising
e _____ _____ personality
f _____ _____ decision-making
g _____ _____ software
h _____ _____ staff

**2** What other adjectives of this type do you know?

## Listening

### The invoice

In the context of international trade, the invoice provides information about goods exchanged between the exporter and the importer. It is prepared by the exporter and includes a description of the goods, their price and the quantity supplied. It can act as proof of purchase, informing the buyer that the goods have been sent.

▭ Listen to an explanation of the invoice below, and complete the missing information.

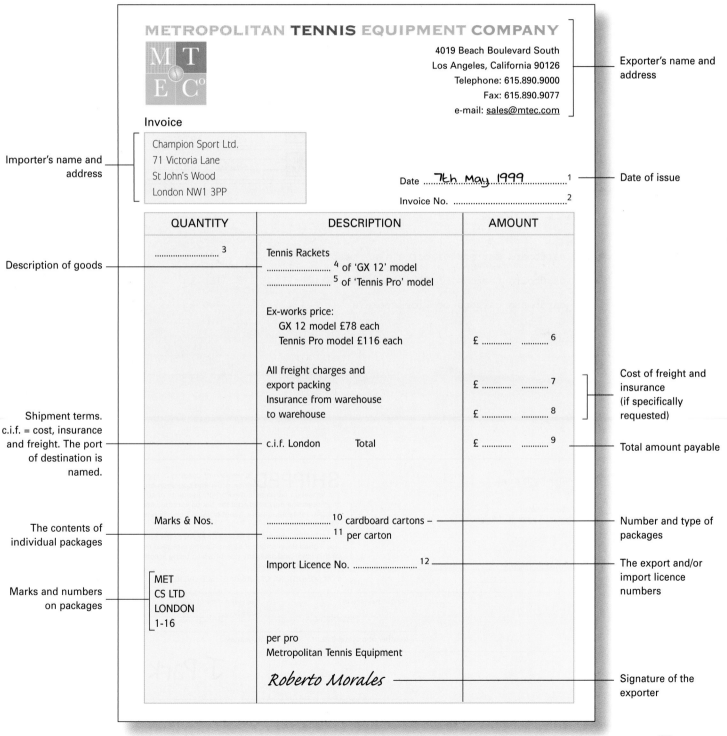

**METROPOLITAN TENNIS EQUIPMENT COMPANY**

4019 Beach Boulevard South
Los Angeles, California 90126
Telephone: 615.890.9000
Fax: 615.890.9077
e-mail: sales@mtec.com

Exporter's name and address

Invoice

Champion Sport Ltd.
71 Victoria Lane
St John's Wood
London NW1 3PP

Importer's name and address

Date .....7th May 1999........ 1 — Date of issue

Invoice No. ........................ 2

| QUANTITY | DESCRIPTION | AMOUNT |
|---|---|---|
| ...................... 3 | Tennis Rackets<br>...................... 4 of 'GX 12' model<br>...................... 5 of 'Tennis Pro' model | |
| | Ex-works price:<br>  GX 12 model £78 each<br>  Tennis Pro model £116 each | £ ............ ............ 6 |
| | All freight charges and<br>export packing<br>Insurance from warehouse<br>to warehouse | £ ............ ............ 7<br><br>£ ............ ............ 8 |
| | c.i.f. London        Total | £ ............ ............ 9 |
| Marks & Nos. | ...................... 10 cardboard cartons –<br>...................... 11 per carton | |
| | Import Licence No. ................ 12 | |
| MET<br>CS LTD<br>LONDON<br>1-16 | | |

Description of goods

Shipment terms. c.i.f. = cost, insurance and freight. The port of destination is named.

The contents of individual packages

Marks and numbers on packages

Cost of freight and insurance (if specifically requested)

Total amount payable

Number and type of packages

The export and/or import licence numbers

per pro
Metropolitan Tennis Equipment

*Roberto Morales* ———— Signature of the exporter

### Reading    The bill of lading

**The bill of lading is a transfer document. The exporter writes the importer's name on the bill of lading, and in this way the importer becomes the legal owner of the goods.**

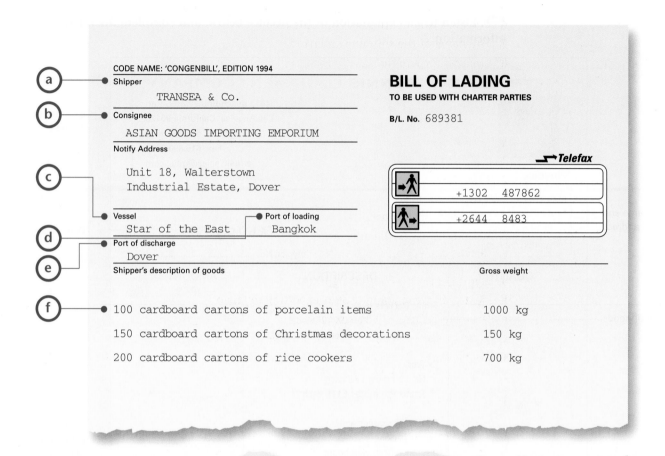

CODE NAME: 'CONGENBILL', EDITION 1994

**(a)** Shipper

TRANSEA & Co.

**(b)** Consignee

ASIAN GOODS IMPORTING EMPORIUM

Notify Address

**(c)** Unit 18, Walterstown
Industrial Estate, Dover

**(d)** Vessel            Port of loading
Star of the East     Bangkok

Port of discharge

**(e)** Dover

Shipper's description of goods

**(f)**

| | Gross weight |
|---|---|
| 100 cardboard cartons of porcelain items | 1000 kg |
| 150 cardboard cartons of Christmas decorations | 150 kg |
| 200 cardboard cartons of rice cookers | 700 kg |

## BILL OF LADING
**TO BE USED WITH CHARTER PARTIES**

B/L. No. 689381

↗ *Telefax*

+1302   487862

+2644   8483

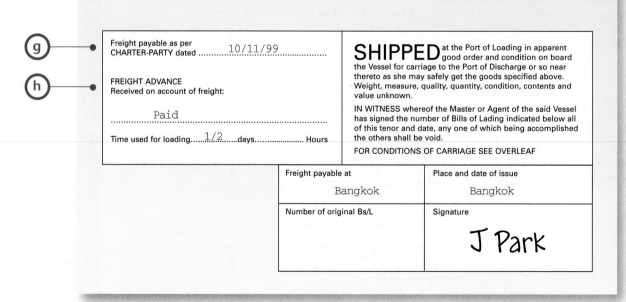

**(g)** Freight payable as per
CHARTER-PARTY dated ............... 10/11/99 ...............

**(h)** FREIGHT ADVANCE
Received on account of freight:

Paid
.................................................................

Time used for loading ....... 1/2 ..... days ..................... Hours

**SHIPPED** at the Port of Loading in apparent good order and condition on board the Vessel for carriage to the Port of Discharge or so near thereto as she may safely get the goods specified above. Weight, measure, quality, quantity, condition, contents and value unknown.

IN WITNESS whereof the Master or Agent of the said Vessel has signed the number of Bills of Lading indicated below all of this tenor and date, any one of which being accomplished the others shall be void.

FOR CONDITIONS OF CARRIAGE SEE OVERLEAF

| Freight payable at | Place and date of issue |
|---|---|
| Bangkok | Bangkok |
| Number of original Bs/L | Signature |
| | J Park |

**Match the parts of the bill of lading opposite with the descriptions below.**

1 The date of the contract between the exporter and the shipping company. 9

2 The name of the importer.

3 Details of the goods.

4 The name of the ship.

5 Money paid to the shipping company before the journey.

6 The place where the goods are unloaded.

7 The name of the shipping company.

8 The place where the goods are loaded.

## *Language Focus*

**The future**

**Which sentence below refers to**

1 a future fact?

2 a prediction not based on present evidence?

3 a degree of probability or certainty?

4 a decision made now?

5 something decided before, an intention?

6 a prediction based on present evidence?

a Is it urgent? OK, I'll do it right now.

b Next year, we're going to start exporting to Japan.

c His overseas trip will be a success.

d Exports are slowing down; there's going to be a recession.

e The market will definitely be there in a few years.

f This company will be 100 years old next year.

▶▶ **For more information on *will* and *going to*, turn to page 167.**

**Practice**

**Complete this dialogue between Steve, an export manager, and Bob, his agent in Australia, using *will* or *going to* and the verbs in brackets.**

> Steve: Hello Bob, I'm phoning to check a few things with you about my trip next week.
>
> Bob: Hold on Steve, I ¹_____ (get) the file out. Right, how can I help you?
>
> Steve: Well, we've had a few problems here in the European office so I've decided to stay and book a later flight. Now I ²_____ (leave) on the 5th, not the 3rd.
>
> Bob: Actually that suits me better, that way I ³_____ (have) time to finish the monthly sales figures before you come.
>
> Steve: Good, I think we ⁴_____ (need) to have a look at those together.
>
> Bob: Don't forget, we ⁵_____ (visit) the Melbourne office when you're here.
>
> Steve: I haven't forgotten, I'm sure it ⁶_____ (be) interesting to see how they run their operation. OK, see you next month.
>
> Bob: Looking forward to it. Bye.
>
> Steve: Bye.

## Describing trends

Unit 1 looked at some of the nouns and verbs used to describe changes in price, quantity and amount, for example:

| Noun | Verb |
|------|------|
| an increase | to increase |
| a rise | to rise |
| a decrease | to decrease |
| a drop | to drop |
| a fall | to fall |

These can be qualified with an adjective or adverb to describe a change more precisely. Complete the table.

| | | Adjective | Adverb |
|---|---|-----------|--------|
| Used to show a small change: | a | slight | *slightly* |
| Used to show a regular movement: | b | gradual | |
| | c | steady | |
| Used to show considerable, striking or unexpected change: | d | sharp | |
| | e | dramatic | |
| | f | sudden | |

## Practice

**1** Complete the descriptions of the following graphs using an appropriate adjective or adverb.

Prices rose ¹ _*steadily*_ from February to October, before falling ² _____ in November.

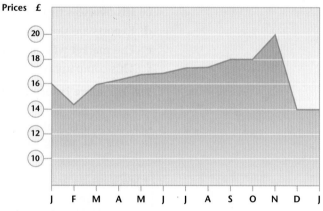

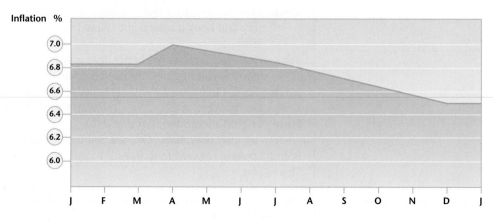

Inflation rose ³ _____ in March, before beginning its ⁴ _____ descent to today's figure of 6.5%.

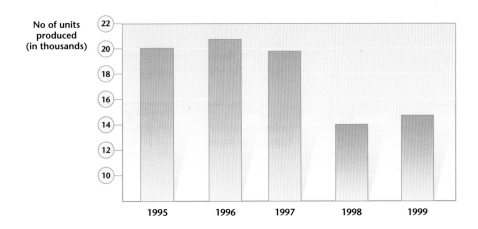

No of units produced (in thousands)

1998 saw a ⁵_____ drop in production, followed by a ⁶_____ recovery in 1999.

**2** Which parts of the following graph would you talk about using each of these expressions?

| | | |
|---|---|---|
| **a** to fluctuate May to Sep | **b** to level off | **c** to remain stable |
| **d** to reach a peak | **e** to stand at | |

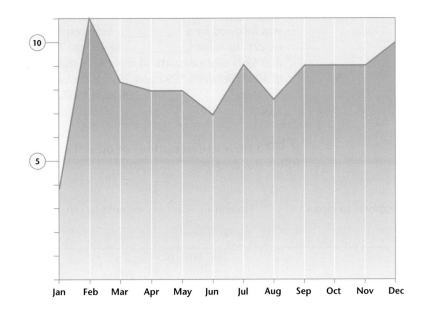

**3** Join expressions from each box to make sentences about the graph.

| | |
|---|---|
| **1** Sales reached a peak | **a** 10,000 in December. |
| **2** Sales fluctuated | **b** from September to November. |
| **3** Sales remained stable | **c** of 11,000. |
| **4** Sales stood at | **d** at about 8,000 in April. |
| **5** Sales levelled off | **e** from May to September. |

## *Skills Focus*

**Writing**

Write a short description of Finnish paper exports to Japan between 1987 and 1997 using the following graph.

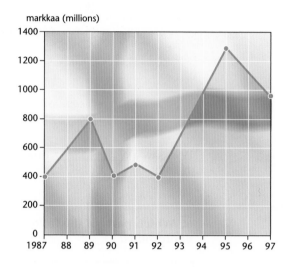

**Finland's** paper **exports to Japan**

markkaa (millions)

**Listening**

**1** 🖭 Listen to a description of the graph above and complete the text.

In 1987 the export figures ¹<u>stood at</u> 400 m Finnish markkaa. There was a ²_____ between 1987 and 1989 when figures ³_____ over 800 m. This was followed by a ⁴_____ between 1989 and 1990 when Finnish paper exports to Japan ⁵_____ to 400 m. There was a ⁶_____ between 1990 and 1991 when exports hit the 450 m mark but they ⁷_____ again to 400 m in 1992. Between 1992 and 1995 there was a ⁸_____ and exports of paper to Japan ⁹_____ of 1,300 m in 1995, before ¹⁰_____ again to under 1,000 m in 1997.

**2** 🖭 Listen to descriptions of other Finnish exports to Japan and complete the following graphs.

**Finland's** wood **exports to Japan**

markkaa (millions)

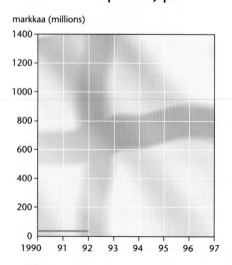

**Finland's** machinery **exports to Japan**

markkaa (millions)

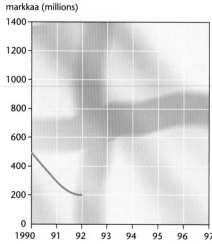

**Finland's** chemical **exports to Japan**

markkaa (millions)

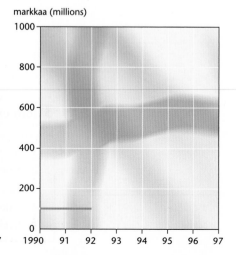

**Speaking**

**1** **Work in pairs. You will each study a graph showing US trade from August 1996 to August 1998. Student A, look at the graph below. Student B, turn to page 160.**

> **Student A**
> The graph below shows US imports of goods and services from August 1996 to August 1998. Describe the information to Student B using the language you have learnt in this unit. Then listen to Student B's description of US exports for the same period and complete the graph using a different colour.

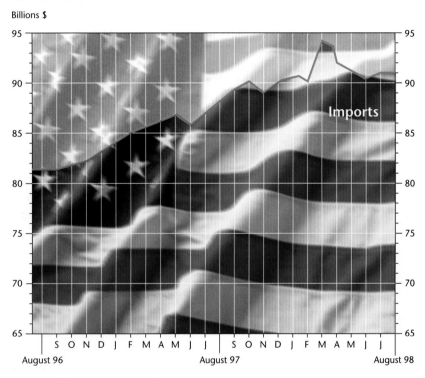

**US International Trade in Goods and Services**

Billions $

**2** A country's **balance of trade** is the difference between the values of its imports and exports. This includes **visible imports / exports** (goods) and **invisible imports / exports** (services). If a country imports more than it exports, it has a **trade deficit**. If it exports more than it imports, it has a **trade surplus**.

**Look at the graph in Speaking 1.**

1   Did the US have a trade deficit or surplus?

2   In pairs, calculate the balance of payments for the following periods.

    **a** May 1997 *deficit of $9 bn*

    **b** October 1997

    **c** March 1998

3 **a** When did the US have the lowest deficit in the period from August 1996 to August 1997?

    **b** When did the US import the most?

    **c** When did the US export the most?

# 10 *Company Performance*

**Key vocabulary**  Companies need to know how they are performing in order to analyse problems, find solutions and make plans for the future. **Management accounts** provide **data** about operational efficiency and **financial accounts** give information about financial performance. These tell the company not only how much it is selling, or how much **revenue** it is receiving, but also what its costs are – how much it has to pay for the different things that it needs in order to operate. With this information a company can then calculate how much money it has made (**profits**) or how much it has lost (**losses**) during a specific period. **Listed companies**, whose shares are sold on the stock exchange, have to present their accounts to the public in an **annual report**.

**Lead-in**   **1** **With the increasing complexity of the modern business world, companies often need to seek the advice of specialist consultants, such as PricewaterhouseCoopers, who can help them improve their performance and prepare for the future.**

# PRICEWATERHOUSECOOPERS 🖼

**Match the departments of PricewaterhouseCoopers below with their functions.**

| | | | | |
|---|---|---|---|---|
| 1 | **FAS** | *(Financial Advisory Services)* | a | check company accounts |
| 2 | **MCS** | *(Management Consulting Services)* | b | provide advice on finance |
| 3 | **TLS** | *(Tax and Legal Services)* | c | advise on performance |
| 4 | **ABAS** | *(Assurance Business Advisory Services)* | d | provide taxation advice |

**2** **You will hear four managers from PricewaterhouseCoopers describing the services their departments provide. Before you listen, decide which department a client would contact to**

1 arrange for an evaluation of its administration.    `MCS`

2 obtain advice about new VAT laws.

3 decide what to do about a subsidiary company that is losing money.

4 look at ways of improving its computer network.

5 decide which aspects of the business to concentrate on in the future.

6 find out the value of a company.

7 certify that the annual accounts are accurate.

📼 **Listen to the managers and check your answers.**

**3** **Read the text below and answer the questions.**

1 What is the purpose of an annual report?

2 What are stakeholders?

# What's an annual report?

An annual report is prepared by the management of a company whose stock is traded publicly. It discusses the company's financial affairs. An annual report performs a useful function in a free market system, transmitting information from the company to its shareholders and investing public. Although the report is addressed to shareholders, other people who have a stake in the business – stakeholders such as employees, suppliers, customers, and lenders – will find it informative.

*MTS Employee Supplement to the 1994 Annual Report*

**Reading**

**1** **Read the text and match the headings to the paragraphs.**

**Paragraphs 1–5**

Report of management
Auditor's report
Management discussion
Financial statements and notes
Selected financial data

**Paragraphs 6–10**

Financial highlights
Letter to stockholders
Corporate message
Board of directors and management
Stockholder information

# Anatomy of an annual report

While most annual reports contain optional elements, all reports contain information required by the Securities Exchange Commission or SEC, the commission that controls and administers the activities of US stock exchanges.

**SEC-required elements include:**

**1** <u>Auditor's report</u> This summary by independent public accountants shows whether the financial statements are complete, reliable, and prepared consistent with generally accepted accounting principles (GAAP).

**2** <u>Report of management</u> This letter, usually from the board chairperson and the chief financial officer, takes responsibility for the validity* of the financial information in the annual report, and states that the report complies with SEC and other legal requirements.

**3** _____ These provide the complete numbers for the company's financial performance and recent financial history. The SEC requires:

• Statement of earnings*
The statement of earnings shows how much revenue a company brings into the business, and the costs and expenses associated with earning that revenue during that time.

• Statement of cash flows*
The statement of cash flows reports the flow of cash into and out of a company in a given year. Cash is a company's lifeblood*. Cash includes currency and deposits in banks. Cash equivalents are short-term, temporary investments that can be quickly and easily converted to cash.

• Statement of financial position*
The statement of financial position reports a company's financial status at a set date. The statement is like a snapshot* because it shows what the company is worth at that set date. The statement shows:

  • what the company owns (assets)
  • what the company owes (liabilities)
  • what belongs to the owners (stockholders' equity)

**4** _____ This information summarizes a company's financial condition and performance over five years or longer, including gross profit and net earnings (net income).

**5** _____ This series of short, detailed reports discusses and analyzes the company's performance. It covers results of operations, and the adequacy* of resources to fund operations.

**Optional elements include:**

**6** _____ This list gives the names and position titles of the company's board of directors and top management team. Sometimes companies include photographs.

**7** _____ This information covers the basics – the company's headquarters, the exchanges on which the company trades its stock, the next annual stockholders' meeting, and other general stockholder service information. It is usually in the back of the annual report.

**8** _____ This may be from the chairperson of the board of directors, the chief executive officer, or both. It can provide an analysis and a review of the year's events, including any problems, issues, and successes the company had. It usually reflects the business philosophy and management style of the company's executives, and it often lays out* the company's direction for the next year.

**9** _____ Some consider this an advertisement for the company. However, it almost always reflects how a company sees itself, or how it would like others to see it. Here, the company can explain itself to the stockholders, using photographs, illustrations, and text. It may cover the company's lines of business, markets, mission*, management philosophy, corporate culture, and strategic direction.

**10** _____ Probably the most often-read section of any annual report, these give a quick summary of a company's performance. The figures appear in a short table, usually accompanied by supporting graphs.

*International Business Machines
Guide to Understanding Financials*

---

*validity: correctness
*statement of earnings (US): profit and loss account (GB)
*statement of cash flows (US): cash flow statement (GB)
*lifeblood: the essential item
*statement of financial position (US): balance sheet (GB)

*a snapshot: information that quickly shows a situation at a point in time
*adequacy: sufficiency, whether there is enough
*to lay out: to present
*a mission: the aim of an organisation

**2** Read the text again. Which section of a company's annual report would you read for information about these things?

1 any difficulties the company has had to face during the last year
2 how the company performed during previous years
3 the company's results for the year
4 whether the report satisfies government requirements
5 the company's plans for the next year

**Vocabulary**

**1** The article includes words for different people who are either directly or indirectly involved with a listed company. Match the words for people from the text with their corresponding definitions.

1 a director
2 a chief executive officer
3 a stockholder
4 a chief financial officer
5 a chairperson
6 an auditor

a has bought shares in the company
b is in charge of the board
c is a member of the board
d is an outside financial specialist
e is responsible for finance
f is responsible for all operations

**2** Find words in the text which correspond to the following definitions.

**Statement of earnings**

1 money received, generally from sales        ( _revenue_ )

2 money that is spent on such things as salaries, rent, office supplies, advertising and taxes        (_____)

**Statement of cash flows**

3 money in general use as cash, such as coins or bank notes        (_____)

4 money or its equivalent paid into an organisation for safe keeping, or as security, or to bear interest        (_____)

5 money that has been invested but that can be rapidly changed into cash        (_____)

**Statement of financial position**

6 anything with money value that a company owns        (_____)

7 a company's debts        (_____)

**Selected Financial Data**

8 the difference between a company's total sales and costs of sales        (_____)

9 a company's total revenue minus total expenses, also known as 'the bottom line'        (_____)

**3** Complete the following extract from the financial highlights section of an annual report using words from Vocabulary 2.

| | |
|---|---|
| a _revenue_ | $1,145,773 |
| b _____ : | |
| Materials and labor | $794,780 |
| c _____ (a – b) | $350,993 |
| d Selling and administration | $230,153 |
| Interest | $14,435 |
| e _____ (c – d) | **$106,405** |

**Vocabulary development: nouns and prepositions**

Some nouns are always followed by the same preposition(s). Look at these examples from the text on page 98.

takes **responsibility for** the validity (para 2)

an **advertisement for** the company (para 9)

**1** Match the prepositions with the nouns below. In some cases it may be possible to use two prepositions.

| with | for | of | on | into | in |
|------|-----|----|----|------|----|

**a** the result … of    **f** satisfaction …

**b** an enquiry …    **g** a percentage …

**c** involvement …    **h** a tax …

**d** an interest …    **i** research …

**e** support …    **j** an effect …

**2** Add a suitable noun after each preposition above.

Example: *The result of the changes.*

## Language Focus

**Fractions and percentages**

We use fractions and percentages to express the relative values of one amount compared to another. Look at the examples.

*More than half of our personnel (51%) already own shares in the company. A quarter (25%) will qualify next year.*

Complete the table.

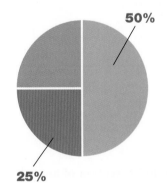

50%

25%

| $^1/_2$ | a half | 50% |
|---------|--------|-----|
| $^-/_3$ | _____ | 66% |
| $^-/_4$ | _____ | 25% |
| $^-/_4$ | _____ | 75% |
| $^-/_5$ | _____ | 40% |
| $^\underline{5}/_6$ | five sixths | 83% |
| $^-/_{10}$ | _____ | 90% |

▶▶ For more information on fractions and percentages, turn to page 168.

**Practice**

We use the following words to give approximations when we are talking about amounts.

| *about* | *approximately* | *nearly* | *roughly* | *around* |

Example: *Approximately one third of our products have been created in the last five years.*

**Which word is different in meaning from the others?**

**Use the information in the two pie charts to complete the extract below from an annual report. Use the appropriate fractions and modifying words where necessary.**

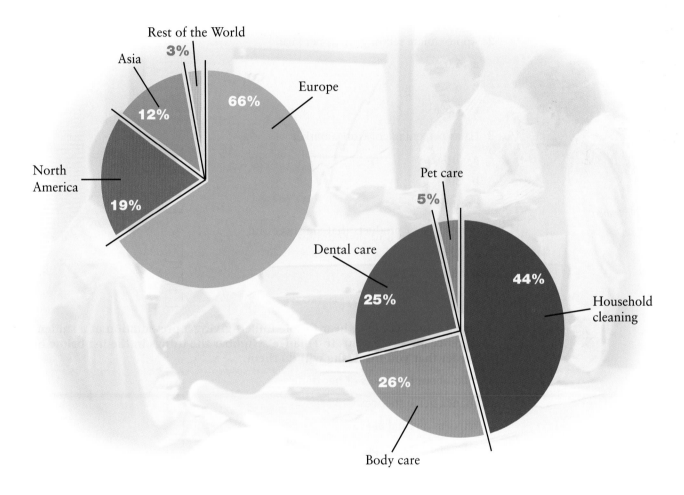

Analysis of our performance during the last year shows that ¹<u>about two thirds</u> of our revenue came from the European markets. The second largest source of sales was North America which accounted for ²_____. In third position, the Asian markets contributed ³_____. The rest of the world provided the remaining 3% of total revenue.
As for products, our leading category was household cleaning which represented ⁴_____. This was followed by body care, accounting for ⁵_____ of turnover. Dental care represented a further ⁶_____ and pet care added an additional 5%.

## Business Skills Focus: Presentations

**Listening**

**1** 🔲 A financial analyst is an expert on a specific business sector, whose opinion is used by investors to decide whether or not to invest in a particular business at a given time. Listen to Carole Imbert, a financial analyst with CPR Finance in Paris, talking about the sector she specialises in. Tick the box next to the correct figure.

**1** Pharmaceutical sector turnover

   **a** 3 billion dollars ☐

   **b** 13 billion dollars ☐

   **c** 300 billion dollars ☐

**2** Approximate sector growth per year

   **a** 5.0% ☐

   **b** 6.5% ☐

   **c** 7.5% ☐

**3** US as percentage of world market

   **a** 50% ☐

   **b** 30% ☐

   **c** 40% ☐

**4** Percentage of products that are successful

   **a** 13% ☐

   **b** 15% ☐

   **c** 50% ☐

*Carole Imbert*

**2** You are now going to hear Carole Imbert giving a presentation at a student conference on 'Professions in Finance'. Number the things in the list below in the order that you think she will do them.

**a** talks about the 'tools of her trade' ☐

**b** thanks her audience ☐

**c** refers to a visual aid ☐

**d** talks about her experience of presenting ☐

**e** talks about how important presentation skills are ☐

**f** describes the plan of her talk ☐

**g** explains what her job involves ☐

🔲 Listen to the presentation and check your answers.

**3** 🔲 Listen to part of the presentation again and complete the definitions that she gives for the terms below.

*listed:*         *by 'listed' we mean* _____

*brokerage firms:*  *which are really* _____

4 [🔊] Listen to the last part of the presentation again. Which visual aid does Carole Imbert actually refer to?

5 Do you think that Carole Imbert is reading her text or speaking from notes? What do you think are the advantages and disadvantages of these two approaches to giving a presentation?

## Speaking

### Giving a presentation

1 When you give a presentation you have to make it as easy as possible for your audience to follow what you are saying. To do this you have to make it clear what you are going to do in each part of your talk, and when you have finished one section and are moving on to the next. Read the tapescript of Carole Imbert's presentation on page 163 and underline the language that she uses to

a  explain the order of her talk
b  repeat something
c  draw attention to visual aids
d  make a transition from one section to another

2 In groups, you are going to give a short presentation (maximum ten minutes) of a company's results, based on the financial highlights section of an annual report. The objective of the presentation is both to report on the performance of the company in its sector and to explain the different terms that are used.

Group A turn to page 155
Group B turn to page 159
Group C turn to page 161

3 Give your presentations to the other groups. As you listen, take notes to help you complete the writing activity below.

## Writing

You are a researcher for a consulting firm. Write a company report on L'Oréal, using the notes and information from the presentations in Speaking.

# Review 2

## Grammar check

### 1 Underline the correct forms of the words in italics.

The results of the latest supplier audit are [1] *already / <u>still</u>* incomplete. They will [2] *process / be processed*, then we will prepare a full report. However, early analysis shows that some of our suppliers [3] *still / yet* haven't complied with our policy. The companies concerned [4] *will be informing / will be informed* that failure to comply will mean that we [5] *are discontinuing / will discontinue* our dealings with them.

[6] *Although / In spite of* a lot of progress [7] *has been made / has made* to eliminate products containing toxic materials, further work remains [8] *to do / to be done*, which [9] *is going to / will* [10] *enable / let* us to include an ecological label on most of our goods. We [11] *are going to / will* probably be able to do this next year, and guarantee that none of our products [12] *have tested / have been tested* on animals.

As for health and safety and working conditions, we [13] *will produce / will be produced* new guidelines in the near future. A summary of the problem areas [14] *is given / is being given* below. [15] *In spite of / Although* protective clothing is provided, there are too many accidents. Additional training will [16] *allow / let* workers become more familiar with the hazards of different machinery.

Regarding workers' rights, we [17] *have been agreed / have agreed* that companies using unpaid overtime will be removed from our list of suppliers. [18] *Even though / Despite* there are national differences in legislation, we [19] *will / are going to* continue our efforts to introduce minimum working conditions for overseas suppliers.

We expect that this year's survey [20] *is going to / will* enhance the performance of the company and maintain our reputation.

### 2 Complete the sentences with the correct forms of the verbs in brackets.

1  If people (not be) __weren't__ so concerned about the environment nowadays, businesses (not develop) __wouldn't develop__ environmental polices.

2  If they (know) _____ the market was going to expand so quickly last year, they (increase) _____ production accordingly.

3  If UK interest rates (fall) _____ next week, we (switch) _____ our investments into another currency.

4  If they (reduce) _____ tariffs this year as they have promised to, we (do) _____ more business there.

5  If biodegradable materials (not be) _____ still so expensive, we (use) _____ them more often in our manufacturing process.

6  If we (buy) _____ shares before the crash, we (lose) _____ a lot of money. I'm glad we didn't.

7  If sales in the Indian market (increase) _____ as they are expected to, we (expand) _____ our production site there.

8  If we (not cut) _____ costs in production, we (not survive) _____ the last economic crisis.

9  If we (have) _____ the necessary information, we (be able) _____ to make a decision, but at the moment we don't.

10  If they (not deliver) _____ the goods on time tomorrow, we (not use) _____ their services again.

### 3 Correct the information in italics where necessary, using the information in the graph.

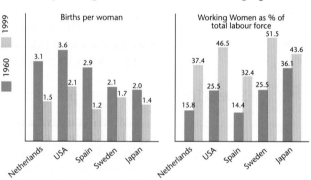

If we look at the chart concerning the number of births per woman, we can see that in the Netherlands, for example, these [1] *~~more than doubled~~* more than halved between 1960 and 1999. In Japan, during the same period, there was [2] *a slight increase* _____ in the number of children born. This was also the case in Sweden where births also [3] *rose* _____. In all countries the birth rate [4] *remained stable* _____ between 1960 and 1999.

As for the number of women in the labour force, we can see that this figure increased by more than [5] *25%* _____ in Sweden, where more than half of the total number of employees in 1999 were women. There was a similar [6] *rise* _____ in Spain. In Japan, however, there was a [7] *big increase* _____ with approximately [8] *7%* _____ more women joining the workforce. In the USA, where only approximately [9] *1/3* _____ of the female population worked in 1960, the total number of female employees reached slightly less than [10] *2/3* _____ of the labour force by 1999.

## Vocabulary check

**1** **Complete the boxes with the words and expressions from the list below that are most commonly associated with each theme.**

| Banking | The Environment |
|---|---|
| _____ | _____ |
| _____ | _____ |
| _____ | _____ |
| _____ | _____ |

| The Stock Market | Import Export |
|---|---|
| _____ | *tariffs* |
| _____ | _____ |
| _____ | _____ |
| _____ | _____ |

| Company Performance |
|---|
| _____ |
| _____ |
| _____ |
| _____ |

| | |
|---|---|
| tariffs | quota |
| chief financial officer | broker |
| balance | sustainability |
| net profit | local subsidiary |
| waste | revenue |
| yield | duties |
| deposit | debit card |
| balance sheet | global warming |
| cashpoint | issue shares |
| dividend | recycling |

**2** **Complete the extract from a letter to shareholders with words and expressions from exercise 1 in the correct form.**

It has been another excellent year for the company as our businesses have continued to grow. As you will see from the [1] _balance sheet_ and the accompanying financial statements, our financial performance has improved significantly. We are particularly proud of our sales record and of the fact that we are able to report a 6% increase in [2] _____ during the period. Thanks to this and to the success of various cost reduction initiatives, our [3] _____ is substantially higher and consequently our shareholders have benefited from a significant rise in [4] _____ per share. Our continuing commitment to the environment, and our policy of ensuring the long term [5] _____ of the resources that we use in manufacturing, have contributed to our recent success in the new export markets in Eastern Europe where concern for the environment is growing. Our performance in toxic

[6] _____ reduction has been significantly improved and we are now on target to meet EU requirements. In the light of our success in the East European markets, we are planning to continue investing there and are moving forward with plans to set up additional [7] _____. However, our performance in some areas has been affected by continuing economic uncertainty and also by the introduction of [8] _____ restricting sales of certain products. On the recommendation of our advisers, we have decided to go ahead with plans [9] _____ on the Stock Exchange. Our [10] _____ will be responsible for implementing this new programme in the second half of the year.

**3** **Complete the sentences using the words in the box.**

| | | | |
|---|---|---|---|
| on (x2) | with | for | of |
| off (x2) | into | out (x2) | |

1  The magazine has a very interesting article __on__ how to measure the environmental impact of consumer products.

2  We're having trouble _____ our agent as he has not met the conditions in the contract.

3  Could you find _____ when the next meeting will take place?

4  We were cut _____ in the middle of the phone call.

5  The arguments _____ increasing our investment in the company are not very convincing.

6  One of the effects _____ the financial crisis has been a drop in consumer spending.

7  We are doing research _____ the possibility of opening a new office in Poland.

8  The launch of the new version has been called _____.

9  A tariff is a tax _____ imported goods.

10  The speaker pointed _____ that the information was incomplete.

# *Setting Up a Business*

**Key vocabulary** Many large businesses in the UK are **public limited companies (plc)**, which means that the public can buy and sell their shares on the stock exchange. Examples include Marks & Spencer, British Telecom and the National Westminster Bank. The minimum share capital for a public limited company is £50,000, so many new businesses are likely to take one of the following forms.

### Sole Trader or Sole Proprietor (UK)
The simplest way of starting a business. You are self-employed and entirely responsible for all aspects of the management of your business.

### Partnership (UK)
Two or more people starting a business together can set up a partnership. All partners are responsible for the debts of the partnership, and profits and losses are shared between them.

### Private Limited Company (UK)
A company can be formed with a minimum of two people becoming its shareholders. They must appoint a director and a **company secretary**. If the company goes out of business, the responsibility of each shareholder is limited to the amount that they have contributed; they have **limited liability**. Such a company has **Ltd** (**Limited**) after its name.

In the US, businesses take the same basic forms. However, American companies are registered or **incorporated** with the authorities in the state where they have their headquarters. The abbreviations **Inc** and **Corp** refer to such companies. To sell shares to the public they must apply to the Securities Exchange Commission.

*Discount New/Used*
*Fishing Tackle Specialist*

## The Tackle Exchange

Proprietor
M J Schofield

29 Church Street
Walton-on-Thames
Surrey
Tel 01932 24377
Mobile: 0875 435731

ACCOLADE

Liz Morris
Marketing Assistant

Accolade Europe Ltd.
Bowling House, Point Pleasant,
Wandsworth, London SW18 1PE

Tel 0181 977 0880
Fax: 0181 977 1880
email: Accolade@btinternet.com

Hoskyns Group plc

**Jonathan Grinsted**
*Project Systems Division*

Hoskyns Group plc
South Bank
95 Wandsworth Road
London
SW8 2LX

Telephone 0181 735 0800
Fax: 0181 735 8943
email: Jonhosk@ndirect.co.uk

FREEDSTONEGOODMANSolicitors

*Charles Goodman*

14 & 15 Craven Street, London WC2N 5AD
Telephone 0181 926 0303  Fax: 0181 926 0334
This firm is registered by the Law Society in the conduct of Investment Business

**Lead-in**

**1** In pairs, decide which of the advantages and disadvantages below you would associate with the following forms of business. In some cases there may be more than one correct answer.

a sole trader    a partnership    a private limited company

**Advantages**

1  You have total control of your business.
2  This is a good way of sharing the pressure and work of starting a business.
3  The financial risks that you are taking are restricted.
4  You can increase your capital by selling shares.

**Disadvantages**

1  There is a danger that conflicts of personality could ruin your business.
2  It may be difficult to expand.
3  You may have to sell your possessions if the company goes into debt.

**2** In pairs, prepare a short checklist of the questions that you would need to ask yourselves before starting a business.

Example: *How much money will I need?*

**Reading**

**1** Before you read the text on the next page about a computer entrepreneur, answer the questions.

1  What computer and software companies do you know?
2  Which company below did each of these people create?

①
*Roger Foster*

②
*Bill Gates*

③
*Steve Jobs*

④
*Scott McNealy*

ⓐ

ⓑ

ⓒ

ⓓ

ⓔ

ⓕ

# The idea man

1  Here's a few of the most prolific* entrepreneurs in computer history: Steve Jobs, Bill Gates, Roger Foster.

## Roger who?

2  Admittedly, this British entrepreneur is no household name* – but if history had any justice he would be. For more than 30 years, with his ventures, Foster has always been able to spot the next big wave in the industry.

### Borrowed start

3  He left school at 16, but qualified as a chartered accountant five years later. It was during his first job at GKN PLC, that 'the light dawned'. Computers were expensive and cumbersome, yet increasingly companies were using them to run back-office* operations such as payroll.

4  So in 1965, with two colleagues and loans from their parents he set up ACT, designing software systems and offering computer programming services to corporate accounting departments.

5  After two years, ACT started making a profit. In fact, it was so successful that it became, in 1979, the first British software company to be listed on the Stock Exchange.

6  Soon after, however, Foster decided that the future lay in hardware. A little chip company called Intel Corp. had launched the first microprocessors not long before, and a few entrepreneurs saw a future in small, personal computers made from them.

7  After distributing a US-made PC called the Sirius for a couple of years, ACT started manufacturing its own version in 1982. The result, the Apricot, was a phenomenal success.

8  Between 1983 and 1985, ACT sold between 40,000 and 50,000 Apricots a year, more than anyone else in the UK, including IBM. At the company's height, recalls Peter Horne, one of Apricot's co-founders, 'We couldn't make enough to satisfy demand.'

### Bad bite

9  But ACT let the advantage slip.

10  In 1985 ACT introduced a $7 m advertising campaign to launch Apricot in the US and steal market share from Apple Computer Corp. The campaign flopped and the US sortie cost ACT $14 m in 14 months of operation.

11  And one trend Foster failed to spot proved fatal: the rise of IBM-compatible computing. Apricot, which ran a version of Microsoft's MS-DOS operating system, had a hardware architecture peculiar to itself. Foster concedes being late in shifting to the IBM standard; 'If we got the timing wrong, it was six to nine months, not a year,' he says.

12  But it was too late. Margins on the Apricot computer began to be squeezed following the rise of cost-efficient, PC-clone manufacturers like Compaq Computer Corp. Sales stagnated in 1986 at around £100 m ($164 m), the high set in 1985. ACT's profit of more than £10.5 m in 1985 turned into a loss of £15 m in 1986, as the company abandoned its non-IBM-compatible inventory*.

13  In the end, ACT was forced to sell the Apricot business. Foster had plans to pursue. Financial software was the next wave to catch. He went on a buying spree*, adding three financial software companies. ACT's sales soared to £200 m in the early 1990s – making it one of the biggest players in its niche.

### Fleeting victory

14  The company's financial products division was in trouble, mostly due to poor sales. ACT embarked on* restructuring. The move led to two sudden profit warnings in 1995; the company's shares slumped. The boardroom was paralysed by infighting between Foster and his managing director, Mike Hart.

15  Seeing ACT's weak financial position, Misys PLC, a UK software house, stepped in, and bought the company for £212 m in 1995.

16  Foster's latest brainchild is Financial Objects, founded in October 1995. The company is compiling a library of software components that companies can then slot together as they wish, something like Lego software.

17  Foster claims: 'In 10 to 15 years, software will be a commodity*, just like the PC now. We want to be the company with the largest set of banking components in the Microsoft world. We can be dominant for ten years if we do it.'

18  The company is the second-largest in its field in the UK, behind Misys – but that's a pretty small field. Last year, it posted sales of £15.5 m and made a small profit. Foster remains confident – but he stresses that he doesn't need the money: 'It's my swansong*. I don't want other directorships and to go to a board meeting every other month.'

19  Would he ever leave Financial Objects in the same way he left Apricot and ACT? 'Financial Objects has the potential to grow at 30% to 40% as far as the eye can see, and I want to take it all the way,' he predicts. But he adds, 'maybe there is a size at which it is time to move.'

*The Wall Street Journal Europe's Convergence*

The Apricot Computer Show 1986

apricot COMPUTER SHOW

---

| | |
|---|---|
| *prolific: producing a lot | *a buying spree: a short, intensive period of buying |
| *a household name: a very famous person | *to embark on: to start |
| *back-office: administrative | *a commodity: a product that can be sold |
| *an inventory: the stock a company has at a particular time | *a swansong: a person's last piece of work |

**2** Below is a list of some of the things that Roger Foster did at different stages in his career. Read the text and number these events in the order in which they happened.

a ☐ created ACT  f ☐ bought financial software companies

b ☐ sold Apricot  g ☐ reorganised ACT

c ☐ produced a PC  h ☐ started Financial Objects

d ☐ moved into the US market  i ☐ 1 worked for GKN

e ☐ changed to a new computer architecture

**3** Read the text again and find one example of

a an innovation that Roger Foster has been responsible for.

b an opportunity that he has taken.

c a mistake that he has made during his career.

**Vocabulary**

**1** Find words in the text which correspond to the following definitions.

1 developing new ideas for products and software (*para 4*)

*designing*

2 writing (and entering) sets of instructions for computers (*para 4*)

3 selling a product made by someone else (*para 7*)

4 making a product in a factory (*para 7*)

5 sell a product for the first time (*para 10*)

6 reorganising (*para 14*)

**2** Match the words from the text with their corresponding definitions.

1 phenomenal (*para 7*)  a to have problems

2 to flop (*para 10*)  b to stop changing

3 fatal (*para 11*)  c to be unsuccessful

4 to stagnate (*para 12*)  d the maximum point reached

5 a high (*para 12*)  e very unusual and impressive

6 to soar (*para 13*)  f having a very serious effect

7 to be in trouble (*para 14*)  g to go down suddenly

8 to slump (*para 14*)  h to go up quickly

**3** Use the following words from the text to complete the passage below.

entrepreneurs (*para 1*)    ventures (*para 2*)    industry (*para 2*)    demand (*para 8*)
advantage (*para 9*)       founded (*para 16*)    predicts (*para 19*)

Andrew Klein, the director of Spring Street Brewing Company, <sup>1</sup> founded his
company in 1993 with the idea of bringing a Belgian beer, Wit Beer, to the
American market. However, his original approach to finding the necessary capital,
by using the Internet, soon made him a pioneer in this new field. He was one of the
first to understand the <sup>2</sup>_____ of using the Internet as a means to attract
investment capital for new business <sup>3</sup>_____. For just $200 a month, Klein was
able to rent a site, present his products and contact investors all over the world.
Following in his footsteps, many other <sup>4</sup>_____ have been able to finance and
promote their own businesses in a similar way.

Today, Wit Beer can be found in several major cities in the US and Andrew Klein
<sup>5</sup>_____ that consumer <sup>6</sup>_____ for his company's products will continue to
rise. Indeed Wit Beer already outsells some of the more exotic beers which compete
in the <sup>7</sup>_____ .

## Vocabulary development: prefixes

Prefixes can sometimes be added to words to change their meanings. In the text on
page 108, the word *co-founder* (*para 8*) means 'a person who founded a company
with someone else'.

**1**    Match the following prefixes with their corresponding definitions.

| 1 inter- e | 2 post- | 3 bi- | 4 pre- | 5 multi- | 6 ex- |
|---|---|---|---|---|---|

a    more than one; many

b    later than; after

c    before; in preparation

d    former and still living

e    between; among a group

f    two; twice; double

**2**    Match the prefixes from exercise 1 with the words below. Use your dictionary to
help you.

a    ..bi...lingual              e    ........director
     multi..lingual              f    ........graduate

b    ........date                g    ........personal
     ........date                h    ........husband

c    ........arranged            i    ........annual

d    ........national

     ........national

**3**    What other words do you know that can be used with these prefixes?

## *Language Focus*

**Relative clauses**

Look at the following sentences from the text on page 108. The relative clause is in bold.

A *The company is compiling a library of software components **that companies can then slot together**. (para 16)*

B *Apricot, **which ran a version of Microsoft's MS-DOS operating system**, had a hardware architecture peculiar to itself. (para 11)*

**Complete the sentences.**

1 The relative clause in sentence ( _____ ) is a **defining clause**. It is essential to the meaning of the sentence.

2 The relative clause in sentence ( _____ ) is a **non-defining clause**. It gives us extra information. This information is not essential to understand the main point of the sentence.

The two types of clauses are different in terms of grammar and punctuation.

▶▶ For more information on relative clauses, turn to page 168.

**Practice**

**1** Look at the following sentences and decide whether they are defining (D) or non-defining (N) relative clauses.

1 The design that we selected was in fact the most expensive. `D`

2 Wayne Calloway, who is from our Glasgow office, will be making a presentation of the new project. ☐

3 The new investment plan, which was announced on Wednesday, will take five years to complete. ☐

4 The manager who made the mistake lost his job. ☐

5 This is Jane Stewart, whose company manufactures computer software. ☐

6 The Marketing Department is the one whose contribution has been the most significant this year. ☐

**2** Join each pair of sentences using a defining relative clause.

Example: We signed an agreement. It will give us exclusive rights to several products.
*The agreement **which** we signed will give us exclusive rights to several products.*

1 We use videos for training purposes. This is one of them.
This is one of _____.

2 I left a report on your desk last night. Have you read it?
Have you _____?

3 We interviewed some candidates. They were highly qualified.
The candidates_____.

4 A secretary's computer crashed last week. What's her name?
What's the name _____?

5 A woman introduced me to Mr Ross. She was Australian.
The woman _____.

**From which sentences could the relative pronoun be omitted? Why?**

**3** Choose the non-defining relative clause which best completes each of the sentences below.

1 The firm's 300 employees, ..c.., decided to go on strike

2 The report, ..., contained many interesting ideas on how to promote our new products.

3 The firm, ..., intends to expand its presence in Eastern Europe.

4 The new machinery, ..., is not as efficient as we had hoped.

5 Professor Harding, ..., will be the main speaker at this year's conference.

6 KBJ Optics, ..., has over a hundred patented products.

7 The Chairman, ..., maintains close relations with the company's major investors.

a whose engineers are among the most brilliant in the country

b which cost the company over £2 m

c whose salaries had not been increased

d who was elected to the Board last year

e which was written by our Marketing Manager

f which has recently signed a contract with a Polish manufacturer

g who is a specialist in American management techniques

## Skills Focus

**Speaking**    Do the questionnaire, then compare your answers with a partner.

# How do you rate as an *entrepreneur?*

**H**ave you got what it takes to run your own business?
For each of the following questions, tick the answer which
comes closest to what you feel about yourself.

**1   Are you a self-starter?**
- a  *I only make an effort when I want to.*
- b  *If someone explains what to do, then I can continue from there.*
- c  *I make my own decisions. I don't need anyone to tell me what to do.*

**2   How do you get on with other people?**
- a  *I get on with almost everybody.*
- b  *I have my own friends and I don't really need anyone else.*
- c  *I don't really feel at home with other people.*

**3   Can you lead and motivate others?**
- a  *Once something is moving I'll join in.*
- b  *I'm good at giving orders when I know what to do.*
- c  *I can persuade most people to follow me when I start something.*

**4   Can you take responsibility?**
- a  *I like to take charge and to obtain results.*
- b  *I'll take charge if I have to but I prefer someone else to be responsible.*
- c  *Someone always wants to be the leader and I'm happy to let them do the job.*

**5    Are you a good organiser?**
- ❏ a   I tend to get confused when unexpected problems arise.
- ❏ b   I like to plan exactly what I'm going to do.
- ❏ c   I just like to let things happen.

**6    How good a worker are you?**
- ❏ a   I'm willing to work hard for something I really want.
- ❏ b   I find my home environment more stimulating than work.
- ❏ c   Regular work suits me but I don't like it to interfere with my private life.

**7    Can you make decisions?**
- ❏ a   I am quite happy to execute other people's decisions.
- ❏ b   I often make very quick decisions which usually work but sometimes don't.
- ❏ c   Before making a decision, I need time to think it over.

**8    Do you enjoy taking risks?**
- ❏ a   I always evaluate the exact dangers of any situation.
- ❏ b   I like the excitement of taking big risks.
- ❏ c   For me safety is the most important thing.

**9    Can you stay the course?**
- ❏ a   The biggest challenge for me is getting a project started.
- ❏ b   If I decide to do something, nothing will stop me.
- ❏ c   If something doesn't go right first time, I tend to lose interest.

**10   Are you motivated by money?**
- ❏ a   For me, job satisfaction cannot be measured in money terms.
- ❏ b   Although money is important to me, I value other things just as much.
- ❏ c   Making money is my main motivation.

**11   How do you react to criticism?**
- ❏ a   I dislike any form of criticism.
- ❏ b   If people criticise me I always listen and may or may not reject what they have to say.
- ❏ c   When people criticise me there is usually some truth in what they say.

**12   Can people believe what you say?**
- ❏ a   I try to be honest, but it is sometimes difficult or too complicated to explain things to other people.
- ❏ b   I don't say things I don't mean.
- ❏ c   When I think I'm right, I don't care what anyone else thinks.

**13   Do you delegate?**
- ❏ a   I prefer to delegate what I consider to be the least important tasks.
- ❏ b   When I have a job to do I like to do everything myself.
- ❏ c   Delegating is an important part of any job.

**14   Can you cope with stress?**
- ❏ a   Stress is something I can live with.
- ❏ b   Stress can be a stimulating element in a business.
- ❏ c   I try to avoid situations which lead to stress.

**15   How do you view your chances of success?**
- ❏ a   I believe that my success will depend to a large degree on factors outside my control.
- ❏ b   I know that everything depends on me and my abilities.
- ❏ c   It is difficult to foresee what will happen in the future.

**16   If the business was not making a profit after five years, what would you do?**
- ❏ a   give up easily.
- ❏ b   give up reluctantly.
- ❏ c   carry on.

**Scoring:**  *Use the key on page 160 to calculate your score. Then check on the next page to see how you rate as an entrepreneur.*

**44 or above**
You definitely have the necessary qualities to become the director of a successful business. You have a strong sense of leadership, you can both organise and motivate and you know exactly where you and your team are going.

**between 44 and 22**
You may need to think more carefully before setting up your own business. Although you do have some of the essential skills for running a business, you will probably not be able to deal with the pressures and strain that are a part of the job. You should perhaps consider taking some professional training or finding an associate who can compensate for some of your weaknesses.

**below 22**
Managing your own business is not for you. You are better suited to an environment where you are not responsible for making decisions and taking risks. To operate successfully you need to follow well defined instructions and you prefer work that is both regular and predictable.

## Listening

**Cargolifter is a company that is producing a new generation of airships for cargo transportation. You will hear a company spokesman answering questions about the different stages that were involved in starting the company.**

**1** Before you listen, number the different stages of the project in the order in which you think they happened.

**a** Conduct a feasibility study.
**b** Get the idea of using an airship to transport heavy goods.
**c** Identify the market.
**d** Construct the assembly plant.
**e** Seek investment from major companies.
**f** Identify a problem.
**g** Create the company.
**h** Invite private investors to join the project.

**2** 📼 Listen to the cassette and check your answers.

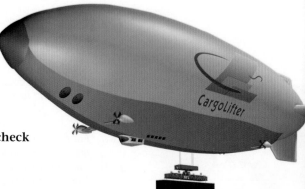

## Writing

Setting up a successful business requires careful preparation and planning but also involves a degree of risk-taking. There are a number of questions that all entrepreneurs must ask themselves concerning the products or services that they intend to sell, the competition that they will face, the structure of the business itself and the sources of finance that they will need to open their new venture. This means that all of these parameters must be defined in a **business plan**: a document that shows how the entrepreneur will organise his or her business, how much he or she expects to sell and where the capital will come from. Once this information has been put down on paper, the entrepreneur can then choose an appropriate form for the company, **register** it with the authorities and open for business.

**1** Read these extracts and decide which sections of the checklist they come from.

(a)
At first I will be concentrating on getting the business into profit. But if I am successful I would then consider looking for other sites in the city area and expanding the management team. Eventually it might be possible to set up shops in different locations around the country.

(d)
Retail outlet selling a wide range of specialist teas and tea-related giftware. Sales will be made direct to customers and also by mail order.

(g)
It is not easy to give a precise estimate but it would seem to be essentially passing trade within the shopping area. The target consumer is middle-aged and with a comfortable income. There is no competition in the area as the concept for this type of shop is new and comparable products are not currently available in other outlets.

(e)
I plan to advertise on local radio and in the local press and free press. This will be complemented by flyers distributed directly through letterboxes to residents in the area.

(b)
The Tea Set. Initially the business will be registered as a limited company with ten shareholders.

(c)
In a street with pedestrian access only, which leads into the main shopping area and market square in a town of 70,000 inhabitants. The shop is also close to the station, which is used by several thousand commuters daily. The surface area is 45 square metres at a rent of 1000 euros per month.

(f)
I have already worked as an employee in two different companies, where I was involved in both marketing and customer service at junior management level.

(h)
Two full-time sales staff for the shop. One personal assistant to do secretarial work and general office administration.

## Business plan checklist

**1 Details of the business**
Name of business
Type of business (limited company, partnership etc.)

**2 Personal details**
Relevant work experience

**3 Personnel**
Number of people / job function

**4 Product / service**
Description

**5 Market**
Describe your market.
Who are your customers?
Is your market growing, static or in decline?
Who are the main competitors?
What are the advantages of your product or service over the competition?

**6 Marketing**
What sort of marketing or advertising do you intend to do?

**7 Premises / machinery / vehicles**
Where do you intend to locate the business and why?
What sort and size of premises will you need?
What machinery / vehicles do you require?

**8 Objectives**
What objectives do you have for the business?

**2** Work in small groups. You have decided to set up your own business together and have approached the bank for advice. They have asked you to prepare a business plan. Decide what type of business you are going to set up, then discuss each of the points listed in the business plan. When you have finalised all the details of your business, prepare a written plan to give to the bank.

# 12 Corporate Alliances and Acquisitions

**Key vocabulary** 🔲 As business and the world economy become increasingly competitive, more and more companies have to strengthen their operations to remain profitable. Companies can go about this in a number of ways, including the following.

**Joint venture:** Two or more companies agree to collaborate and jointly invest in a separate business project. This type of deal allows the partners to combine their strengths in one specific area.

**Merger:** Two companies, often in the same industry, come together to form one company. Companies merge for many reasons, for example, to increase market share and cut costs in certain areas, such as research and development.

**Acquisition** or **takeover:** One company accumulates enough of another company's shares to take over control and ownership.

**Lead-in**  **1** Read the following extracts from the financial press. In pairs, decide whether each one refers to (a) a joint venture, (b) a merger or (c) an acquisition.

① Walt Disney Co., Hearst Corp and Peterson Publishing Co. are discussing a deal that would combine their considerable influence in the publishing world to launch a weekly magazine to compete with 'Sports Illustrated' next year.

② General Motors is to start building its Chevrolet Blazer, a sports utility vehicle, in the factories of Elabuga Avtomobilny Zavod (EIAZ) in Tartarstan, an autonomous part of Russia. This business project will be owned by EIAZ and GM, which plans to invest as much as $250 m in the plant.

③ Poland may call off talks on the sale of newsstand chain Ruch to France's Hachette distribution service if it fails to make a firm financial offer soon.

⑤ Just as Daewoo Electronics chairman Bae Soon-Hun thought he had agreed a deal to buy Thomson Multimedia, the consumer electronics arm of Thomson, he heard that it had refused his offer.

④ Bank Inicjatyw Gospodanczych (BIG) and Gdanski are planning to work together on a new deal. They will form one new bigger and stronger bank and together they will control 4% of Polish banking assets.

**2** 🔲 You will hear Margareta Galfard, Director of Communication for Volvo in France, talking about why the merger between the major automotive companies, Renault and Volvo, failed. Listen and decide if the following statements are true (T) or false (F).

1  The reasons why the merger failed are very simple to understand.  ☐

2  The shareholders were afraid that Volvo would lose its Swedish identity.  ☐

3  The shareholders feared that Renault was trying to take over their company.  ☐

4  The Swedish management were keen for the merger to go ahead.  ☐

**3** **Can you think of any other reasons why a merger might fail?**

# When egos* collide

## In the acquisitions jungle, alpha* males are deal-breakers

Perhaps business schools should add anthropology* to the curriculum; the parallels between the behaviour of corporate executives and that of great apes are uncanny*. The spectacular collapse of the supposed alliance of drug giants GlaxoWellcome and SmithKline Beecham is a textbook example.

There was a clear business logic to the union of the two pharmaceuticals giants. The deal gave the companies a drugs research and development budget more than twice the size of their closest rivals, Novartis and Merck, and the combination of their complementary research technologies could have left them streets ahead of* the competition; cost-cutting alone could have saved $1 bn. But because these two great beasts of the jungle (the CEOs of the corporations) chose to throw sand in each other's faces, the deal is off, at least for now.

Corporate egos cause problems but they seem to be inevitable in a business culture that prizes drive, determination and leadership above all. Having the strength of personality and the ability to outmanoeuvre* others is a fundamental prerequisite to climb to the top of the corporate ladder. So with a power-hungry alpha male at the top of each company, it is not surprising that every time a mega-merger is announced, there's a high probability of a boardroom bust-up. Nicholas Bates, head of Human Resources Management at the European Business School, says many senior businessmen actually go off the top of the scale on personality tests. 'Some of them are almost psycho-pathological and would have no hesitation taking everyone down with them. Some are verging on* paranoid.' Nevertheless these are precisely the sorts of personalities that companies want because they can transform a business; the problems only appear when they have to get together with peers in their organisation who don't share their views. Then clashes are inevitable.

Europe's most spectacular and public bust-up was between automotive giants Volvo and Renault. In September 1993 Volvo and Renault announced they were to tie the knot, with Volvo holding a minority 35% stake. However, three months later Volvo shareholders and senior management rejected the marriage plans because of concerns that the deal undervalued Volvo, and was turning into a Renault takeover, without Renault paying the acquisition premium. Simmering* resentment over chairman Pehr Gyllenhammer's dictatorial management style at Volvo added spice to the management revolt. The divorce is reputed to have cost Volvo several hundred million dollars and forced the resignation of Gyllenhammer after more than two decades in the driving seat. Egos play such a large role when two giant corporations come together that it is hard to make them work unless one personality is prepared to take a back seat or step down. The $26 bn marriage between Swiss giants Ciba and Sandoz to form Novartis in 1996 is often held up as a textbook example of how mega-mergers can work. It is successful, but much of that success is dependent on the fact that key personnel were ready for retirement, or were prepared to relinquish* old roles in favour of new opportunities in other scenarios.

Compromise* is essential if mergers between two powerful corporations are to work to the advantage of both parties and their shareholders. Otherwise friendly discussions break down and can easily turn into all-out war. In the corporate jungle, the question is now whether the imperatives of shareholders can control the egos of managers, to force through deals that deliver them the financial return they expect. This is where independent directors ought to play a part, although they rarely do.

*The European*

---

*an ego: a person's opinion about him / herself
*alpha: the highest mark in an exam
*anthropology: the study of people
*uncanny: strange and difficult to explain
*streets ahead of: much better than

*to outmanoeuvre: to gain an advantage by having a better plan
*verging on: almost, nearly
*simmering: just hidden below the surface
*to relinquish: to let s.b. else take
*compromise: agreeing, while accepting some things you don't like

**Reading**

**1** Read the text opposite about failed mergers, which uses the Volvo–Renault deal as an example, and see if it mentions any of your suggestions from Lead-in 3.

**2** Read the text again and answer the questions.

1 According to the author, why should GlaxoWellcome and SmithKline Beecham have gone ahead with their alliance?

2 Why didn't the deal go through ?

3 What does Nicholas Bates say about the personalities of many senior businessmen?

4 What reason does the author give for the success of the Ciba–Sandoz merger?

5 What according to the author makes a successful merger?

**Vocabulary**

**1** Choose the best definition for the word in italics in the sentences from the text.

1 The *parallels* between the behaviour of corporate executives and that of great apes are uncanny. (*line 3*)

  **a** similarities   **b** differences   **c** distinctions   *a*

2 The spectacular collapse of the supposed alliance of drug giants GlaxoWellcome and SmithKline Beecham is a *textbook* example. (*line 9*)

  **a** unusual   **b** interesting   **c** perfect

3 The deal gave the companies a drugs research and development budget more than twice the size of their closest *rivals*. (*line 17*)

  **a** competitors   **b** partners   **c** friends

4 Corporate egos cause problems but they seem to be *inevitable* in a business culture that prizes drive, determination and leadership above all. (*line 30*)

  **a** unavoidable   **b** impossible   **c** likely

5 Having the strength of personality and the ability to outmanoeuvre others is a fundamental *prerequisite* to climb to the top of the corporate ladder. (*line 36*)

  **a** step   **b** problem   **c** requirement

6 The problems only appear when they have to get together with *peers* in their organisation who don't share their views. (*line 57*)

  **a** people who hold higher positions     **b** people who hold lower positions
  **c** people who hold similar positions.

7 Then *clashes* are inevitable. (*line 59*)

  **a** solutions   **b** strong differences of opinion   **c** long discussions

8 In the corporate jungle, the question is now whether the *imperatives* of shareholders can control the egos of managers. (*line 109*)

  **a** urgent demands   **b** instructions   **c** strong personalities

**2** Expressions normally associated with marriage are often used to describe mergers. Read the text again and find three examples.

**3** Find the following idioms in the text. In pairs, discuss what they mean.

1 to throw sand in each other's faces (*line 26*)
2 to climb to the top of the corporate ladder (*line 36*)
3 a boardroom bust-up (*line 42*)
4 in the driving seat (*line 83*)
5 to take a back seat (*line 88*)

## Vocabulary development: phrasal verbs 2

**1** In the following examples from the text, are the verbs in bold

    a transitive (followed by an object)?

      or

    b intransitive (not followed by an object)?

    *...... unless one personality is prepared to take a back seat or* **step down**. *(line 89)*

    *...... otherwise friendly discussions* **break down** *...... (line 106)*

**2** Replace the words in italics with a verb from A and a particle from B, in the correct form.

| A | | B | |
|---|---|---|---|
| catch | get | up (x2) | ahead |
| stand | go (x2) | on (x2) | by |
| speak | look | down | under |
| end | | | |

a The company had hoped that the new sportswear designs would be a success but in fact they never really *became popular*. caught on

b They *finished by* having to abandon the idea altogether.

c Following the recent takeover of his company the chairman has announced his intention to *resign*.

d I'm afraid I can't hear what you are saying. Could you *talk louder* please?

e He's new here, but he seems to be *making progress*.

f Many businesses *fail* in their first year.

g We need to *think of the future* and decide where we want to be in five years.

h It's a pity we let that opportunity *pass*; we need more orders like that.

**Discussion**
Read these profiles of some senior business people. Which of the characteristics do you think are essential, useful, not useful and dangerous? In pairs, discuss your answers.

# Danger ego out of control

## Seven warning signs

1 Dominates conversations, commandeers meetings, interrupts and finishes off sentences of others. Competitive in all aspects of life, not only business but tennis, squash or drinking.

2 Bold, doesn't worry about going into new situations and meeting new people.

3 Has a high opinion of himself and his abilities and he always thinks he's right.

4 Loves pressure. He likes tight deadlines, is impatient to get ahead and does several things at once.

5 Must be the centre of attention at meetings, parties, social gatherings, and can't do without attention or flattery.

6 Loves power and the trappings. Couldn't bear to be without a chauffeur-driven car, panelled office, secretaries and trips on Concorde.

7 Has abnormal energy levels, is always on the go, needs little sleep, and is constantly restless.

## Language Focus

**Modal verbs of obligation**

Look at the following examples from the text on page 118.

*Perhaps business schools **should** add anthropology to the curriculum. (line 1)*
*This is where independent directors **ought to** play a part. (line 114)*

In both these examples a modal verb is used to express mild obligation or advice. What do the following verbs express?

| | |
|---|---|
| 1 have to a | 5 needn't |
| 2 should / shouldn't | 6 must / mustn't |
| 3 ought to | 7 need to |
| 4 don't have to | 8 don't need to |

a obligation or necessity

b advice

c absence of obligation or necessity

▶▶ For more information on modal verbs, turn to page 168.

**Practice**

Look at the Discussion text again. What does the person need to change / not change? Write eight sentences using modal verbs of obligation.

Example:
*He **should** be competitive in some aspects of his life but he **has to** stop being competitive about drinking.*

## Business Skills Focus: Meetings

**Listening**

It is generally agreed that successful meetings make successful companies. However, many professionals complain that meetings are often unproductive and too long. Discussions are regularly dominated by participants with large egos and hours of talking ends without any clear result. Consequently, many companies get help from specialised consultants, who give advice on how to make meetings more effective.

**1** 📼 You will hear a consultant giving advice about meetings. Listen and take notes to help you complete the passage below.

**2** In groups, use your notes to complete the passage.

---

If a meeting is to be productive it should have ¹ <u>a clear and stated purpose</u> that all the participants know and understand. You should appoint a
² _____ who manages and controls the meeting.
You must write an ³ _____ , or list of items to be discussed and send it
⁴ _____ . They should ⁵ _____ and come to it with ideas to contribute.
You have to ⁶ _____ to each point, otherwise there is a risk that some of the items will not be dealt with at all.
You ought to ⁷ _____ . If not you have to ⁸ _____ into the agenda.
You don't need to ⁹ _____ . But you should send other senior staff members ¹⁰ _____ , or summary of what was discussed.
The minutes should include ¹¹ _____ you don't have to
¹² _____ . However, you need to include ¹³ _____
decided upon at the meeting. Lastly, the minutes should ¹⁴ _____ .
It is essential to keep the ¹⁵ _____ clear in everyone's mind.

---

**Speaking**

**1** Match the expressions a–j below to the following things that a chairperson should do.

1 open the meeting
2 keep things moving
3 keep an eye on time
4 make sure everyone stays focused
5 invite contributions
6 summarise regularly
7 seek clarification
8 summarise agreed action points
9 allocate action points and establish deadlines
10 close the meeting

a Has everyone got that?
b Shall we move on?
c As I see it, we seem to be saying …
d Could you let us have the exact figures for Friday?
e What exactly do you mean?
f So what we've finally decided on is …
g We'll have to move on I'm afraid.
h Thanks for coming everyone.
i What do you think of that, Mr …?
j Thanks very much everyone, that was very useful.

**2** Match the expressions a–l below to the following things that participants should do.

1 express agreement
2 express disagreement
3 make suggestions
4 summarise arguments
5 ask for clarification
6 present arguments

a I'm convinced that …
b How about …
c I'm all in favour of that.
d Why don't we …
e I'm afraid I don't accept that at all.
f So what you are suggesting is …
g Could you explain that in more detail?
h I'm sorry but I don't agree at all.
i I quite agree.
j The way I see it is …
k Am I right in thinking that …?
l In other words you are saying …

**3** What other expressions do you know?

**Role-play**

**1** Read the text and make notes about the situation.

> Your company is negotiating an alliance with a company which insists that employees only work 35 hours per week. If your company goes ahead with the alliance, the employees will not have to take a salary cut but they will not be allowed to work overtime. Ordinary workers, who often work overtime to earn extra money, will therefore lose some of their earning potential. Executives in the company who are not paid overtime will be less concerned about that, but the 35-hour week will have other consequences for them. If they don't have enough time to complete their projects, they will have to share power and control with new employees who will need to be brought in to meet work demands.

**2** In groups, you will be given a role to play. Read the agenda and your role carefully. Then prepare how you will express your opinions and suggestions at the meeting. Be prepared to agree and disagree with the other participants.

## AGENDA

**1** The chairperson will bring everybody up to date on the negotiations concerning the alliance. If it goes ahead we will be obliged to adopt their policy of working a 35 hour week. (5 mins.)

**2** Each person will be invited to put forward his/her views on this situation. (5 mins. per person)

**3** A general discussion period will follow, where each member will put forward suggestions and recommendations to help reach a satisfactory compromise. Action points will be decided upon. (20 mins.)

**4** The chairperson will appoint people to be responsible for the various action points. (5 mins.)

**3** In groups, conduct the meeting. Every member should take notes in order to write a full report on the meeting later. Feel free to add other opinions and recommendations.

**Writing**

Using the notes you took at the meeting, write the minutes.

Remember the minutes of a meeting should include:
- a summary of the chairperson's introduction
- a summary of the opinions and suggestions made by the participants
- the action points that were decided upon
- the people involved in carrying out the action points
- the deadlines that were fixed
- the date and time of the next meeting

# 13 *Marketing*

**Key vocabulary** 💬 **Marketing** is the term given to all the different activities intended to make and attract a profitable demand for a product. This involves:

- identifying consumer needs and wants in order to develop the **product**.
- setting the **price**.
- deciding on the best **place** to sell the product.
- deciding on how best to **promote** the product.

These four factors are often referred to as '**The Four Ps**' or the **marketing mix**.

**Lead-in**

**1** In unit 12 you saw how metaphors of marriage are often used to describe corporate alliances. It is also very common to use *military metaphor* in business: we talk about management *strategy* and *tactics*, and takeover deals are often described as *coups* and *raids*.

💬 Listen to a marketing manager talking about her company. Complete the passage below.

It's true that we've been deeply affected by our competitor's latest
¹ s_____ s_____ . A new plan of action must be developed as soon
as possible. ² L_____ have been particularly high in every foreign
³ c_____ . We have lost ⁴ m_____ m_____ in Russia and
Venezuela. Even in the home market we ⁵ c_____ c_____ . However
we are not going to ⁶ g_____ u_____ . We are developing a new
⁷ m_____ p_____ which will help us regain some of our market
share. The war will ⁸ c_____ for some time yet but we are confident that
we can still win.

**2** Replace the words and phrases 1–8 with military expressions from the box.

| | | | |
|---|---|---|---|
| surprise attack | casualties | are outgunned | campaign |
| territory | surrender | key strongholds | rage on |

**3** In pairs, make a list of the different techniques that companies can use for market research.

# Hello to the **good buys**

*A new marketing campaign promising hassle\*-free and faster fuel buying for customers is under way in America. Suzanne Peck reports on the 18-month research project which involved Shell Oil researchers 'moving in' with their customers to test their buying habits.*

1 Three years ago when Sam Morasca asked his wife what could be done to exceed her expectations when buying gasoline\*, her answer 'that I would never have to think about it any more' made him pause and think. The marketing people from Shell Oil Products, of which Sam is vice-president, were desperately seeking ways to increase the business, and to come up with a strategy which would put them clearly ahead of their competition by differentiating\* the Shell Oil brands in the eyes of consumers. 'We are big business for Shell Oil, contributing US $7 bn of revenue, and the leading retailer of gasoline, but it is a fragmented market and the mission was to profitably expand the business,' said Sam.

2 Today, after 18 months of cutting edge research, Shell Oil is on track to make buying fuel at their 8,900 service stations clearly different with a new brand initiative. Its aim is to deliver through facilities, systems upgrades\*, and new operating practices, a hassle-free fueling experience targeted at specific customer segments.

3 Over the past few years, the company has been developing detailed knowledge of consumer needs and attitudes, which formed the basis for the new brand initiative. Team leader Dave Yard, manager of Strategy and Planning – Marketing, picks up the story. 'We began with a customer segment study of 55,000 people, who we stopped in shopping malls in six cities for a 45-minute interview into their attitudes, especially regarding driving and cars. The result was that everyone wanted three things from a service station: competitive price, a nearby location and good quality fuel – something they all believed was already being delivered by the industry.'

4 This meant their buying decisions were influenced by other factors – some wanted full-serve outlets like the old days, some chose a service station depending on whether it looked safe or not. 'There were ten different segments with different needs, and we wanted a better understanding of each of these audiences.'

5 A focus group was set up for each segment; an anthropological study was carried out, which involved team members spending waking hours with people from each segment, watching them at home and accompanying them on shopping trips to see their buying habits; and a clinical psychologist was hired to create a psychological profile of each segment.

6 The study indicated that three groups, which comprised 30% of the driving public, should be targeted:
• Premium Speeders – outgoing, ambitious, competitive and detail orientated. They drive upmarket cars which make a statement\* about them. Efficiency rules, plus fast pumps, quick access and payment.
• Simplicity Seekers – loyal, caring and sensitive, frustrated with complexities of everyday life. Want simple easy transactions.
• Safety Firsters – control orientated, confident people, like order and comfort of the familiar. Higher value on relationships and go out of their way\* to stations that make them feel comfortable. Prefer to stay close to cars.

7 'The common thread was that they all wanted a faster and easier service than anything already available,' said Dave, 'so the study ended and the launch began.'

8 The field organisation and Shell Oil retailers combined forces to determine how to eliminate the little hassles that customers sometimes face, such as improved equipment and clearer instructions at the pump. New innovations are currently being test marketed. A new advertising campaign was launched and a sophisticated measurement system introduced to monitor satisfaction, behavior and perception of the brand. 'Fueling\* a car is a necessity of life and I believe we are ahead of the game – but we won't allow ourselves to stop and be caught up.'

*http://www.shell.com*

---

| | |
|---|---|
| \*hassle: problems | \*to make a statement about s.b.: to show |
| \*gasoline (US): petrol (GB) | what kind of person s.b. is |
| \*to differentiate: to show how products are different from each other | \*to go out of one's way: to make an effort |
| \*an upgrade: making s.th. work better, and do more | \*fueling (up) (US): filling up (GB) |

**Reading**

**1** Read the text opposite which describes how Shell Oil developed a new brand image, and see if it mentions any of the market research methods that you listed in Lead-in 3. What techniques did Shell Oil use?

**2** Read the text again and number the different stages in the research project in the correct order.

**a** They analysed the results, which showed that there were 10 different consumer segments. ☐

**b** Focus groups studied the 10 segments. ☐

**c** Shell Oil's marketing team decided to differentiate the Shell brand from the other brands on the market. ☐ 1

**d** Shell launched a new advertising campaign. ☐

**e** They interviewed 55,000 people about their attitudes to driving and cars in general. ☐

**f** Work started on improving products and services. ☐

**g** They carried out a detailed study of the market over 18 months. ☐

**h** Three groups were chosen as the target markets. ☐

**3** Find words and expressions in the text relating to 'The Four Ps' of the Shell marketing mix.

Example: *Product – good quality*

**Vocabulary**

**1** Match the words from the text with their corresponding definitions.

| | | |
|---|---|---|
| 1 | to exceed (*para 1*) | **a** a part or section |
| 2 | a mission (*para 1*) | **b** a group of interested people |
| 3 | an initiative (*para 2*) | **c** an important new plan with a particular aim |
| 4 | a segment (*para 2*) | **d** an assignment or task |
| 5 | an audience (*para 4*) | **e** to find out / to discover |
| 6 | a profile (*para 5*) | **f** to check at regular intervals |
| 7 | to determine (*para 8*) | **g** to be more than |
| 8 | to monitor (*para 8*) | **h** a description of the characteristics of someone or something |

**2** Find words and expressions in the text which correspond to the following definitions.

1 Many different types of consumer who buy the same product (*para 1*)

f ragmented   m arket

2 The most advanced and up to date (*para 2*)

c_____ e_____

3 Conclusions people reach about which products to purchase (*para 4*)

b_____ d_____

4 An informal discussion group used for market research (*para 5*)

f_____ g_____

5 A shared characteristic (*para 7*)

c_____ t_____

6 A method of evaluation (*para 8*)

m_____ s_____

**3** Complete the passage using words from Vocabulary 1 and 2. Change the form of the words where necessary.

> As more and more industries are making products specifically adapted to particular ¹ segments of the market, market researchers are being asked to conduct studies and to compile more detailed ² _____ of consumer groups. Broad classifications based on sex, age and social class are not sufficient for companies operating in highly competitive and ³ _____ _____. Questionnaires are carefully designed to ⁴ _____ the exact needs and demands of consumers as well as establishing what affects consumer ⁵ _____ _____ when they choose one product instead of another. Advertising campaigns can then be targeted to appeal to the identified ⁶ _____. Finally, marketing people must ⁷ _____ the success of the campaign and modify it if necessary.

## Vocabulary development: compound adjectives 2

Some compound adjectives can be formed by combining two words with no hyphen. In the text on page 126, *upmarket* (*para 6*) means 'for the richer section of the market'.

1 Replace the words in italics with a compound noun made of a word from A and a word from B. Use some words more than once.

**A**

| up | under |
|---|---|
| down | out |
| over | |

**B**

| due | worked |
|---|---|
| drawn | priced |
| market | paid |
| staffed | dated |

a The invoice still hasn't been paid. It's now two weeks *late*. overdue

b Some of our customers are complaining that our products are *too expensive*.

c Our latest policy is to introduce more luxury products. This means that we will phase out our *less sophisticated* brands.

d During the Christmas period many employees will be on vacation and as a result the company will be *short of personnel*.

e The only catalogue I could find is from last year but I'm afraid that the information in it is *no longer valid*.

f For the last few weeks I've been staying late to get everything finished; I really feel that I've been *doing too much*.

g The database is two years old and needs to be *changed to include the latest information*.

h The workers claim that they are *not earning enough*.

i My bank account has been *in debit* for the last two months.

2 What other compound adjectives can you make from the words in A and B?

## Discussion

1 Consumers allowed Shell marketing people to 'move in with them' in order to observe their habits and routine. In pairs, discuss the questions.

1 What are the advantages of this type of research over the more conventional data collecting processes?

2 Would you agree to participate (as a potential consumer) in this type of research? Why (not)?

3 Why do you think some people do accept?

2 Read this description of a Shell TV ad called 'Stealth' and discuss the questions in pairs.

> 'Stealth' – A driver in a sporty Jaguar presses a button to avoid road obstacles, and is refuelled by a Draken jet aircraft while travelling at speed between skyscrapers.

1 Which of the target profiles described in the text would it appeal to most? Premium Speeders, Simplicity Seekers or Safety Firsters?

2 What sort of advertisements do you think would appeal to the other two target profiles?

## Language Focus

**Comparison**

**Look at this sentence from the text on page 126.**

*'The common thread was that they all wanted a **faster** and **easier** service **than** anything already available,' said Dave. (para 7)*

How do we form the comparative of adjectives with one syllable? How do we form the comparative of adjectives with two or more syllables?

▶▶ **For more information on forming comparatives, turn to page 169.**

The use of quantifiers before an adjective can make it more precise.

*'The common thread was that they all wanted a **much faster** and **easier** service **than** anything already available' said Dave.*

Put these quantifiers in the correct column.

slightly              a little              considerably              significantly
moderately          far                  somewhat                 much

| **a**  *a small degree of difference*<br><br>slightly | **b**  *a degree of difference* | **c**  *a large degree of difference* |
| --- | --- | --- |
|  |  |  |

**Practice**

**Rewrite the following sentences using a quantifier and a comparative form of the adjective in brackets.**

Example:
We have a very large market share in comparison to our competitors. (big)
*Our market share is much bigger than our competitors'.*

1  This year's sales figures increased by only 1% on last year's figures. (high)
   *This year's sales figures are* ................................................................ .

2  In recent years a few advertising laws concerning children have been relaxed. (easy)
   *Advertising to children has become* ................................................................ .

3  Our products only cost a bit more than our competitors' products. (expensive)
   *Our products are* ................................................................ .

4  In comparison to the US, advertising laws in Europe are very complex. (complicated)
   *Advertising laws in Europe are* ................................................................ .

5  We can see a small improvement in our market share this year. (good)
   *This year's market share is* ................................................................ .

6  It is interesting to learn other languages, but English is the international language of business. (useful)
   *English is* ................................................................ .

## Reported speech

In the text on page 126 there are many examples of direct speech or quotes of the exact words used by someone.

*'We are big business …' said Sam. (para 1)*

*Team leader Dave Yard … picks up the story.*
*'We began with a customer segment study …' (para 3)*

**The author could have used reported speech.**

*Sam said that they were big business.*
*The team leader explained that they had begun with a customer segment study.*

**What are the main rules when changing direct speech to reported speech? Think about tenses, pronouns, punctuation and word order.**

▶▶ For more information on reported speech, turn to page 169.

## Practice

**1** Notice how the tenses change in the following examples, and complete the table.

| Direct speech | Reported speech | Examples | |
|---|---|---|---|
| Present simple | Past simple | 1 'Where do you work?' → | He asked me where I worked. |
| Present continuous | | 2 'We're expanding rapidly.' → | She said that they were expanding rapidly. |
| | Past perfect | 3 'Prices went up in 1999.' → | He said that prices had gone up in 1999. |
| Present perfect | | 4 'Have you finished the report?' → | She asked if I had finished the report. |
| | would | 5 'I'll probably be late.' → | She said that she would probably be late. |
| can | | 6 'I can't afford it.' → | He said that he couldn't afford it. |

**2** Below are the answers given by a shopper during a market research survey. Write the shopper's answers in reported speech.

Example:

I wash my hair more than twice a week.
*She said she washed her hair more than twice a week.*

1 I don't always buy the same shampoo.
2 The price influences my decision most.
3 I have been using my present brand for two years.
4 I had used the previous brand for three years.
5 I have never used hair colour.
6 I like my natural colour.
7 I would use hair colour if it were as easy as shampoo.
8 I would be willing to pay £5 for hair colour.
9 I will accept the free sample.
10 No, you can't telephone me next week.

*Skills Focus*

**Reading**

**Direct mail marketing** involves sending publicity material to people directly by mail. It is highly successful for selling magazine subscriptions, insurance and financial services. The letters contain

- a very personalised first sentence designed to ensure that the reader continues reading.
- a persuasive and clear sales message, adapted to a specific market segment.
- direct and convincing language, intended to appeal to the chosen audience.

**1** The profiles below are based on the results of several hundred interviews conducted in a shopping centre by a major insurance company. Following the survey, the company decided to concentrate its direct marketing sales efforts on two specific products: a life insurance plan for young couples and a pension plan for slightly older couples. Read the profiles and match the letter extracts below to the profiles.

### 1 Profile for life insurance

Young married couples who have just had their first baby. They are aged between 25 and 30 and have fairly good salaries but are very careful about their spending. They have never considered insurance before and are put off by the complicated documents. They are suspicious of insurance sales people and would not agree to spending hours going over figures with them. They would respond if the insurance plan was inexpensive and looked easy to take out.

### 2 Profile for private pension

Couples aged between 35 and 45 who are just beginning to have some financial stability. They have never considered pensions until now because they felt they couldn't afford it and that they were too young to think about retirement. They are a little anxious as they realise that they have left it very late, and would like to discuss their financial situation with 'an expert' who could advise them on the best plan.

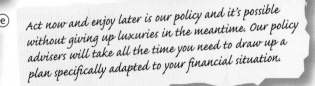

(a) *Our new policy is guaranteed to give you the best value for money currently available. There is no red tape, just a simple application form which takes two minutes to complete.*

(b) *It's still not too late to join the club and dream about the future. Just pick up the phone and make an appointment and you can start saving straightaway. The sooner you start the more you have to look forward to!*

(e) *Act now and enjoy later is our policy and it's possible without giving up luxuries in the meantime. Our policy advisers will take all the time you need to draw up a plan specifically adapted to your financial situation.*

(c) *Of course most parents recognise that it is important to provide insurance cover for the family, but many of the schemes around are confusing and too expensive.*

(f) *They have no worries about whether they will be able to afford holidays, presents for their grandchildren and all those little extras that make life easy and comfortable in later years.*

(d) *Offered direct to you – no sales commission, no insurance broker to pay and no pushy sales people in your living room.*

(g) *Just return the attached enquiry card. There's no postage to pay and we will send full details to your home address so you can read at your leisure.*

**2** Complete the two letters below, using the extracts a–g.

Dear Parent

The arrival of a new baby is such an important time,
it is almost impossible to think about the practical
side of being a parent … however, I know that you'll
agree that nothing matters more than your baby's
future.

1 **c**

We feel that now is the right time to tell you about a
plan which has been designed especially for young
people like you. Interested? Read on.

2

So you see it really is your type of plan.

3

4

Don't miss this opportunity to provide financial
protection for your family at a low cost.
I look forward to receiving your enquiry card.

Yours faithfully

Dear John and Mary

Have you ever wondered how lucky you really are?
Have you ever wondered what the future has in
store? Our policy holders are looking forward to the
future and planning how they will spend all the
money they have saved.

5

6

So relax, the situation is under control.

7

Looking forward to hearing from you very soon.

Sincerely

**3** Do the completed letters contain all the necessary elements of a good direct
mail marketing letter? Refer back to the description on the opposite page.

**Writing**

**1** You work for an insurance company which has decided to use direct mail
marketing to sell retirement pensions to young, single business graduates, who
have just started their first job.

1 In groups, complete the target profile below. Add in other headings you may
wish to include.

2 Make a list of persuasive arguments to convince them that a little less cash
now means a more comfortable retirement (for example, one less outing to a
night club per week).

Age: ................................................
Salary: ................................................
Likes: *nightclubs*, ................................................
**Proportion of income which goes towards**
rent: ................................................
clothes: ................................................
food: ................................................
entertainment: ................................................
holidays: ................................................
savings: ................................................

**2** Write the letter. Make sure your opening sentence attracts their attention.

# Product and Corporate Advertising

**Key vocabulary**  **Product advertising** is an important part of the marketing mix. Its aim is to increase sales by making a product or service known to a wider audience, and by emphasising its positive qualities. A company can advertise in a variety of ways, depending on how much it wishes to spend and the size and type of audience it wishes to **target**. The different **media** for advertising include television, radio, newspapers, magazines, the Internet and direct mail. The design and organisation of advertising campaigns is usually the job of an advertising agency.

**Corporate advertising** is not directly concerned with increasing sales of a particular product or service, but more with the **brand image**, or picture, a company wants to present to the public. **Public relations (PR)** experts specialise in organising activities and events which generate positive **publicity** for companies. Unusual advertising campaigns sometimes get extra publicity for the company by way of media reports about the campaign.

**Lead-in** **1** In groups, what other methods of advertising do you know?

**2** As consumers get more used to advertising, companies have to come up with better ways of ensuring that people pay attention to their ads. In pairs, say what you think of these recent experiments in advertising. Can you think of any new and innovative ways to advertise?

- Interrupting telephone conversations with advertising messages (in exchange for free phone calls).
- Talking ads at bank cash machines.
- Ads on toilet walls.
- Advertising on small television screens on supermarket shopping trolleys.

**3** Many advertisements contain a **slogan** or short phrase to attract the consumer's attention. Effective slogans are usually short, easy to remember, easy to repeat and easy to translate for international markets.

1 Read the texts about translations of slogans and brand names, and note the problem in each case.

ⓐ
In Taiwan, the translation of the Pepsi slogan 'Come alive with the Pepsi generation' came out as 'Pepsi will bring your ancestors back from the dead.'

ⓑ
When Parker marketed a pen in Mexico, its ads were supposed to say 'It won't leak in your pocket and embarrass you.' However, the company translated 'embarrass' as 'embarazar', which means 'to become pregnant'. So the ads said 'It won't leak in your pocket and make you pregnant.'

ⓒ
In Italy, a campaign for Schweppes Tonic Water translated the name as Schweppes Toilet Water.

ⓔ
When Braniff Airlines translated a slogan for its comfortable seats, 'fly in leather' it came out in Spanish as 'fly naked'.

ⓓ
Colgate introduced a toothpaste in France called Cue, the name of a French pornographic magazine.

2 In groups, write down five popular slogans in your language. Try to translate them into English. Read them out to the other groups and see if they can guess which products your translated slogans refer to.

**4** The Italian clothing retail company Benetton is one of the most successful European franchisors. Its advertising has been highly successful but also extremely controversial, and has been banned in some countries.

In pairs, discuss the advertisement below.

1 What is it advertising?
2 What do you think of it? Does it shock you?
3 Do you think it was a successful advertising campaign? Why? / Why not?

# Sacrilege

### By Stephen Armstrong

1 Is Volkswagen bold or stupid? Across France, workmen have been busy scraping off 10,000 billboard advertisements for its new Golf following furious complaints from the Catholic Church. In a series of posters, the German carmaker's model was likened to a religious revelation; one that showed Jesus at the last supper recommending the car to his disciples.

2 VW's agency DDB Needham doubtless thought its advertising was ironic and extremely up-to-date. After all, the admen presumably figured, if outrageous* advertising worked for the likes of Benetton, it could work to revive the image of the Golf, which is frankly rather old-fashioned.

3 After the Catholic Church threatened to sue* for Ffr 3.3 m ($550,000) to obtain reparation for the damage suffered by Christians, the agency and the carmaker confessed to their sins and agreed to remove the ads. 'We have no disrespect for the fundamental values of society nor for the beliefs of the faithful,' said a spokesperson for DDB Needham. 'We decided to retract the posters immediately in order to show our respect for the faith and the feelings expressed by certain believers.' The agency's penance* has included making a substantial donation to a Catholic charity.

4 European consumers are exposed to hundreds of commercial messages a day, but the vast majority of these are ignored, so ads which shock have become more popular with advertisers. It is believed that these ads force consumers to listen to their message. But some adland thinkers argue that it's a little more complicated than that.

5 Virginia Valentine, director of advertising's foremost cultural analysis company, Semiotic Solutions, argues that brands can no longer expect consumers to take sales messages at face value*. Consumers challenge everything they are told, she believes, and will prefer brands that give them something back, rather than the old-style 'here's our product ain't it great!' philosophy which has dominated advertising since its inception. Thus ads can deal with social issues and refer to the news agenda these days. Inevitably, though, it can go horribly wrong. 'The risk is, and I think this is true in the case of Volkswagen, that if you use images of faith and prostitute them, people will take offence. It's all very well if you give them something back, but it is clear that Jesus could not have benefited from that poster campaign.'

6 The ad agency, however, may well have done. The VW campaign might look like a marketing disaster, but increasingly ad agencies are selling to clients not simply their ability to write ads but their ability to write ads that generate PR. Some clients ask all agencies pitching for their business to demonstrate their ability to garner* extra publicity.

7 A deliberately shocking ad is the simplest way to get additional media coverage, and even if the media coverage is negative, it can still help to sell the product as advertisers like Benetton have already proved.

8 One supporter of Benetton's work is Leon Jaume, Deputy Creative Director of ad agency Ogilvy & Mather, who believes its success lies in knowing its target. 'In marketing terms the only real taboo is upsetting the people you want to buy your product,' he says. 'As long as it's legal and the client is OK with it, you can offend anyone else and in many ways you should. I'd normally see outrageous advertising as a youth proposition though, and I think VW's mistake may have been in selling a product that isn't a youth product with this kind of style. Young people are receptive to taboo-breaking as they are more open-minded than older people. I think they positively welcome advertising that annoys their parents.' Some agency creatives argue that young people today are fundamentally different from previous generations in their internationalism, and young consumers in Tel Aviv are closer to their counterparts* in Paris, New York and Sydney than they are to their parents.

9 As this generation grows up, the argument goes, they will continue to be more broad-minded than their parents and will see the shattering of taboos as the norm. So outrageous advertising will no longer be limited to those products which target youth.

10 Perhaps Volkswagen was just ahead of its time, advertising to a market that wasn't broad-minded enough in a country that still gets nervous when Church and State are challenged. Or perhaps VW's collision with Catholics shows that for all their claimed acumen*, ad agencies are less in touch* with the public mood than they claim.

*The European*

---

*outrageous:* very shocking
*to sue:* to claim money because you have been harmed
*penance:* suffering to show you are sorry
*to take s.t.h at face value:* to accept s.th. without thinking

*to garner:* to collect
*a counterpart:* a similar person in a different place
*acumen:* the ability to make good judgments
*to be in touch with:* to understand

**Reading**

**1** Read the text opposite about controversial advertising. Do you think the VW campaign was successful?

**2** Read the text in more detail and choose the best answer.

1 Which of the following is **least** likely to be one of the reasons why Volkswagen ran a deliberately provocative campaign?

   a   to generate media coverage of the campaign.

   b   to shock some members of society.

   c   to show their lack of respect for the Catholic Church.

2 Using taboo images in advertising has become popular with advertising executives mainly because

   a   they only want to target young people.

   b   consumers have stopped paying attention to conventional advertising.

   c   products are becoming more international and sophisticated.

3 According to the text, shocking advertising is

   a   always damaging for the advertiser.

   b   always damaging for the ad agency.

   c   the simplest way to get media coverage.

4 According to Leon Jaume, the young generation of consumers like ads

   a   with an international flavour.

   b   that offend them.

   c   that offend their parents.

5 The author of the text suggests that

   a   perhaps Volkswagen isn't broad-minded enough.

   b   admen are not doing enough market research before running campaigns.

   c   Volkswagen wanted to break taboos in France.

**Vocabulary**

**1** Find words or expressions in the text which correspond to the following definitions.

1 a public space reserved for advertisers to put their ads on (*para 1*)

   b illboard

2 large pictures or notices put up in a public place to advertise something (*para 1*)

   p_____

3 human interest subjects (*para 5*)

   s_____ i_____

4 people or companies who pay for a professional service (*para 6*)

   c_____

5 try to win a business deal (*para 6*)

   to p_____ f___ b_____

6 time and space given by the media to a particular news item (*para 7*)

   c_____

7 the person in charge of developing ideas for advertising campaigns (*para 8*)

   C_____ D_____

8 a social custom which means a particular activity or subject must be avoided (*para 8*)

   t_____

**2** RXV, a major electronics company, has decided to advertise its latest digital camera. It has asked several advertising agencies to submit proposals for a campaign. An executive at one of these agencies has made a list of tasks to be completed before submitting its proposal to RXV.

Complete the executive's list using words from Key vocabulary and Vocabulary 1. Change the form of the words where necessary.

- Obtain complete market information about the ¹___client___'s product; advantages, disadvantages, competitors, which groups of consumers the advertiser wants to ²_____. Define marketing objectives and plan an overall advertising strategy.
- Meet with the media department to select the most appropriate means of advertising: media or posters on ³_____ .
- Meet with the ⁴_____ _____ to work on the design and ideas of the campaign. Point out that these should fit in with the overall ⁵_____ _____ the company wants to project. Explain that we must be careful not to generate any negative ⁶_____ by offending anyone.

## Vocabulary development: uses of *like*

Look at the following examples from the text on page 136.

**A** *The German carmaker's model **was likened to** a religious revelation. (para 1)*

**B** *…if outrageous advertising worked for **the likes of** Benetton, it could work to revive the image of the Golf. (para 2)*

**C** *The VW campaign might **look like** a marketing disaster … (para 6)*

**D** *… it can still help to sell a product as advertisers **like** Benetton have already proved. (para 7)*

**1** In which of the examples above are the words in bold used:

**a** as a synonym for 'to appear'? C

**b** to give an example?

**c** to refer to a type of person or group of people?

**d** as a verb to compare one thing to another?

**2** Complete the sentences using the correct form of the expressions with *like*.

**1** TV advertising is too expensive for small computer software companies, only the likes of IBM can afford it.

**2** Aggressive bosses are sometimes _____ great apes by the media.

**3** Advertising for products _____ alcohol is banned in some countries.

**4** The new perfume bottle is designed to _____ a sculpture.

What other uses of the word *like* do you know?

## Discussion

The text begins with the question 'Is Volkswagen bold or stupid?'. What do you think? In groups, discuss whether the company was right to launch such a controversial campaign.

## Language Focus

**Gerund and infinitive**

**Look at the following sentences from the text on page 136.**

A *The agency's penance has included **making** a substantial donation. (para 3)*

B *We decided **to retract** the posters immediately. (para 3)*

1 What form is the verb in bold in sentence A? Why?

2 What form is the verb in bold in sentence B? Why?

3 In which sentence is the verb like a noun?

▶▶ For more information on the gerund and infinitive, turn to page 169.

**Practice**

**Complete the following passage using a gerund or infinitive. Use the verbs in the boxes.**

| A | | B | | C | |
|---|---|---|---|---|---|
| build | set up | decide | reflect | return | change |
| put | bring | appear | create | expand | launch |
| make | transform | | | drink | |

Tanto deliziosa

SARI MARITZA entertains CARY GRANT with true hospitality..Ice Cold Coca-Cola

---

## Coca-Cola and its advertising

(A) John S. Pemberton invented Coca-Cola in 1886. His partner suggested ¹ _putting_ an advertisement for the drink in *The Atlanta Journal* that very year. In 1888, Asa Chandler bought the Coca-Cola business and decided ² _____ the product known through signs, calendars and clocks. The company began ³ _____ its global network when Robert Woodcruff was elected president of the company in 1923. He succeeded in ⁴ _____ Coca-Cola into a truly international product by ⁵ _____ a foreign department, which exported Coca-Cola to the Olympic Games in Amsterdam in 1928. During World War Two, he promised ⁶ _____ Coca-Cola to every soldier in every part of the world.

(B) Coca-Cola's advertising has always attempted ⁷ _____ changing contemporary lifestyles. ⁸ _____ an international advertising campaign requires the talents of professionals in many areas, and extensive testing and research are always done before ⁹ _____ which advertisements will finally be used. Celebrity endorsements have featured heavily — Cary Grant, Ray Charles and Whitney Houston are just three of the big name stars who have agreed ¹⁰ _____ in Coca-Cola commercials.

(C) After ¹¹ _____ Diet Coke in 1982, the company saw its sales grow quickly. The drink is now the third most popular in the world. In 1985, the company tried ¹² _____ the secret formula of Coca-Cola, but realised that Americans were very attached to the original recipe. The company listened to its consumers and quickly responded by ¹³ _____ the original formula to the market as 'Coca-Cola Classic'. Today, people in more than 160 countries around the globe enjoy ¹⁴ _____ Coca-Cola. It is asked for more than 524 million times a day in more than 80 languages. The company intends ¹⁵ _____ its global presence even further in the twenty-first century, particularly in developing markets.

**The article**

**1** Read the advertisement opposite for BP Solarex, part of the leading international petrochemical company, BP Amoco. What brand image is BP Solarex trying to project?

**2** Read the advertisement again and identify which form of the article is used with each of the nouns below. The definite article (*the*), the indefinite article (*a/an*), or no article? Can you explain why?

| | | | |
|---|---|---|---|
| 1 power no article | 2 world | 3 electricity | 4 sun |
| 5 need | 6 difficulty | 7 range | 8 living standards |

▶▶ For more information on the article, turn to page 170.

**Practice**

Complete the following passage about the mineral water company Perrier, putting in the correct form of the article where necessary.

> In February 1990, Perrier, one of [1] __the__ most famous mineral water companies, faced [2]_____ serious image problem when small quantities of benzene were found in some bottles. [3]_____ company decided to take 160 million bottles, worth $70 m, off the market. [4]_____ spokesperson from [5]_____ communications department made [6]_____ statement to the press saying that this did not present [7]_____ health problem but he did admit that for [8]_____ product known for purity, it was definitely [9]_____ mistake.
>
> [10]_____ independent environmental consultant carried out [11]_____ inspection at the Perrier plant and identified and corrected [12]_____ fault. [13]_____ same consultant said that a person spilling one drop of [14]_____ lead-free petrol on their hand would absorb more benzene than if they drank a bottle of Perrier every day for a year. In this instance Perrier's policy of [15]_____ honesty and its concern for [16]_____ consumers saved its image and good name.

# BP S⬤LAREX

Solar Energy from BP Amoco

## Power for Rural Communities

Nearly two billion people in the world have no electricity; 70% of them have difficulty obtaining clean drinking water. Many live in widely scattered and remote rural communities, with little hope of connection to national electricity grids. Their need is not simply for electricity, but for stand alone power systems that are long-lasting, reliable and simple to maintain. Above all, they need a constant and cheap source of fuel, like the sun.

## BP Solarex - Meeting the need

BP Solarex has over twenty-five years experience working in remote areas, not only in developing countries but also in the developed world. This experience has allowed us to build an unrivalled understanding of local needs. We have put that experience to good use, to build a range of packaged products designed to enhance living standards anywhere grid-connected electricity is unavailable.

## Skills Focus

**Listening**

### Designing a television commercial

A TV **commercial** generally consists of a short film **sequence** of between 30 and 60 seconds with an accompanying **soundtrack** which includes a mixture of **live recordings** (what people actually say in the commercial), a **voice-over** (the voice of someone who does not appear on screen) and music and sound **effects**. Various techniques are used in commercials to convince the viewer of the value of the product or service that is being advertised. One of the most common of these is 'dramatisation' where a short story is developed around the product or service. The original ideas behind a commercial of this type are developed from a **scenario**, a written document that summarises the action, the atmosphere, the characters and the scene where the sequences of the commercial will be filmed. An artist then produces a **storyboard**, or series of pictures, to show how the commercial will look.

**1** **Look at the storyboard opposite for a Gillette anti-perspirant TV commercial. In pairs or small groups, discuss these questions.**

1 What do you think the 'story' is about?
2 Do you think the characters say anything? If so, what do they say?
3 What do you think the voice-over says?
4 What do you think the slogan is?

**2** 🔲 **Listen to a description of the commercial and compare it with what you discussed.**

**3** 🔲 **Listen again and make notes about:**

1 the characters
2 the setting
3 the action
4 the different camera positions
5 the final slogan

**Which tense is used to describe what happens? Why?**

**Discussion**

In groups, choose a product or service to prepare a scenario for. Discuss your ideas and agree on a scenario and slogan for a TV commercial using the dramatisation technique.

**Writing**

In groups, prepare a complete written scenario for your product or service. Follow the model of the description of the advertisement in Listening 2.

**Speaking**

Present descriptions to the rest of the class. Discuss which scenario is the most effective.

# 15 *The Business Media*

**Key vocabulary** The business community relies on various media to provide news, **information** and **data**. The **print media** (newspapers, books and magazines) supply this in written form through the **press** (people who write for newspapers and magazines) and **publishing** companies, which produce them. Radio and television **channels** or **stations** produce and distribute audio and audio-visual programmes or **broadcasts** which cover the main events and developments in business. Recently there has been considerable expansion of **multimedia** businesses which provide integrated media services containing sound, pictures and text, accessed by **audiences** around the world through **networks** such as the Internet.

SMITH – WESSON MERGER OFF ++ DAVIDSON SHARES REACH ALL TIME HIGH ++ FTSE CLOSES UP 38 AT 6678 ++

**Lead-in** Listen to an executive from Bloomberg, a multimedia information network, describing the different types of information that the organisation supplies. Make notes about the four products that he talks about, using these three headings.

• Services    • Audience(s)    • Media

Bloomberg News

The Bloomberg Service

Bloomberg Television

Bloomberg Personal

**Reading**

**1** Before you read the text opposite about Michael Bloomberg, the founder of Bloomberg, write three questions you would like to ask about the man, and three about his company.

**2** Read the text and see if you can find the answers to your questions. Can you guess the answers to your other questions?

# A Man And His Information Machine

*By Lisa Napoli*

Ubiquity*, says Michael Bloomberg, was never his intention. Nonetheless, his name seems to be everywhere these days. A new deal with AT&T,
5 announced on Monday, will plaster the Bloomberg name on Internet cell phones. An autobiography, *Bloomberg by Bloomberg*, is out in stores this week. He owns a news
10 wire service and a satellite television network. He also syndicates* radio programming, publishes a consumer financial magazine and maintains a Web site that he says gets 45,000
15 visitors a day.

None of these, however, represents the core business of this 55-year-old from Medford, Massachusetts; they are all parts of a multimedia empire
20 founded in 1981 when Bloomberg left Salomon Brothers with $10 m and an idea centred on the most basic and valuable of late 20th century commodities: information.
25 Bloomberg set to work, with the money and a small group of computer programmers, to come up with an analytical system that would be simple for brokers to use. With
30 some initial financial backing from Merrill Lynch, he built his network to deliver stock and bond information, a database of corporations' histories and analysis. And he named it
35 Bloomberg.

Today, Bloomberg terminals, for which subscribers pay $1,200 a month, sit on the desks of 75,000 financial analysts around the world. He has
40 turned his original concept into a reported $1 bn-a-year multimedia news and information empire. Bloomberg's name has become a one-man brand, prominent
45 throughout the investment and news-

gathering industries. Yet, unless you travel in the financial world, you may not have seen his empire growing. Rupert Murdoch and Ted
50 Turner probably have vaster holdings, but Bloomberg, with his privately held company, may exert more autocratic* control than any one man in the information
55 business.

A recent visit to Bloomberg world headquarters on Manhattan's Park Avenue found people crowding into and through the lobby* as if it were
60 the trading floor of the New York Stock Exchange. On this day, many of the young employees were carrying advance copies of *Bloomberg by Bloomberg*, a clear
65 demonstration of what one outsider described as the 'cultish' devotion employees seem to have for the man, his empire and his vision. These are impressive offices by any
70 newsroom standards, and there are perks. A veritable convenience store of soft drinks and chocolates and other snacks, all free, draws an endless stream of workers.
75 The premises are crowded, but no one, not even Bloomberg, has a private office. Although his desk is off to one side, right next to a small glass-enclosed sitting area, nearby
80 employees can easily hear him on the phone.

Surrounded by state-of-the-art digital equipment which powers his information network, this Johns
85 Hopkins-educated engineer with an MBA from Harvard keeps a slide rule* on his desk. ('Other people must be smarter than I am, because they can use calculators

90 and see relationships; I think calculators mask.') He says he wrote his book on a yellow pad.

He disdains critics who predict that the Internet will displace the need for
95 the 'Bloomberg box'; the Internet, he asserts, is nothing more than a delivery system – and an unreliable one at that. 'Our long distance bills, hardware, depreciation and money
100 sent to phone companies, is about $100 m a year,' he said. 'If the Internet really worked and I could get our customers to come to us through the Internet, we'd save $100 m.
105 'Why can we charge $1,200 a month and these other idiots can't get away with anything?' he asks. 'Because on the Internet, when you try to charge for anything, usage goes to zero. The
110 data that we have is publicly available, but the value added is in the categorization and the utilities that let you do something with it.'

Though Bloomberg has fewer
115 subscribers than Reuters and Dow Jones / Telerate, his competitors in the financial information business, his system is growing faster and is often praised as easier to use. Bloomberg
120 claims he doesn't pretend to know the direction he'll go. What happens next, as Bloomberg figures it, is equal parts luck and design.

'There are many reasons why some
125 succeed and others don't,' Bloomberg writes. 'Three things separate the winners from the losers over the long term: time invested, interpersonal skills and plain old-fashioned luck.'

*New York Times*

*ubiquity:* seeming to be everywhere
*to syndicate:* to sell to other media
*autocratic:* giving orders without asking others' opinions
*a lobby:* a large entrance hall in a public building
*a slide rule:* a kind of ruler with moving parts, for calculating

**3** Read the text again and decide if the following statements are true (T) or false (F).

1 Originally the Bloomberg service was designed to provide news reports. ☑ F

2 The main customers of Bloomberg are professionals in the field of finance. ☐

3 You can buy shares in Bloomberg on the Stock Exchange. ☐

4 Bloomberg employees seem to like working for the company. ☐

5 Only Michael Bloomberg has a private office. ☐

6 Michael Bloomberg believes that the Internet will provide serious competition for his company. ☐

7 Michael Bloomberg believes that using the Internet would help him to reduce company costs. ☐

8 Bloomberg provides tools to analyse information that is freely available. ☐

9 Bloomberg has more customers than its competitors. ☐

10 Michael Bloomberg believes that success in business is principally a question of luck. ☐

**4** What do you think are the advantages / disadvantages of working in an office like the one described in the article?

## Vocabulary

**1** **Match the words from the text on page 145 with their corresponding definitions.**

| | | | |
|---|---|---|---|
| 1 | core business (*line 17*) | **a** | a quantity of shares held by one owner |
| 2 | backing (*line 30*) | **b** | a computer program that is used to record and list data |
| 3 | a database (*line 33*) | | |
| 4 | a subscriber (*line 37*) | **c** | a benefit for an employee in addition to salary |
| 5 | a concept (*line 40*) | | |
| 6 | a holding (*line 51*) | **d** | the fall in the value of something as it becomes older |
| 7 | a perk (*line 71*) | | |
| 8 | premises (*line 75*) | **e** | the building where a company is located |
| 9 | state-of-the-art (*line 82*) | **f** | newest or most sophisticated |
| 10 | depreciation (*line 99*) | **g** | central activities of a company |
| | | **h** | support |
| | | **i** | an idea or a thought |
| | | **j** | a person who pays regularly for a service |

**2** **Complete the passage about WorldSpace Inc using words from Key vocabulary and Vocabulary 1. Change the form of the words where necessary.**

Noah Samara, an Ethiopian born lawyer, has a new media ¹ *concept* that he says will bring news, ²_____ and education to millions of people in Asia, the Middle East, Africa and Latin America. His company, whose headquarters are located in Washington DC, plans to use satellites to transmit digital radio ³_____ to 'under-informed' ⁴_____ in these areas of the world. Potentially that means that more than three hundred million listeners could soon be tuning in, using special radios that may ultimately cost as little as $50. To get his business off the ground, Noah Samara has raised $850 m receiving the ⁵_____ of investors from the regions where WorldSpace will operate. Most of the programming will be provided free although some services will be reserved for ⁶_____. The company has recently signed a deal with media tycoon Michael Bloomberg who will supply business news to WorldSpace listeners.

**WORLDSPACE**
CORPORATION
*Yes, we go there.*

Digital Sound Broadcasting for the 21st Century

## Vocabulary development: phrasal verbs 3

In the following examples from the text on page 145, are the phrasal verbs in bold transitive or intransitive?

*Bloomberg set to work, with the money and a small group of computer programmers, to* **come up with** *an analytical system that would be simple for brokers to use. (line 27)*

*'Why can we charge $1,200 a month and these other idiots can't* **get away with** *anything?' (line 106)*

Three-part phrasal verbs are transitive and consist of a verb, an adverb particle and a preposition.

**1** Replace the words in italics with three-part phrasal verbs. Use a word from each box in the correct form.

| A | B | C |
|---|---|---|
| cut | over | on (x2) |
| live | along | for |
| go | forward | with (x2) |
| come | out | to (x5) |
| miss | round | |
| get (x3) | back | |
| look | down | |
| move | in | |
| | on | |
| | up | |

**a** I'm *very excited about* retiring next year. looking forward to

**b** She is not an easy person to *have a friendly relationship with*.

**c** The director has *received* a lot of criticism lately.

**d** Our sales of this product have failed to *meet* our expectations.

**e** We have decided to *accept* the report's recommendations.

**f** Now that everyone has been introduced, perhaps we can *start discussing* business.

**g** They still haven't given us the contracts to sign. When do you think they will *finally do* it?

**h** If we don't submit an offer, we may *fail to take advantage of* a good opportunity.

**i** The company will *adopt* the new accounting procedures at the end of the year.

**j** If the situation does not improve, the company will have to consider *reducing* personnel.

**2** What other examples of three-part phrasal verbs do you know?

## *Language Focus*

**could have +
past participle**

**Look at the statement about Michael Bloomberg and choose the correct rule,
A or B.**

*He **could have invested** his ten million dollar payment from Salomon and he **could
have lived** quite comfortably from the income. Instead he chose to risk it all creating his
company.*

We use *could have* + past participle to talk about something which

A was possible in the past and which was done.

B was possible in the past and which was not done.

▶▶ **For more information on *could have* + past participle, turn to page 171.**

**Practice**

**1 For each of Michael Bloomberg's actions write an alternative, using *could
have.***

Example: After graduating from Johns Hopkins University, he did an MBA at
Harvard Business School.
*He could have started work after graduating from Johns Hopkins University.*

1 He accepted a job at Salomon despite being offered a better paid position with
another company.

2 He set up Bloomberg offices in the most expensive parts of London and New
York.

3 He chose open plan offices for all of his staff.

4 He arranged for free food and drinks to be made available to all employees.

5 He refused to open a Bloomberg office in South Africa during apartheid.

6 He wrote his autobiography himself.

7 He donated the profits from his book to charity.

8 He decided to keep Bloomberg as a private company.

**2 Write three things you have done in your life, when you had a choice. Write
an alternative for each, using *could have*.**

Example: *I went to the USA. I could have gone to England.*

**Nouns**

**Match the nouns in bold, from the text on page 146, with the descriptions below.**

1 the young **employees** were carrying advance copies (*line 62*)

2 the **premises** are crowded (*line 75*)

3 **equipment** which powers his information network (*line 83*)

a a countable noun which can be singular or plural.

b an uncountable noun which can only be used in the singular form.

c a plural noun which cannot be used in the singular form.

▶▶ **For more information on nouns, turn to page 171.**

**Practice**

**1 Which category does each noun belong to?**

| | | | |
|---|---|---|---|
| 1 information b | 5 business | 9 bond | 13 education |
| 2 backing | 6 goods | 10 luck | 14 network |
| 3 magazine | 7 intelligence | 11 logistics | 15 depreciation |
| 4 earnings | 8 cash | 12 knowledge | 16 money |

**2 Check your answers in a dictionary.**

## *Skills Focus*

**Listening**

**1** Before you listen to a radio business news bulletin from EBNW (The European Business Network), decide the order in which these categories of business news would appear.

**a** latest news about specific companies and markets

**b** trading results on international exchanges

**c** a general economic news item

**2** Listen to the news bulletin to check your answers.

**Reading**   You are going to prepare a short radio business news bulletin. Read the articles that your teacher gives you, and note the key points.

**Speaking**   In groups, give a brief summary of your texts and decide on the order in which they would appear in a radio news report.

**Writing**   **1** Number the guidelines in the correct order.

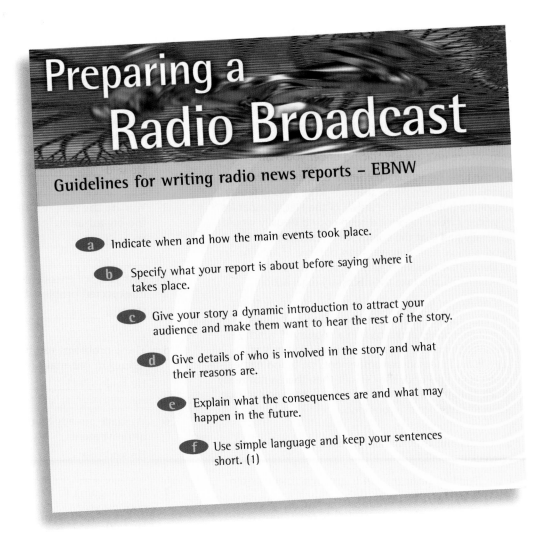

# Preparing a Radio Broadcast

## Guidelines for writing radio news reports – EBNW

**a** Indicate when and how the main events took place.

**b** Specify what your report is about before saying where it takes place.

**c** Give your story a dynamic introduction to attract your audience and make them want to hear the rest of the story.

**d** Give details of who is involved in the story and what their reasons are.

**e** Explain what the consequences are and what may happen in the future.

**f** Use simple language and keep your sentences short. (1)

**2** In groups, write the introductions to your reports and the text of the summaries that will follow.

**3** Decide who will speak and in what order and make sure that your script makes clear links between the different speakers.

**Role-play**   Present your reports to the other students.

# Review 3

## Grammar check

### 1 Complete the passage below by choosing the correct forms of the words in italics.

The latest dilemma [1] *who / which* faces thousands of businesses all over the world is yet another result of [2] *an / the* explosive growth of the Internet. But this time the question [3] *that / whose* executives are asking is 'How can I get my company's name on the Net?'.

The fraudulent use of company and brand names on the Net, [4] *which / that* is technically no different from normal trademark infringement, has become [5] *a / the* problem of global proportions. As executives [6] *which / whose* companies have been slow to set up on the Web are finding out, [7] *setting up / to set up* an official site on the Web doesn't necessarily mean that someone somewhere isn't already trading under your name.

For the time being [8] *a / the whole* issue of trademark piracy is one [9] *that / who* seems [10] *to be / being* totally out of control. Before the arrival of the Net, companies [11] *whose / which* logos had been copied illegally would generally find that the copies were restricted to one geographical region. It was then possible [12] *identifying / to identify* the people [13] *who / which* were behind the infringement and take the necessary legal action.

It is no longer that simple today when the only things [14] *which / whose* pirates need are some computing [15] *powers / power* and a base in a country [16] *which / whose* government has no intention [17] *to sign / of signing* any international agreements on brand name protection. And once they've got that, there's not really much [18] *that / who* anyone can do [19] *stopping / to stop* them [20] *using / to use* your logo.

### 2 Underline the mistake in each sentence, and correct it.

1   Our European market is growing ~~more~~ faster than our Asian one.

2   Our products are marketed to the children as well as adults.

3   We chose a TV campaign but we could have did a print one as well.

4   We carried out a full study and collected a lot of informations.

5   Advertisers as Benetton have very provocative campaigns to get publicity.

6   He needs lots of equipments for his new business.

7   This is a no smoking area; we don't have to smoke here.

8   The mergers do not always work out the way top executives plan them.

9   Advertising on the Internet is cheaper as advertising on TV.

10   A product as ours is always successful on the American market.

### 3 Rewrite the extracts from a speech made by a chief executive officer, using reported speech. Make any other necessary changes.

1   We are making every effort to improve our financial performance.
    He said ___they were making every effort to improve their financial performance___ .

2   We expect to be in a position to resume dividend payments next year.
    He said _____ .

3   You are the people who will decide the future of the organisation.
    He said _____ .

4   Last year we encountered a number of unexpected problems.
    He said _____ .

5   These problems resulted in disappointing sales figures in our main market.
    He said _____ .

6   We have already started to work on improvements.
    He said _____ .

7   We are going to have two main objectives in the coming year.
    He said _____ .

8   We must improve customer satisfaction.
    He said _____ .

9   We will have to innovate in new areas of business.
    He said _____ .

10   We can then re-establish our company as market leader.
    He said _____ .

## Vocabulary check

**1** Complete the boxes with the words and expressions from the list below that are most commonly associated with each theme.

| Setting up a business | Corporate Alliances |
|---|---|
| _____ | _____ |
| _____ | _____ |
| _____ | _____ |
| _____ | _____ |

| Marketing | Advertising |
|---|---|
| _____ | _____slogan_____ |
| _____ | _____ |
| _____ | _____ |
| _____ | _____ |

| The Business Media |
|---|
| _____ |
| _____ |
| _____ |
| _____ |

slogan                          entrepreneur
takeover                        Creative Director
subscribe                       acquisition
billboard                       segment
networks                        research
joint venture                   sole trader
limited liability               merger
consumer profile                broadcast
terminal                        commercial
focus group                     partnership

**2** Replace the words and expressions in italics with words from exercise 1 in the correct form.

Nowadays, [1] *people who have started companies*
___entrepreneurs___ can access important information
through various [2] *channels which distribute information*
_____. There are numerous TV and radio
[3] *programmes* _____ and the Internet
allows companies to do all kinds of [4] *studies*
_____ quickly and efficiently without
leaving the office. Businesses can look for potential
[5] *companies to buy* _____ and get
essential market data about specific [6] *parts*
_____ of their market at the push of a
button. Professional business media companies provide
specialist material exclusively to people who [7] *pay a fee*
_____. They also earn money by running
[8] *audiovisual advertisements* _____ for
various products and services. Companies can also get
market information directly from the public in [9] *informal*

*discussion sessions* _____, which can help
them to build up [10] *pictures of typical customers*
_____.

**3** Complete the passages below, using words from A and B in the correct form.

A

| under |
|---|
| bi |
| over |
| break |
| pre |
| up |
| out |
| catch |
| inter |
| post |

B

| on |
|---|
| national |
| graduate |
| down |
| planned |
| paid |
| worked |
| market |
| dated |
| lingual |

The trade unions are fighting for salary increases and a shorter working week. The Managing Director, however, has rejected this proposal, saying that the workers are already [1] ___overpaid___ and [2] _____. It looks very much like negotiations are about to [3] _____. A strike seems increasingly likely.

Ours is a truly [4] _____ company, we are active in markets throughout the world. Most of our managers are [5] _____ and are encouraged to learn a third language as well as studying for [6] _____ diplomas in business.

The range we introduced in the 1990s has now become [7] _____ and we are losing our market share. We have decided to launch a new product range which will include more expensive [8] _____ lines. Our marketing department is confident that these will [9] _____ and bring the success we would like. We expect the launch to go well as it has all been carefully [10] _____.

# Communication Activities

## Unit 1 Speaking 1

**Student B** (Giancarlo Peretto)
Read your profile. Prepare the questions that you will need to ask Student A (Susan Robertson) in order to complete her profile.

Example: *How long have you been with your present company?*
*What are you responsible for?*

Answer Student A's questions. Then interview Student A and complete the profile.

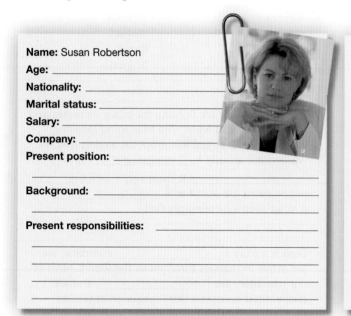

**Name:** Susan Robertson
**Age:** _____
**Nationality:** _____
**Marital status:** _____
**Salary:** _____
**Company:** _____
**Present position:** _____
_____
**Background:** _____
_____
**Present responsibilities:** _____
_____
_____
_____
_____
_____

**Name:** Giancarlo Peretto
**Age:** 48
**Nationality:** Italian
**Marital status:** Married, 3 children
**Salary:** $160,000 per annum
**Company:** The Milan Bank of Commerce
**Present position:** Chief Financial Officer
Reports to the Managing Director
**Background:**
• Studied at the London School of Economics
• Joined the accounts department in 1985
**Present responsibilities:**
• Leads a team of senior executives working on various aspects of financial management
• In charge of planning the bank's financial strategy

## Unit 12 Role-play

### The chairperson

- You should prepare a short introduction about the proposed alliance. You have to convince the participants that the alliance is a positive move for your company.
- Explain the 35-hour week situation.
- Study the language of chairing a meeting carefully and be ready to fulfil your role as the organiser of the meeting. Invite each person to speak and summarise what they've said before moving onto the next speaker.
- You will accept some of the compromise suggestions put forward and delegate the organisation of these 'action points' to the relevant people. Fix a date and time for the next meeting to discuss progress on the action points.

## Unit 3 Speaking

### Student A

# Unit 10 Speaking

## Group A

(All figures are in French francs. Source: *L'Oréal Annual Report 1998*)

**Breakdown of share ownership at 31 December 1998**

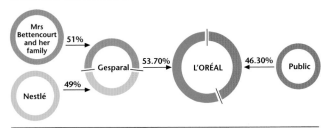

**L'Oréal share performance**

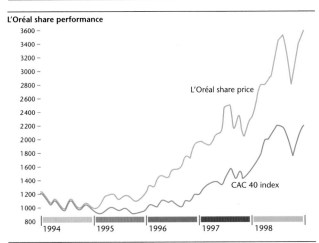

The L'Oréal Group is the world leader in the cosmetics industry with international brands such as: L'Oréal, Laboratoires Garnier, Maybelline, Redken, Lancôme, Helena Rubinstein, Biotherm, Vichy, Ralph Lauren Perfumes and Giorgio Armani Perfumes.

Research is one of the keys to L'Oréal success and has been at the core of the company's strategy since its foundation by a chemist in 1907. L'Oréal has built up its own cutting edge research by investing £1.2 billion in this area in the last 10 years.

**Shares (monthly settlement market)**

| | | 1994 | 1995 | 1996 | 1997 | 1998 |
|---|---|---|---|---|---|---|
| Final adjusted closing price | | 990 | 1,191.82 | 1,954 | 2,355 | 4, 040 |
| Dividend per share and investment certificate for the year | Net dividend | 11.09 | 12.09 | 14.00 | 16.00 | 18.50 |
| | Tax credit | 5.55 | 6.05 | 7.00 | 8.00 | 9.25 |
| | Total value | 16.64 | 18.14 | 21.00 | 24.00 | 27.75 |

**Fully diluted earnings per share and investment certificate (before capital gains and losses, after minority interests)**

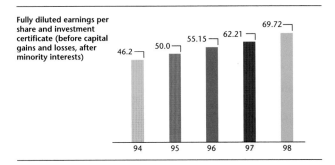

**Comparison of absolute P/Es**

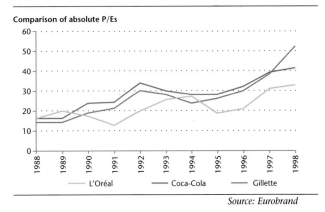

*Source: Eurobrand*

# Unit 1 Speaking 2

## Student B

**Read the company profile. Ask Student A about the company he or she has read about, and complete the notes below.**

**Motorola** maintains sales, services and manufacturing facilities throughout the world, conducting business on six continents. Its major business areas are: advanced electronic systems, components and services, two-way radios, paging and data communications, automotive, defence and space electronics and computers. It has the largest portfolio in the world of cellular phones. The CEO is Christopher Galvin and the headquarters are situated in Chicago. Sales in 1999 were $30.2 bn.

Name of company _____

Headquarters _____

Chairman _____

Business activities _____

_____

Main markets _____

_____

Sales in 1999 _____

# Unit 4 Speaking

**Student A**     Expense Reduction Analysts

### Expense Reduction Analysts International Ltd.

**Description:**
Cost management consulting to small and medium sized businesses.

**Activities:**
Helping clients (businesses) to reduce overheads. ERA analyses existing costs in areas such as office supplies, telephone and cleaning services. It then suggests cheaper solutions where necessary. Payment is on a percentage basis with ERA receiving 50% of any savings made during the first six months. The ERA Intranet has databases of suppliers and clients.

**Training:**
Full training and ongoing support, one week's initial training followed by monthly meetings and training. Dedicated mentor to assist you getting started. ERA Intranet holds all copyrighted materials and systems allowing you to keep in close contact with other franchisees. Training certified to ISO9001 standard.

**Qualifications:**
Need to have business management, consulting, or executive background. Possess strong communication skills, have an analytical mind, and like working as a team player.

**Company Details:**
Business established in: 1983
Franchised since: 1994
# of franchised units: 472
Company owned: 1

**Financial information for franchisees:**
Startup cash required: £12,500
Investment required: £18,900

Ongoing fees per month:
Year 1 – £100; year 2 – £300; year 3 – £400

**Contact Information:**
Address:
Richmond House,
PO Box 374,
St. Anne's Place,
St. Peter Port,
Guernsey,
Channel Islands.
GY1 2NU.

Phone: 44-7000-372-000
Fax: 44-1481-713-654
Primary Contact: Frederick Marfleet
Secondary Contact: Bo Sjoholm
WWW: http://www.expense-reduction.net
E-mail: info@expense-reduction.net

# Unit 2 Discussion

### INSTRUCTIONS

In this example you are given a block of four statements: A, B, C and D. Choose the statement which you think is most true or typical of you in your everyday behavior and then choose the one which is least true or typical of you. Indicate your choices by writing 'M' (for most) in one box, and 'L' (for least) in another.

**I am the sort of person who ...**

| | | | | |
|---|---|---|---|---|
| 1 | **A** has a wide circle of friends | ❏ | 3 **A** has lots of new ideas | ❏ |
| | **B** enjoys organising people | ❏ | **B** feels calm | ❏ |
| | **C** relaxes easily | ❏ | **C** likes to understand things | ❏ |
| | **D** seeks variety | ❏ | **D** is easy to get on with | ❏ |
| 2 | **A** helps people with their problems | ❏ | 4 **A** enjoys organising events | ❏ |
| | **B** develops new approaches | ❏ | **B** sometimes gets angry | ❏ |
| | **C** has lots of energy | ❏ | **C** is talkative | ❏ |
| | **D** enjoys social activities | ❏ | **D** resolves conflicts at work | ❏ |

## Unit 6 Role-play

**Student B**

You are an experienced journalist and you want to create a new magazine entitled *The Security Gazette*. The magazine will be aimed at professionals from the security industry. It will cover all subjects related to the protection of people and property and will be distributed nationally. The target audience consists of the employees of private companies in this sector, which is growing at 10 % annually. It is also designed to appeal to public sector organisations such as the police, and also to the general public.

Use the information below to help you to prepare your negotiation. Remember that you should convince the banking representative that you have:

- the right character
- a serious commitment to the business
- the capacity to manage it
- enough collateral or security to use as a guarantee

### Business plan

**Product description:** Full colour magazine, A4 format, 80 pages
**Market size:** Potential - 7,000 issues per month
**Competition:** Fragmented; more specialist publications
Sales forecast: 84,000 issues p.a. @ 3.75 euros = 315,000 euros

| Sales: | euros |
|---|---|
| Sales | 315,000 |
| Cost of sales | 63,500 |
| **Gross margin** | **251,500** |

**Operating expenses:**

| | |
|---|---|
| Advertising | 15,400 |
| Travel | 10,000 |
| Public relations | 10,000 |
| Payroll | 74,800 |
| Leased equipment | 6,000 |
| Utilities | 6,000 |
| Insurance | 9,000 |
| Rent | 12,600 |
| Logo, concept design | 10,300 |
| Miscellaneous | 3,500 |
| Total operating expenses | 157,600 |
| **Profit before taxes** | **93,900** |
| **Personal investment** | **70,000** |

Collateral / security:
Own house ........................................95,000

**Credit history:**
No previous business loan, only mortgage for house and consumer credit.

## Unit 3 Speaking

**Student B**

## Unit 12 Role-play

**The Human Resources Manager**

**Opinions**
In principle you disagree with the 35-hour week but believe in the necessity of the alliance. You feel the company will not survive without it. You should prepare arguments to convince the others of this.

**Suggestions**
Training seminars to develop team spirit and power sharing practices for executives.

**Attitude**
Open to other suggestions; you want to reach a compromise.

## Unit 12 Role-play

### The Finance Director

**Opinions**
You think the 35-hour week is an excellent idea. In any case, the alliance must be formed at any cost. The 35-hour week will save the company money, as part-time workers will cost less than present overtime costs. The alliance will bring a new customer base and improve the overall financial health of the company.

**Suggestions**
• people should think about the long term not the short term.
• they should think about the company not themselves!
• they should try to see the advantages of only working 35 hours per week.
• perhaps improved profits will bring salary increases for everyone in the long term.

**Attitude**
If necessary you will agree to the possibility of a long term salary increase. You will argue against the other proposed solutions and only agree with a compromise after much argument.

## Unit 8 Speaking 2

| 52 weeks High | Low | Stock | Price | Chg | Yld | P/E |
|---|---|---|---|---|---|---|
| **FOOD PRODUCERS** | | | | | | -1.252% |
| 287 | 115 | Acatos & Hutch | 151.0 | 12.0 | ... | ... |
| 39 | 6 | Albert Fisher | 7.0 | 0.0 | ... | 5.8 |
| 91 | 27 | Anglo East | 43.5 | 0.0 | 9.2 | 4.5 |
| 668 | 433 | **Assc Brit Fds** | 615.0 | -23.0 | 3.2 | 20.8 |
| 300 | 155 | Banks Syd C | 205.0 | -2.0 | 7.0 | 8.7 |
| 513 | 379 | Barr A G | 445.0 | 1.0 | 6.7 | 8.6 |
| 188 | 83 | Bertam Hldgs | 87.5 | 0.0 | 5.9 | 7.0 |
| 360 | 60 | Booker | 64.0 | -1.5 | 38.9 | 3.5 |
| 1078 | 537 | Brake Bros | 685.0 | 0.0 | 2.1 | 18.7 |
| 993 | 591 | **Cadbury-Schw** | 924.0 | 0.5 | 2.0 | 25.1 |
| 245 | 183 | Rob Wiseman | 200.0 | 3.5 | 3.4 | 13.4 |
| 99 | 48 | Rowe Evans | 50.5 | 0.0 | 8.6 | 4.0 |
| 585 | 256 | Tate & Lyle | 373.0 | -15.5 | 4.6 | 16.5 |
| 153 | 94 | Terranova Fds | 95.5 | 0.0 | ... | ... |
| 739 | 428 | Unigate | 496.0 | -3.0 | 5.6 | 10.7 |
| 712 | 437 | **Unilever** | 645.0 | -5.0 | 1.7 | 41.6 |
| 299 | 180 | Utd Biscuits | 242.0 | 0.0 | 5.5 | 41.7 |
| 63 | 43 | WT Foods | ... | ... | ... | 17.5 |
| **GAS DISTRIBUTION** | | | | | | -1.145% |
| 61 | 47 | Carlo Grp | 59.4 | -0.6 | 1.3 | 19.3 |
| 127 | 81 | **Centrica** | 121.3 | -0.8 | | |
| 450 | 268 | **BG** | 429.5 | 4.5 | 2.4 | ... |
| 147 | 99 | Intl Energy Grp | 133.5 | 0.5 | 3.7 | 12.5 |
| **HEALTH CARE** | | | | | | 2.449% |
| 603 | 315 | Alliance UniChem | 562.5 | 3.0 | 2.2 | 24.9 |
| 1025 | 688 | Bespak | 856.5 | 0.0 | 2.0 | 21.6 |
| 647 | 62 | Biocompatibles | 96.5 | -1.0 | ... | ... |
| 167 | 78 | Biotrace Intl | 107.5 | -5.0 | 59.7 | |
| 248 | 133 | Care UK | 207.5 | 1.5 | 0.8 | 26.6 |
| 93 | 22 | Celsis Intl | 28.5 | -2.5 | ... | ... |
| 551 | 388 | Comnty Hosp | 432.5 | 0.0 | 3.8 | 14.6 |
| 130 | 54 | Drew Scientific Gp | 90.0 | -1.5 | | ... |
| 173 | 128 | Gyrus Grp | 136.5 | 2.5 | | ... |
| 244 | 131 | Huntleigh | 233.5 | 1.0 | 1.7 | 25.4 |
| 593 | 425 | Isotron | 550.0 | 27.5 | 1.6 | 17.0 |
| 232 | 145 | London Intl | 209.5 | 0.0 | 1.5 | 41.9 |
| 390 | 160 | Nestor-BNA | 388.5 | 0.0 | 1.3 | 41.8 |
| 577 | 305 | **Nyce Amersham** | 386.0 | -6.3 | 1.3 | ... |
| 867 | 455 | Seton Scholl | 849.0 | 0.0 | 2.0 | 29.3 |
| 810 | 280 | Shield Diagn | 535.0 | 0.0 | | 232.6 |
| 229 | 97 | Sinclair Montrose | 98.5 | 0.0 | 0.3 | 35.2 |
| 200 | 118 | Smith & Neph | 166.5 | -3.5 | 4.1 | 15.3 |
| 68 | 13 | Tepnel Life | 19.0 | 0.0 | ... | ... |
| 413 | 254 | Westm H'care | 274.0 | 0.0 | 3.2 | 18.3 |

| High | Low | Stock | Price | Chg | Yld | P/E |
|---|---|---|---|---|---|---|
| **HOUSEHOLD GOODS** | | | | | | -1.949% |
| 178 | 71 | Airsprung | 71.5 | 0.0 | 12.9 | 3.7 |
| 220 | 165 | Alba | 175.0 | 0.0 | 4.6 | 9.4 |
| 167 | 82 | Alexandra | 106.5 | 0.0 | 8.2 | 9.9 |
| 188 | 79 | Allied Text | 101.0 | 5.0 | 10.6 | 6.1 |
| 233 | 146 | Aquarius Grp | 162.5 | 0.0 | 7.0 | 9.0 |
| 25 | 7 | Armour Tst | 11.3 | 0.0 | ... | ... |
| 286 | 101 | Baird (Wm) | 113.5 | 0.0 | 11.6 | 5.7 |
| 422 | 233 | Black (Peter) | 286.5 | 0.0 | 3.1 | 14.9 |
| 150 | 95 | Black Arrow | 94.5 | 0.0 | 6.6 | 7.3 |
| 495 | 69 | Churchill China | 99.5 | 0.0 | 15.6 | 2.5 |
| 89 | 13 | Claremont | 18.3 | 0.0 | ... | ... |
| 115 | 25 | Coats Viyella | 26.0 | -1.0 | 9.6 | ... |
| 133 | 71 | Colefax & Fowler | 76.5 | 1.5 | 4.6 | 95.6 |
| 183 | 69 | Cornwell Pkr | 78.5 | 0.0 | 6.4 | 5.2 |
| 203 | 165 | Pifco A | 180.0 | 0.0 | 4.2 | 9.2 |
| 320 | 160 | Portmeirion | 165.0 | 0.0 | 10.0 | 4.7 |
| 48 | 23 | Readicut | 25.5 | 0.0 | 12.6 | 7.2 |
| 1333 | 820 | **Reckitt & C** | 861.0 | -3.0 | 3.0 | 16.2 |
| 620 | 280 | Relyon | 298.5 | -1.5 | 6.5 | 9.6 |
| 228 | 76 | Royal Doulton | 87.5 | -2.5 | 14.3 | 12.9 |
| 48 | 27 | Sherwood Gp | 38.0 | 0.5 | 11.8 | 9.5 |
| 285 | 165 | Silentnight | 187.0 | 0.0 | 8.0 | 7.5 |
| 71 | 51 | Sirdar | 56.5 | 0.0 | 12.5 | 6.8 |
| 53 | 22 | Stirling | 22.0 | 0.0 | 14.2 | 4.1 |
| 262 | 85 | Stoves | 86.0 | -3.5 | 9.3 | 5.6 |
| 279 | 64 | Swallowfield | 64.0 | -1.5 | 13.5 | 3.0 |
| 165 | 68 | Vymura | 76.5 | 0.0 | 9.0 | 5.4 |
| 75 | 40 | Walker GBank | 52.5 | 0.0 | ... | 8.0 |
| 106 | 48 | Waterfd Wedg | 57.0 | 3.0 | 2.4 | 72.1 |
| 73 | 57 | Worthington Grp | 58.5 | -0.5 | 6.6 | 8.0 |
| 142 | 78 | Yorklyde | 77.5 | 0.0 | 6.2 | 12.3 |
| **INSURANCE** | | | | | | 1.695% |
| 900 | 461 | **Allied Zurich** | 826.0 | 0.0 | | |
| 150 | 96 | Amlin Ordinary | 112.5 | 0.0 | 12.2 | ... |
| 162 | 105 | Benfield & Rea | 125.0 | 2.0 | 6.5 | ... |
| 78 | 34 | Bradstock Gp | 44.0 | 0.5 | 13.6 | 5.9 |
| 1297 | 733 | **CGU** | 1030.0 | 12.0 | 3.3 | 19.9 |
| 278 | 199 | Charles Taylor | 219.5 | 1.5 | 2.7 | 24.4 |
| 167 | 121 | CLM Insur Fnd | 123.5 | 0.0 | 13.2 | ... |
| 525 | 228 | Cox Insce | 364.5 | 13.5 | 1.1 | 27.9 |
| 555 | 430 | Dom & Genl | 527.5 | 0.0 | 2.6 | 18.0 |
| 168 | 97 | Euclidian | 126.0 | 0.0 | 14.9 | 4.2 |
| 162 | 116 | GoshawkinsurHldgs | 117.5 | 0.0 | 3.1 | 11.8 |
| 494 | 229 | **GRE** | 344.0 | -6.5 | 3.8 | 5.3 |

*The Independent*

# Unit 10 Speaking

## Group B

(All figures are in French francs. Source: *L'Oréal Annual Report 1998*)

### Consolidated cosmetics sales (1)

**Consolidated net cosmetics sales 1998**
(FF millions)

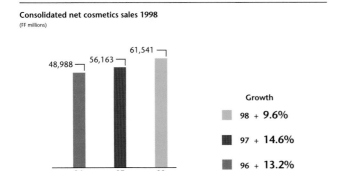

| | Growth |
|---|---|
| 98 | + **9.6%** |
| 97 | + **14.6%** |
| 96 | + **13.2%** |

**Breakdown of 1998 cosmetics sales by sector**

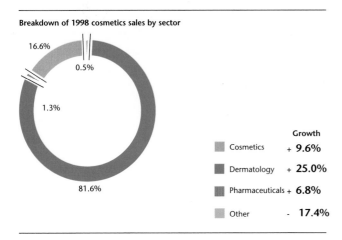

| | Growth |
|---|---|
| Cosmetics | + **9.6%** |
| Dermatology | + **25.0%** |
| Pharmaceuticals | + **6.8%** |
| Other | - **17.4%** |

**Breakdown of 1998 consolidated cosmetics sales by geographical zones**

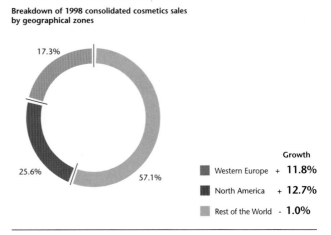

| | Growth |
|---|---|
| Western Europe | + **11.8%** |
| North America | + **12.7%** |
| Rest of the World | - **1.0%** |

**Breakdown of 1998 consolidated cosmetics sales by division**

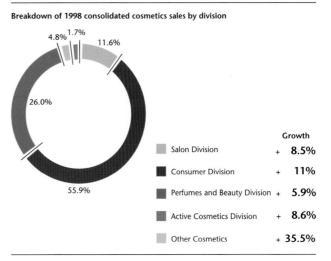

| | Growth |
|---|---|
| Salon Division | + **8.5%** |
| Consumer Division | + **11%** |
| Perfumes and Beauty Division | + **5.9%** |
| Active Cosmetics Division | + **8.6%** |
| Other Cosmetics | + **35.5%** |

The L'Oréal Group is the world leader in the cosmetics industry with international brands such as: L'Oréal, Laboratoires Garnier, Maybelline, Redken, Lancôme, Helena Rubinstein, Biotherm, Vichy, Ralph Lauren Perfumes and Giorgio Armani Perfumes.

Research is one of the keys to L'Oréal success and has been at the core of the company's strategy since its foundation by a chemist in 1907. L'Oréal has built up its own cutting edge research by investing £1.2 billion in this area in the last 10 years.

## Unit 9 Speaking 1

### Student B

The graph below shows US exports of goods and services from August 1996 to August 1998. Listen to Student A's description of US imports for the same period and complete the graph using a different colour. Then describe the information in your graph to Student A using the language you have learnt in this unit.

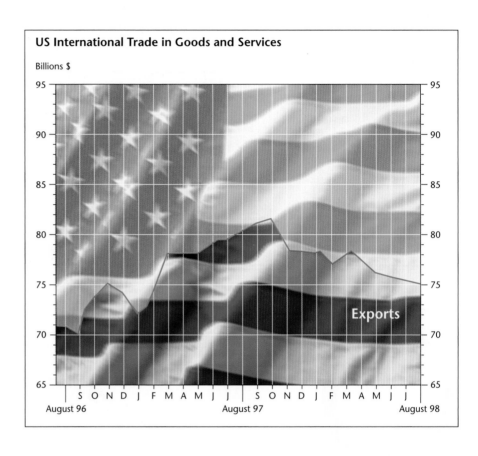

**US International Trade in Goods and Services**

Billions $

Exports

S O N D J F M A M J J    S O N D J F M A M J J

August 96          August 97          August 98

---

## Unit 12 Role-play

### The Trade Union Representative

**Opinions**
You strongly disagree. You believe salaries are too low and the loss of overtime will be a real problem for the workers. You should prepare your arguments and try to convince the others of your opinion.

**Suggestions**
You would reluctantly accept performance related bonuses and other perks, such as longer paid holidays and better health insurance, as a compromise.

**Attitude**
You will not be able to convince the workers to accept the 35-hour week if you don't obtain some of the above compromises.

## Unit 11 Speaking

**Key**

| | | | |
|---|---|---|---|
| 1 | a = 0 | b = 2 | c = 4 |
| 2 | a = 4 | b = 2 | c = 0 |
| 3 | a = 0 | b = 2 | c = 4 |
| 4 | a = 4 | b = 2 | c = 0 |
| 5 | a = 2 | b = 4 | c = 0 |
| 6 | a = 4 | b = 0 | c = 2 |
| 7 | a = 0 | b = 4 | c = 2 |
| 8 | a = 2 | b = 4 | c = 0 |
| 9 | a = 2 | b = 4 | c = 0 |
| 10 | a = 0 | b = 2 | c = 4 |
| 11 | a = 0 | b = 4 | c = 2 |
| 12 | a = 2 | b = 4 | c = 0 |
| 13 | a = 2 | b = 0 | c = 4 |
| 14 | a = 2 | b = 4 | c = 0 |
| 15 | a = 0 | b = 4 | c = 2 |
| 16 | a = 4 | b = 2 | c = 0 |

# Unit 10 Speaking

## Group C

(All figures are in French francs. Source: *L'Oréal Annual Report 1998*)

| Total number of employees | | |
|---|---|---|
| 1997 | | 47,242 |
| 1998 | | 49,665 |

Production and logistics investment in cosmetics (FF millions)

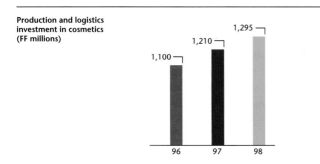

Treatment of transportable waste 1998

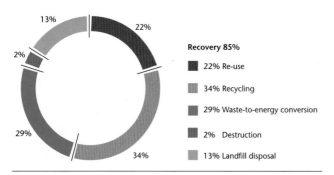

Recovery 85%

■ 22% Re-use

■ 34% Recycling

■ 29% Waste-to-energy conversion

■ 2% Destruction

■ 13% Landfill disposal

The L'Oréal Group is the world leader in the cosmetics industry with international brands such as: L'Oréal, Laboratoires Garnier, Maybelline, Redken, Lancôme, Helena Rubinstein, Biotherm, Vichy, Ralph Lauren Perfumes and Giorgio Armani Perfumes.

Research is one of the keys to L'Oréal success and has been at the core of the company's strategy since its foundation by a chemist in 1907. L'Oréal has built up its own cutting edge research by investing £1.2 billion in this area in the last 10 years.

Cosmetology and research sectors budget (FF millions)

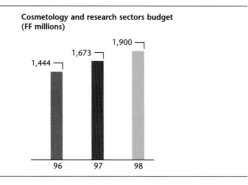

Number of employees cosmetics and dermatology sectors in research

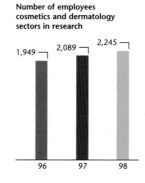

---

# Unit 4 Speaking

## Student B    Mad Science

### Description:
Science education and entertainment for children

### Activities:
Mad Science provides children (from 4 to 14) with the opportunity to discover and understand science through a series of practical exercises and spectacular scientific experiments. The concept combines fun with learning.

### Training:
11-day training period

### Qualifications:
No specific qualifications required

### Company details:
Founded: 1994

### Financial information for franchisees:
Initial investment:
Our franchise fee for domestic franchises is $23,500
The equipment package is $25,000
Working capital $15,000–$20,000
A total investment of $55,000–$60,000
Ongoing fees: 8% royalty

### Contact information:
Address:
Mad Science Group Inc,
3400 Jean Talon, West Suite 101,
Montreal, Quebec. H3R-2E8.
Tel: (514) 344-4181
E-mail: franchise@madscience.org

## Unit 6 Role-play

### Student A

You are a member of the small business loan department of a bank. You have a first meeting with a businessperson who is interested in applying for a loan from your bank in order to set up a business. Evaluate the risks involved in the project that he / she presents and decide whether the person has the right profile to succeed as an entrepreneur. This means that you must be convinced that he / she has:

- the right character
- a serious commitment to the business
- the capacity to manage it
- enough collateral or security to use as a guarantee

Remember that 33% of the total project cost should be covered by a personal investment and that four out of five new businesses fail within the first three years!

## Unit 12 Role-play

### The Production Manager

**Opinions**
You are very much against the 35-hour week. You are worried about meeting production deadlines. This will involve recruiting large numbers of part-time workers who you will have to train. You are also worried about the effect this will have on the workers' morale.

**Suggestions**
You would reluctantly accept a 'changeover' from the current situation where present workers could continue to earn overtime while they trained the new part timers to do their jobs.

**Attitude**
You want the workers to be happy and you will support any reasonable suggestion to do that.

## Business Loan Table

**10 years**

| Interest Rate | | 10,000 euro | 25,000 euro | 50,000 euro | 100,000 euro |
|---|---|---|---|---|---|
| 3% p.a. | Annual repayment | 1,172.31 | 2,930.76 | 5,861.53 | 11,723.05 |
| | Total cost | 11,723.05 | 29,307.63 | 58,615.25 | 117,230.51 |
| 5% p.a. | Annual repayment | 1,295.05 | 3,237.61 | 6,475.23 | 12,950.46 |
| | Total cost | 12,950.46 | 32,376.14 | 64,752.29 | 129,504.57 |
| 7% p.a. | Annual repayment | 1,423.78 | 3,559.44 | 7,118.88 | 14,237.75 |
| | Total cost | 14,237.75 | 35,594.38 | 71,188.75 | 142,377.50 |

**20 years**

| Interest Rate | | 10,000 euro | 25,000 euro | 50,000 euro | 100,000 euro |
|---|---|---|---|---|---|
| 3% p.a. | Annual repayment | 672.16 | 1,680.39 | 3,360.79 | 6,721.57 |
| | Total cost | 13,443.14 | 33,607.85 | 67,215.71 | 134,431.42 |
| 5% p.a. | Annual repayment | 802.43 | 2,006.06 | 4,012.13 | 8,024.26 |
| | Total cost | 16,048.52 | 40,121.29 | 80,242.59 | 160,485.17 |
| 7% p.a. | Annual repayment | 943.93 | 2.359.82 | 4,719.65 | 9,439.29 |
| | Total cost | 18,878.59 | 47,196.46 | 94,392.93 | 188,785.85 |

# Tapescript for Unit 10

## *(for complete tapescripts see Teacher's Book)*

### Unit 10

**Business Skills Focus: Presentations**

#### *Listening 2*

Before I start I'd just like to thank you all, both for inviting me to deliver this talk but also, and for me this is the really important thing, for actually coming along to listen to me. This is actually the first time that I have addressed a group of students like yourselves but not the first time that I have made a public presentation. Indeed being able to present is one of the really important skills that you need to have if you want to be successful in my line of business: financial analysis. But it is not the only one, as I hope I will be able to show you during this short presentation.

I think I will begin by answering the one question that I'm sure is at the back of all your minds, 'What exactly does a financial analyst do?'. Once I've explained that, I will go on to describe how analysts actually do their work and talk a little bit about some of the tools of the analyst's trade, define a few of the key terms and then, to finish, I will give you my views about what I think is the best preparation for a career in this field. After that, if I have got the timing right, we should be able to fit in a ten minute question and answer session.

I suppose that the answer to that first question 'what does an analyst do?' is really quite obvious because just as the name suggests, he or she does exactly that, analyses the financial results of companies that are listed, on the Stock Exchange. By 'listed' we mean that these are companies in which you and I can invest, they are open to the public and, of course, they are therefore also open to the professional investors and the managers of investment funds. Today most analysts are employed either by banks or by brokerage firms, which are really just companies specialised in buying and selling different types of financial investment. In fact we, the analysts, are really a key element in the relationship between brokers and investment managers because it is the analysis that we produce on a particular company that is the signal that the professional investor can use to decide whether to make, keep or sell an investment in that company.

I'm going to give you an example of the sort of work that I produce for the sector that I am specialised in, which is the pharmaceutical and cosmetics industry. If you look at the transparency, you can see some of the different types of analysis that we have to do. In this particular case this is part of a report that I made about the French company L'Oréal. At the top here, we have a simple table showing comparative figures for turnover and operating profit over the last three years. Then, next to it, we have a graph where we can see the evolution of the share price over the last five years. Below that we have a bar chart which illustrates the evolution of the company's margins and at the bottom there is a short summary of some of my recommendations to investors. As I said before, I actually prepared this as part of a written report but I think it's also a good example of the sort of information that I normally include when I'm making an oral presentation to investors.

If we now move on to look at the different tools that we use, I have drawn up a short list so that you can see what these are ...

# Grammar Reference

## UNIT 1
### Present perfect and past simple (page 9)
### Present perfect

- We use the present perfect to talk about:

1 the present result of something that happened at an unspecified time in the past.

   *He's **decided** to look for a new job.* (he's looking now)
   *I'm afraid I've **forgotten** your name.* (I don't remember it now)

2 actions or situations which started in the past and continue in the present.

   *How long **have** you **worked** here?* (you work here now; when did you start?)
   *She's **been** away on business since last week.* (she went last week; she's away now)
   *I **haven't seen** him for several years.*

- We use the present perfect + *for* to show the duration of an action, and the present perfect + *since* to show when an action began.

*Since*

↑
←——— *for* ———→ - - - - - - - →
Past           now          future

*I've known her* | **for** *three months.*
                 | **since** *July.*

- We often use the present perfect with these adverbs:

| *just* | *ever* | *never* | *lately* | *so far* | *up to now.* |

   *They've **just** signed an important contract.*
   *Have you **ever** used this type of machine?*
   *I've **never** seen such a well organised office!*
   *We've had good results **lately** / **up to now** / **so far.***

### Past simple
- We use the past simple to talk about actions and events which happened in a finished period of time in the past.

   *Pasteur **made** important medical discoveries.* (when he was alive)
   ***Did** you **go** to the meeting yesterday?*
   *She **worked** in Paris for five years before moving to Rome.* (eg 1994–1999, not now)

## UNIT 2
### Present simple and present continuous
*(page 19)*
### Present simple

- We use the present simple to talk about:

1 habitual actions.
   *She usually **stays** at the Hilton, but it was fully booked.*

2 permanent situations.
   *He **works** in the Personnel Department of a large multinational company.*

3 things which are generally true.
   *Metals **expand** when heated.*

### Present continuous

- We use the present continuous to talk about:

1 actions happening around the time of speaking.
   *Angela's in London at the moment. She's **staying** at the Hotel Intercontinental.*
   *We're **expanding** our operations in the Far East.*

2 temporary situations.
   *I'm **working** in a bookshop during the summer holidays.*

- Some verbs are not normally used in a continuous form.
   *I **know** London.* (NOT *I am knowing*)
   *I **like** my job.* (NOT *I am liking*).

   Common verbs of this type include:

| Verbs of feeling | | | |
|---|---|---|---|
| like | dislike | want | appreciate |
| love | hate | prefer | |

| Verbs of thinking | | |
|---|---|---|
| know | understand | think (= have an opinion) |
| believe | forget | remember |
| recognise | realise | mean |

| Verbs of senses | | | | |
|---|---|---|---|---|
| see | taste | smell | hear | feel |

| Other verbs | | | |
|---|---|---|---|
| belong | own | be | have ( = possess) |
| consist of | contain | include | exist |

## Present tenses with a future meaning
*(page 19)*

### Present simple
- We use the present simple to talk about timetabled or programmed future events.
  *The meeting **starts** at 3 o'clock.*
  *Our flight **arrives** at 6 p.m.*

### Present continuous
- We use the present continuous to talk about future arrangements and plans.
  *I'**m attending** a meeting tomorrow afternoon.*
  *We'**re flying** to Hamburg next week.*

# UNIT 3

## *Make* and *do* *(page 30)*

- We use *do*:

1 to talk about activities without mentioning exactly what they are.
  *What's she **doing**?*
  *Are you **doing** anything tonight?*

2 to talk about work or a task.
  *Have you **done your homework** yet?*
  *It was a pleasure **doing business** with you.*

3 with a determiner (eg *the, some*) + *ing*, to talk about activities that are repeated or take some time.
  *Could you **do some photocopying** for me please?*
  *We need a temp to **do the filing**.*

- We use *make*:

1 to talk about creating or constructing.
  *We **made** new plans for the store based on his suggestions.*
  *The company **makes** photographic equipment.*

2 with nouns connected with talking about sounds.
  *I'd like to **make a complaint / an enquiry**.*
  *Those machines **make** too much **noise**.*

3 with nouns connected with travel.
  *The regional manager is **making a visit** next week.*
  *We had to **make a long journey** to find this place.*

- There are many other expressions with *make* and *do* which do not follow these guidelines. It is best to learn these or use a dictionary if you are unsure.

| Do |
|---|
| good    your    best    harm    (someone) a favour |

| Make |
|---|
| an appointment    arrangements    an attempt |
| a choice    money    progress |
| a start |

# UNIT 4

## Adverbs *(page 38)*

- We use adverbs to give extra information about verbs, adjectives and other adverbs.

- We usually add *-ly* to an adjective to form an adverb.
  *She was **definite** about coming. (adj)*
  *She said she was **definitely** coming. (adv)*
  *He is very **efficient**. (adj)*
  *He works **efficiently**. (adv)*

- We add *-ally* to adjectives ending in *-ic*.
  *There has been a **dramatic** drop in interest rates. (adj)*
  *Interest rates have dropped **dramatically**. (adv)*

- Some adverbs are 'irregular' and are not formed with *-ly*.
  *He is a **good** speaker of English. (adj)*
  *He speaks English **well**. (adv)*
  *She is a **fast** typist. (adj)*
  *She types **fast**. (adv)*
  *He is a **hard** worker. (adj)*
  *He works **hard**. (adv)*

- Some adverbs ending in *-ly* have a different meaning from the adjective.
  *He is a **hard** worker. (adj. He does a lot of work.)*
  *He **hardly** works. (adv. He does not do much work.)*

- Some words ending in *-ly* are adjectives and not adverbs.
  *The new manager seems very **friendly**. (adj)*
  *There is a **lovely** view from our office window. (adj)*

## Frequency *(page 38)*

- We can rank expressions of frequency from *always* (100% of the time) to *never* (0% of the time).

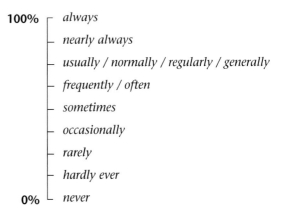

| 100% | *always* |
|---|---|
| | *nearly always* |
| | *usually / normally / regularly / generally* |
| | *frequently / often* |
| | *sometimes* |
| | *occasionally* |
| | *rarely* |
| | *hardly ever* |
| 0% | *never* |

*We **always** try to meet our deadlines.*
*We are **hardly ever** late.*
*We **occasionally** have problems with our suppliers and this **sometimes** causes delays.*

- We can use more precise expressions of frequency.
  *Once / twice / three times a day / week / month / year*
  *Every hour / day / week / month / year*
  *Hourly / daily / weekly / monthly / yearly*

  *We hold departmental meetings **once a month**.*
  *The individual teams meet **every week**.*
  *We update the sales figures **monthly**.*

- We can use *hourly, daily, weekly, monthly* and *yearly* as both adjectives and adverbs.
  *We hold **weekly** meetings. (adj)*
  *We hold meetings **weekly**. (adv)*

## Used to (page 39)

- We use *used to* + infinitive to talk about things that happened regularly in the past but have changed now.

  *They **used to live** in London. Now they live in Madrid.*
  *I **used to go to** work by bus. Now I take my car.*

## Be/Get used to (page 39)

- We use *be used to* to talk about things we don't mind doing because we have become familiar with them.
  *I'm **used to** office work. (I don't mind it now, but it was strange at first)*

- When *be used to* is followed by a verb it takes the *ing* form.
  *I'm **used to working** in an office.*

- We use *get used to* to talk about the process of becoming familiar with something that is new.
  *I quickly **got used to working** in an office.*

# UNIT 5

## The imperative (page 49)

- The imperative has the same form as the infinitive without *to*.

- We use the imperative to give orders, instructions and strong advice.
  ***Complete** this form and **send** it by e-mail.*
  ***Make** sure that you take your passport with you.*

- We use the auxiliary verb *do* to form emphatic and negative imperatives.
  ***Do visit** us again.*
  ***Don't be** late.*

- We can use question tags with imperatives.
  Check the records, ***would you?***
  ***could you?***
  ***will you?***

## Adjectives and nouns of nationality (page 50)

- To talk about the inhabitants of a country collectively, we use a noun which is the same as the adjective of nationality.
  *Private space for **the Japanese** is virtually non-existent.*

- To talk about individual inhabitants, we may:

1 use the adjective of nationality.
  *a Japanese, an American, two Canadians*
2 add *man* or *woman* to the adjective.
  *a Frenchwoman, three Irishmen*
3 use a different word.
  *a Pole, a Spaniard, some Finns*

- To talk about a language, we use the same form as the adjective.
  *In Holland most people speak **Dutch**, **English** and **German**.*

# UNIT 6

## First and second conditional (page 62)

### First conditional

- We use the first conditional to talk about the consequences of something which may possibly happen in the future.
  *If you transfer your money to a deposit account, you'll earn more money.*
  *I'll give you a five per cent discount if you pay cash.*

- We use a present tense in the *if* clause, and a future tense in the main clause.

### Second conditional

- We use the second conditional to talk about something which we think is unlikely to happen, or to refer to an imaginary situation.
  *What would you do if you lost your credit card?*
  *If I had more money, I'd invest it on the Stock Exchange.*

- We use a past tense in the *if* clause and *would* + infinitive in the main clause.

- When the *if* clause contains the verb *be*, we usually use *were* not *was*, especially after *I*.
  *If I **weren't** so tired I would gladly help you.*

- We often use the expression *If I were you* to give advice.
  *If I **were you**, I would take travellers' cheques, not cash.*

# UNIT 7

## Expressing contrast *(page 70)*

- There are several ways of expressing contrast in English.

| although<br>even though<br>though | + subject + verb |
|---|---|

He enjoys his job, **although** he would like more responsibility.
**Even though** she works long hours, she still finds time for other things.
She's never been to Russia, **though** she's fluent in Russian.

| despite<br>in spite of | + noun<br>or<br>+ verb + -*ing* |
|---|---|

**Despite** the recession, we achieved record profits.
They still think they'll win the election, **in spite of** the recent opinion polls.
I haven't finished that report yet, **despite** working overtime last night.

- We can also say *despite the fact that* or *in spite of the fact that*, followed by a clause.
**Despite the fact that** I worked overtime last night, I haven't finished that report.

## The passive *(page 70)*

- When we use an active verb form, we are more interested in the person or thing doing the action (the agent).
*Anita Roddick* **opened** *the first branch of The Body Shop in 1976.*

- When we use a passive verb form, we are more interested in the person or thing affected by the action.
*The first branch of The Body Shop* **was opened** *in 1976.*

- If we want to mention the agent we use *by*.
*The first branch of The Body Shop was opened* **by** *Anita Roddick in 1976.*

- The agent is often not important.
*Our products* **are made** *entirely of recycled materials.*
*Maria* **has been promoted**.

- We use the verb *be* + past participle to form the passive. There are passive forms of most verb tenses.

| Present simple | Every item **is checked** for quality. |
|---|---|
| Present continuous | Whole forests **are being destroyed.** |
| Present perfect | Nothing **has been touched** since you left. |
| Past simple | The company **was founded** in 1903. |
| Past continuous | The machinery **wasn't being used** efficiently. |
| Past perfect | A decision **had** already **been made.** |

# UNIT 8

## The third conditional *(page 79)*

- We use the third conditional to talk about actions or events which did not happen in the past, and the imaginary consequences.
*If you had bought shares in Norcros, (but you didn't) you would have made a lot of money.* (but you didn't)

*The employees would not have gone on strike (but they did)*
*if the company had improved their pension scheme.* (but they didn't)

- We use the past perfect tense in the *if* clause, and *would have* + past participle in the main clause.

- We can 'mix' clauses from second and third conditional sentences to talk about:

1 present consequences of past actions.
*If I had bought more shares (but I didn't, in the past) I would be rich.* (but I'm not, now)

2 possible past consequences of imaginary present situations.
*If I lived in Germany (but I don't, now) I would have got a better interest rate last year.* (but I didn't, then)

# UNIT 9

## The future *(page 91)*

- We use *will*:

1 to express a decision made at the time of speaking.
*Have you booked the hotel?*
*No.* **I'll do** *it now.*

2 to make a prediction.
*Our products* **will sell** *well on the Japanese market.*

3 with adverbs of certainty, probability and possibility.
*We* **will probably have** *to adapt our advertising strategy for the export market.*

**4** in the main clause of a first conditional sentence.
*If they increase import duties, **we won't be able to**
**manufacture competitively.***

**5** to talk about a future fact or part of a process.
*Next year, this company **will be** fifty years old.*
*First the export manager **will talk** about the market*
*possibilities in general and then **he'll give** us some*
*figures.*

• We use *going to*:

**1** to talk about a decision already made, an intention.
*Next year, we **are going to invest** in a new plant.*

**2** to make a prediction based on the present
situation.
*Prices **are going to go up** because import duties are*
*rising.*

See page 165 for more information on present
tenses with future meaning.

# UNIT 10
## Fractions and percentages *(page 100)*

### Fractions

• Most fractions are expressed using ordinal numbers.
*a third (⅓)     a fifth (⅕)     a sixth (⅙)*

***A third** of all our employees are women.*
***Four fifths** of our customers are satisfied with our*
*products.*

• There are some exceptions.
*a half (½)*
*a quarter (¼)*
*three quarters (¾)*
*three and a half (3½)*
*two and three quarters (2¾)*

***Three quarters** of the working population are men.*

### Percentages

• When talking about interest rates we say
*The Central Bank raised / lowered interest rates by **a***
***quarter of one percent**. (0.25%)*
*Interest rates are up / down **half(of)a percentage***
***point**. (0.5%)*

# UNIT 11
## Relative clauses *(page 111)*

### Defining relative clauses

• We use defining relative clauses to add essential
information to a sentence.
*Which company are you talking about?*
*I mean the company **that made an offer for mine**.*

• We use these relative pronouns to introduce a
defining relative clause.

|  | To refer to people | To refer to things |
|---|---|---|
| **Subject** | who, that | which, that |
| **Object** | (who, that, whom*) | (which, that) |
| **Possessive** | whose ||

*\*Whom is mainly used in formal, written English.*

• We can omit the relative pronoun when it is the
object of the relative clause.
*Some of the applicants **(who/that)** we interviewed were*
*very highly qualified.*
*The job **(that/which)** they asked us to do was almost*
*impossible.*

### Non-defining relative clauses

• We use non-defining relative clauses to add non-
essential information to a sentence.
*The company, **which was started in 1983**, is reducing*
*its workforce.*

• We use these relative pronouns to introduce a non-
defining relative clause.

|  | To refer to people | To refer to things |
|---|---|---|
| **Subject** | who | which |
| **Object** | who, whom | which |
| **Possessive** | whose ||

• We cannot use the relative pronoun *that* in a non-
defining relative clause.

• We cannot omit the relative pronoun in a non-
defining relative clause.

• We usually use commas to separate a non-defining
relative clause from the rest of the sentence.
*The manager, **who was in his late fifties**, accepted*
*early retirement.*

# UNIT 12
## Modal verbs of obligation *(page 121)*

• These modal verbs can be used to express different
degrees of obligation.

| Obligation or necessity | Mild obligation or advice | Absence of obligation or necessity |
|---|---|---|
| have to must/mustn't need to | should/shouldn't ought to | don't have to don't need to needn't |

- We use *must* to talk about what we personally consider to be important.
*I **must** finish this report today.* (I would like to start working on a new project tomorrow.)

- We use *have to* to talk about an obligation imposed by someone else.
*I **have to** attend a meeting.* (The boss has asked me to attend a meeting.)

- We use *mustn't* to indicate that it is important not to do something, for example because it is forbidden.
*You **mustn't** adjust the screen.* (Don't adjust the screen.)

- We use *don't have to / needn't* to indicate that there is no obligation to do something – you can do it if you want to, but it is not necessary.
*You **don't have to / needn't** come in early tomorrow.* (You can if you want, but it isn't necessary.)

# UNIT 13
## Comparison *(page 130)*

- We add *-er* to one-syllable adjectives to form the comparative.
*high    high**er***
*low    low**er***

- We add *-est* to one-syllable adjectives to form the superlative.

*high**est***
*low**est***

*Demand for our products is **high** in India, **higher** in China but the **highest demand** is in Japan.* (note that we use the definite article *the* with superlatives)

- We add *-ier* and *-iest* to adjectives ending in *-y*.
*wealthy    wealth**ier**    the wealth**iest***
*easy    eas**ier**    the eas**iest***

- There are 'irregular' comparatives and superlatives.
*good    better    the best*
*bad    worse    the worst*

- We add *more / less* and *the most / the least* to adjectives of two or more syllables.

*important*
*more / less important*
*the most / least important*
*interesting*
*more / less interesting*
*the most / least interesting*

*India is one of **the most exciting** long-term market opportunities in the world – and one of **the most complex**.*

- We use *than* to compare two or more things.
*On a first visit, India seems **easier than** Japan or China because people speak English.*

## Reported speech *(page 131)*

- A number of changes take place when converting direct speech into reported speech.

Direct speech: *'We are totally committed to product quality,' said the Marketing Manager.*
Reported speech: *The Marketing Manager said that they were totally committed to product quality.*

The present tense verb *are* in direct speech becomes a past tense verb *were* in reported speech. Such tense changes take place when the reporting verb (e.g. *said, told, asked*) is in the past.

| Direct speech | Reported speech |
|---|---|
| Present simple ⟶ | Past simple |
| Present continuous ⟶ | Past continuous |
| Past simple ⟶ | Past perfect |
| Present perfect ⟶ | Past perfect |
| Past perfect ⟶ | Past perfect |
| will ⟶ | would |
| can ⟶ | could |

# UNIT 14
## Gerund and infinitive *(page 139)*

### Gerund

- We use the gerund:

1 after certain verbs, for example:

| | |
|---|---|
| admit | imagine |
| appreciate | involve |
| avoid | postpone |
| consider | propose |
| delay | risk |
| enjoy | stop |
| finish | suggest |

*The department head **proposed organising** a meeting for all staff members.*
*This job **involves analysing** our sales figures.*

2 as the subject of a sentence.
***Breaking** into new markets was the key to the company's success.*
***Developing** new products will be our main objective next year.*

3 after prepositions, for example:

| | | |
|---|---|---|
| after | by | while |
| before | when | without |

*They launched the product **without doing** the necessary research.*

4 after verbs and expressions followed by prepositions, for example:

| | |
|---|---|
| to be interested in | to think of/about |
| to be good at | to look forward to |
| to be fond of | to succeed in |
| to be for/against | to approve of |
| to be used to | to insist on |
| instead of | to object to |
| to feel like | |

*I **am interested in travelling** abroad.*
*We're **looking forward to meeting** the new Manager.*

5 after these expressions.

| | |
|---|---|
| it's no use | it's no good |
| it's not worth | to have difficulty |

*It's **no use trying** to phone him. He's on holiday.*

## Infinitive

- We use the infinitive:

1 after certain verbs, for example:

| | | |
|---|---|---|
| afford | hope | refuse |
| agree | learn | seem |
| choose | manage | tend |
| decide | offer | threaten |
| forget | plan | |
| help | promise | |

*The clients **threatened to go** to a different agency.*
*I **hope to find** a job in marketing.*

2 after modals, either with or without *to*.

| Verb + infinitive with *to*: | | |
|---|---|---|
| have to | ought to | used to |

| Verb + infinitive without *to*: | | |
|---|---|---|
| can | might | should |
| could | must | will |
| may | shall | would |

*They **ought to treat** their staff better.*
*You **might have** problems with e-mail today.*

## Gerund or infinitive?

- Some verbs can be followed by either a gerund or an infinitive.

| | | | | |
|---|---|---|---|---|
| begin | can't bear | continue | hate | like |
| love | remember | start | stop | try |

*I **hate to work** long hours.*
*I **hate working** long hours.*

- Some of these verbs have different meanings depending on whether they are used with the gerund or the infinitive.

*to remember* + gerund = to remember something done in the past
*to remember* + infinitive = not to forget to do something

*I **remember seeing** that advertisement in the newspaper last week.*
*I must **remember to cancel** the order before one o'clock.*

*to try* + gerund = to do something as an experiment, for example to see if it is successful or enjoyable
*to try* + infinitive = to make an attempt to do something

*Try asking Sally. She may be able to help you.*
*I **tried not to laugh**.*

## The article *(page 140)*

### The indefinite article (*a/an*)

- We use the indefinite article *a/an*:

1 to refer to a singular countable noun for the first time.
*I've just been given **a** new company car.*
*Could you book me **a** hotel for next week?*

2 with jobs and nouns of nationality.
*She's **an** accountant.*
*She's **a** Spaniard and her husband is **a** Scotsman.*

### The definite article (*the*)

- We use the definite article *the*:

1 when we already know what is being talked about, or when we are referring to a specific person or thing.
*The car cost nearly $40,000.*
*What's the name of **the** hotel we're staying in?*

2 when the noun referred to is the only one of its kind.
*the sun, the world, the Queen.*

3 when we use an adjective as a noun to refer to a group of people.
*the rich, the old, the unemployed, the homeless, the British, the Spanish.*

4 in superlative constructions.
*the fastest, the most expensive, the best, the worst.*

## No article

- We do not use an article:

1 when we make general statements with plural and uncountable nouns.
*~~The~~ cars are a major cause of ~~the~~ pollution.*
*~~The~~ gas is cheaper than ~~the~~ electricity.*

2 with certain types of nouns, such as school subjects, meals, and abstract nouns.
*I'm studying chemistry.*
*What did you have for breakfast?*
*Loyalty to one's company is very important in Japan.*

3 in certain prepositional phrases.
*at home, at university, in bed, by train, at night.*

# UNIT 15

## *could have* + past participle *(page 149)*

- We use *could have* + past participle to express an opinion about a past action, and describe a possible alternative that was not taken.

*She came at 10 o'clock.*
*She **could have come** earlier.* (But she didn't)

*I went to Spain on holiday.*
*I **could have gone** to Portugal for the same price.* (But I didn't)

- We can also use *could have* + past participle to express a criticism of something that someone has done.

*You **could have** told me that you were going to take a day off.* (Why didn't you tell me?)

## Nouns *(page 149)*

### Proper nouns

- Proper nouns refer to people or places which are unique; they begin with a capital letter.

***Philip Morris** is a very famous company.*
***France** is a member of the **European Union**.*

- Plural names, public institutions and newspapers take the definite article.

| | |
|---|---|
| the United States | the Himalayas |
| the National Library | the European Union |
| *The Times* | *The Independent* |

## Common nouns

- Most common nouns are countable and can take an indefinite, definite or no article depending on the context.

*We bought a new **computer**.*
*The new **computer** isn't working.*
***Computers** don't break down very often.*

- Some common nouns are uncountable and take a singular verb form. They cannot take the indefinite article.

| | | | |
|---|---|---|---|
| information | advice | equipment | traffic |
| progress | work | trouble | furniture |
| machinery | news | money | cash |

*We need the **information** before we make a final decision.*
(NOT *an information*)

- Nouns ending in *-ics* are often singular.

| | | | |
|---|---|---|---|
| economics | politics | ethics | mathematics |

***Politics** is a subject to be avoided.*

- Some common nouns have only a plural form and take a plural verb.

| | | |
|---|---|---|
| arrears | headquarters | premises |
| surroundings | thanks | goods clothes |

*Our **premises** are being renovated at the moment.*
*Our **headquarters** are situated in Amsterdam.*

- Some nouns can have both a countable and an uncountable form:

| | | | |
|---|---|---|---|
| time | experience | adventure | age |
| authority | chocolate | fruit | life |

*That news item will take too much **time**.*
*How many **times** have I heard that?*

- Some nouns can have both plural and singular verb forms.

| | | | |
|---|---|---|---|
| team | government | group | staff |
| public | committee | media | |

*The **media** is / are considering self-regulation.*

- Some nouns look singular but have a plural verb form.

| | | |
|---|---|---|
| police | poultry | clergy |

*The **police** are investigating the allegations.*

# Word List

customer p.13, p.27
customer profile p.33
customer satisfaction p.33
customer service p.29
cut p.122
cut back on p.148
cut-price p.27
cutting edge p.126

## D

data p.58, p.96, p.144
database p.145
deadline p.70, p.124
deal p.27, p.117
debit p.60
debit card p.57
decision-maker p.16
decline (n, v) p.10
decrease (n, v) p.10
deficit p.95
delay p.49, p.87
delegate p.44
delegation p.50
demand p.108, p.125
department store p.25
depend on p.8
deposit p.56
deposit account p.62
depreciation p.145
design p.108
determination p.118
determine p.126
differentiate p.126
digital p.146
diploma p.21
direct p.69
direct debit p.58
direct mail p.132
direction p.69
director p.69, p.99
directory p.69
disagree p.38
discount p.26
display p.32
disrespect p.46
distribute p.108
distribution p.58
distribution system p.27
diversification p.6
dividend p.74
dividends per share p.98
division p.12
do (s.th.) up p.27
do business (with) p.27
donation p.136
dovetail p. 58
download p.58
downmarket p.129
downsize p.16
dramatic p.93
drive (n) p.118
drivers' license (US) p.16
driving licence (GB) p.21

drop (n, v) p.10
duty p.84
duty free p.29

## E

early retirement p.11
earnings p.149
earnings per share p.98
e-commerce p.33
education p.14, 21
effect on p.100
effective p.36
effectiveness p.38
effects p.142
efficient p.67
e.g. p.61
ego p.118
e-mail p.43
emergence p.87
employee p.14
employer p.16, p.20
empower p.46, p.67
end up p.120
end-of-line p.27
energy p.67
enquiry into p.100
enterprise p.45
entrepreneur p.108
entrepreneurial p.16
environment p.65
environmental p.65
environmentalism p.66
environmentally friendly p.66
equipment p.145
equity p.74
establish p.6
etiquette p.46
evaluate p.16
evaluation p.35
exceed p.126
ex-director p.110
exemplary p.67
ex-husband p.110
expenses p.41
experience p.14, 15, 16, 20, 22
exploit p.87
export p.84
extraction p.67

## F

face value p.136
factory p.6, p.27
failure p.16, p.68
fall (n, v) p.10
fax p.61
feasibility p.114
feature p.58
field consultant p.36
figure p.36
fill up (GB) p.126
finance p.4, p.56

financial accounts p.96
financial highlights p.99
fit in p.58
fittings p.40
fixtures p.40
floor manager p.36
fluctuate p.93
focus p.36
focus group p.126
force through p.118
foreign currency p.58
foster p.76
found p.108
founder p.27
fraction p.100
fragmented p.126
franchise p.34
franchise agreement p.34
franchise fee p.34
franchisee p.34
franchising p.34
franchisor p.34
freight p.89
front end fee p.34
fuel (up) (US) p.126
funding p.41
fundraising p.72
funds p.58

## G

garner p.136
gasoline (US) p.126
general public p.25
gesture p.47
get around to p.148
get on p.120
get on with p.148
global warming p.65
go ahead with p.148
go by p.120
go down p.120
go into business p.27
goods p.149
gradual p.93
graduate p.15, 23, 24
grant p.67
graph p.98
graphology p.15
grass roots p.67
green-marketing p.67
Greenwich Mean Time (GMT) p.61
greet p.46
greeting p.47
gross margin p.40
gross profit p.98
growth p. 20, p.102

## H

half p.100
handle p.26
harassment p.16

hardware p.108
hassle p.126
headhunter p.18
headquarters p.6
hierarchy p.44
high p.108
highlight p.22
hire (n, v) p.14, p.16
holding p.145
Human Resources p.4, p.14
hypermarket p.25

## I

icon p.43
i.e. p.61
image p.72
imperative p.118
imperfect p.68
implement p.6
import p.84
Inc p.106
Incorporated p.106
increase (n, v) p.10
inevitable p.118
information p.144
initiative p.44, p.126
innovation p.6, p.126
innovative p.68
installation p.41
intelligence p.149
intern (US) p.15
international p.110
Internet, the p.145
interpersonal p.110
interview p.14, p.22, p.23, p.24
interviewee p.23
inventory p.108
invest p.38
investment p.38, p.75, p.114
investor p.74
invisible imports / exports p.95
invoice p.36, p.89
involve p.10
involvement in p.100
IOU p.61
ironic p.136
issue (n, v) p.63, p.74
(address) issues p.67
IT p.4
item p.26

## J

joint venture p.76, p.86, p.116

## K

keyboard p.57
kit p.87
know-how p.41
knowledgeable p.67

Pearson Education Limited
Edinburgh Gate
Harlow
Essex CM20 2JE
England
and Associated Companies throughout the World.
www.longman.com

First Published in 2000
This edition published 2004
Eighth impression 2010

Set in ITC Stone Serif and ITC Stone Sans

Printed in China  SWTC/08

ISBN 978-0-582-84887-0

Designed by Tony Richardson (The Wooden Ark)

**Illustrations**
Illustrated by David Banks, Ian Dicks (illustrators.co),
Emma Dodd (Black Hat), George Foster, David Hayden,
Joe Hayden, Gavin Reece (New Division) and Three Blind
Mice.

Cover illustration by Sarah Jones (Debut Art)

**Acknowledgements**
The authors would like to thank the following:

Linda Davey and Bernie Hayden for editorial work on the
title and Jo Stevenson for the concept design.

Tracy Byrne, Irina Kahn, James Schofield and Patrizia
Spella, for their invaluable comments on the manuscript.

The staff and students of the language department of *Pole
Universitaire Léonard de Vinci, Paris La Defense* and the staff
of the *Infotech, Paris La Defense* for their help.

Those people who helped with research: Anna Bateson,
Bloomberg; Simon Brace, Abbott Mead Vickers BBDO Ltd;
Kate Chernyshov, BP Solarex; Jeremy Cohen, Philips;
Nicolette Dawson, HSBC Bank; Thomas Golsong, BP
Solarex; Sarah Howell, BP Solarex; Evan Lubofsky, Cognex;
Natalie Morris, Richer Sounds; Vanessa Stein, McDonald's;
Debbie Tadaschnik, Cognex; Jeff Toms, The Centre for
International Briefing.

Those people who allowed themselves to be interviewed
for recordings: Janis Errickson, Dunkin' Donuts; Margareta
Galfard, Volvo France; Pat Guerin, Guinness Ireland;
Carole Imbert, CPR Finance, Paris; Isobel Mendelson;
Janet Moore; Tomomi Moriwake; OECD, Paris; David
Smyth; Eleanor Stevens, HSBC Bank.

We are grateful to the following for permission to
reproduce copyright material:

American Marketing Association for an adapted extract
from 'Proven environmental commitment helps create
committed customers' by Jacquelyn Ottman in *Marketing
News* 2.2.98; Bang & Olufsen for an extract from  Bang &
Olufsen brochure; Bank of Scotland for an extract from
The Bank Of Scotland brochure on 'Corporate Hobs' ™;
Bloomberg Financial Markets for share price information;
Business People Publications for an adapted extract from
'Richer Pickings' by  Nigel Cope in *Business* March 1991;
Dow Jones Inc for an adapted extract from 'The Idea Man'
by Matthew Rose in Wall Street Journal Europe's
*Convergence* Spring 1998. © 1998 Dow Jones & Company,
Inc. All Rights Reserved; The Financial Times Ltd for the
article 'Old India hand plans to stay on' from FT Exporter
Survey in *The Financial Times* 11.6.98; IBM Corporation
for adapted text from Guide to *Understanding Financials*
IBM 1997; Irish Independent Newspapers for an adapted
extract from 'Learning to cope with corporate clashes' by
Bernadette Fallon in *The Irish Independent* 20.3.98; L'Oréal:
Corporate Communications L'Oréal (UK) Ltd.; Editor of
Network and the author for an adapted extract from  'One
Day in My Life ...' by Vanessa Stein, BSc. Warwick in
*Network* Magazine; New York Times Syndicate for adapted
extracts from 'Europeans Log On to Investment Fever' by
John Tagliabue in *The International Herald Tribune* 20.7.98
and 'Fit for Hiring' by Judith H. Dobrzynski in
*International Herald Tribune* 2.9.96; New York Times
Syndicate for an extract from 'Profile: Bloomberg. A Man
and His Information Machine' by Lisa Napoli from *The
New York Times* 29.4.97; Patagonia Europe for job advert
'Prefer a camping trip to a cocktail party?'; Pearson
Education Limited for extracts from *The Longman Business
English Dictionary*; Philips International bv for an extract
from  Philips website (www.philips.com); Prospects Direct
and the author Clarke Hooper for an extract from
*Prospects* magazine May 1995; Richer Sounds for extracts
from *The Richer Way* by Julian Richer. (copies of *The Richer
Way* and *Richer on Leadership* by Julian Richer can be
obtained from tel: 0171 378 9739 or fax: 0171 378 9744);
SHL Group plc for questionnaire 'Making Choices' from
their Personality Questionnaire Introduction on the SHL
Group Website;  Shell UK Ltd for extracts from 'Hello to
the good buys' by Suzanne Peck on the Shell website
(www.shell.com); Workplace Learning Resource Centre for
an adapted extract from the Employee Training Institute
website.

We have been unable to trace the copyright holders of
'Sacrilege' by Stephen Armstrong, and 'When egos collide'
by Cath Blackledge & Nicholas Moss, and would
appreciate any information which would enable us to do
so.

**Photo Acknowledgments**
We are grateful to the following for permission to
reproduce copyright photographs:

Advertising Archive: 108 (RB), 135, 139 (LT), 139 (LB)
Allied Domecq: 42 (LT) American Express: 57 (g) Apple